WARRIOR TRUTH

WARRIOR
TRUTH

Discovering the Power
of the Bhagavad Gita

TED L. COX

Spirit House Yoga Publishing
OKLAHOMA CITY

Warrior Truth: Discovering the Power of the Bhagavad Gita
by Ted L. Cox
Copyright © 2016 by Ted L. Cox

Published by

Spirit House Yoga Publishing, LLC

ISBN: 978-0-9910865-2-8
Library of Congress Control Number: 2016912533

Edited by Martha McQuaid, Misty Boyd, and Jackie Ellis
Cover design and interior design by David Grizzard
Photo by Nate Billings

Ordering Information: Special discounts are available on quantity purchaces by yoga studios, associations, and others. For details, contact the publisher at ted@spirithouseyoga.com.

First Edition

1. Yoga   2. Eastern Philosophy   3. Self Help

Printed in the United States of America

This book is dedicated to Krishna.

Although our eyes are open,

they will not see without Him.

CONTENTS

Preface

During my first yoga teacher training, a fellow student told me about a book she was reading entitled *Power vs. Force – The Hidden Determinants of Human Behavior* by David R. Hawkins, M.D., Ph.D. On page 14, Hawkins writes: *Suddenly, the Bhagavad Gita made complete sense.* That sentence is underlined in my book because I had recently read the *Bhagavad Gita* for the first time and had trouble making any sense out of what I read. I found the *Bhagavad Gita* to be similar to a jigsaw puzzle, I could fit a few pieces together, but I could never see the entire picture. From my first reading of this amazing text, I wanted to understand it completely and see the BIG picture.

Fast forward many years later—my first book was published, *Warrior Self – Unlocking the Promise of the Bhagavad Gita.* What more could I say now about the *Bhagavad Gita* that wasn't written in *Warrior Self?* The research for *Warrior Self* led me in many different directions for several years—the bibliography for that book shows some of that research. Once *Warrior Self* was published, I found myself reading *Power vs. Force* once again. Then I read *Transcending the Levels of Consciousness* and *Truth vs. Falsehood,* all three books by Dr. Hawkins. During this time of reading and studying Dr. Hawkins' books, more of the puzzle was revealed to me in ways I never understood before. *Suddenly, the Bhagavad Gita made complete sense!*

The great gift Dr. Hawkins gave to the world was his discovery on the nature of consciousness and how it can be measured. Consciousness is similar to gravity in that it cannot be seen, but it can be measured. Hawkins understood consciousness in entirely new ways—especially in regard to human behavior. His discovery on the nature of consciousness is no less important than the discoveries of Galileo, Newton, and Einstein in how we understand gravity today. We measure gravity by weight—but what is actually being measured with consciousness is truth. Consciousness responds

decisively between truth and falsehood, or more precisely, lack of truth. Out of this discovery, a whole new definition of truth emerged.

Dr. Hawkins' research and books are certainly controversial—many find the idea of consciousness being measurable an absurd idea. The paradox with consciousness is you have to have a certain degree of consciousness to understand it. Our ability to comprehend truth is dependent on our individual level of consciousness, resulting in a definition of truth that is in harmony with our specific level. What's interesting about Hawkins' work is the *Bhagavad Gita* was explaining the same principles of consciousness more than two thousand years earlier.

Why do we behave the way we do—good and bad? Why do we see life so differently from one another? Why is there so much conflict in the world? These types of questions are endless and we typically don't have answers for them, so we use human reason and make assumptions to explain what we don't understand. Framing human behavior in terms of measurable consciousness can actually provide us with the information that keeps us from being so creative with our lack of knowledge. Our new understanding of consciousness will begin to answer many of the questions we may have about ourselves and others. This knowledge has certainly helped me in my life and relationships and my hope is for it to help you too.

The human body can accurately discern the difference between what is true and what is false. In response to questions or statements that are true, a strong muscle reaction occurs in the body. In response to false questions or statements, a weak muscle reaction occurs. Any question where the answer is clearly a yes or a no—true or false, can be answered through **kinesiology**—a well-established science based on the testing of an all-or-nothing muscle response stimulus—telling us what makes us weak (falsehood) and what makes us strong (truth). Kinesiology is the interface between the material and spiritual dimensions. Truth can be retrieved by using the techniques developed by Dr. Hawkins giving us surprisingly clear answers from consciousness itself. It's important to note that falsehood is not the opposite of truth—only its absence. Truth is not a simple yes or no, but is able to be measured or calibrated over a **logarithmic scale** from 1 to 1,000.

Consciousness is similar to a mirror, impersonally reflecting actuality—it provides the context. That which is *not true* is not recognized by the field of consciousness—we cannot measure anything that isn't a Reality. Everything radiates a specific frequency that remains in the field of consciousness forever. Every person who has ever lived and anything about them—including events, thoughts, actions, feelings, or attitudes is imprinted on consciousness and can be retrieved at any time—the truth has no secrets. It is therefore possible to calibrate levels of truth in regard to spiritual teachings, teachers, texts, and nearly everything else. The highest levels of truth in history were taught by great beings like **Krishna**, whose energy field still impacts humanity today.

Of the unreal, there is no existence.
Of the real, there is no non-existence.
Chapter Two, Verse 16

A basic understanding of the logarithmic scale used to measure consciousness begins with bacteria, lichens, and algae, all calibrating at a 1. The average consciousness of mankind as of the publishing of this book is 207.3. Four out of five people in the world calibrate below 200—which is the critical level where the rights of others are ignored. In the United States, the percentage of those above or below 200 is about fifty percent. The experience of life above 200 is very different than the experience of life below 200. Those measuring below 200 tend to create **problems** and are more selfish and destructive. Those above 200 find **solutions** and are more selfless and constructive. This may be the first time in your life that you've heard of consciousness being measured—a natural reaction is to think it's not possible. What else in the history of mankind was also thought to be impossible?

Two types of people exist in this world –
the divine and the demonic.
Chapter 16, Verse 6

We all know human relationships are challenging—we all struggle from time to time with other people. There really is a difference between those above 200 and those below. It doesn't mean that people below 200 are not intelligent, successful, or somehow diminished from those above 200—their life compass has a different setting pointing to personal survival more strongly than those above 200. People calibrating below 200 want their life and relationships to be on their terms. Because of the tipping point of 200, conflicts between someone above 200 and someone below 200 can often ignite a fire that may be impossible to put out. This is the contrast of **power** and **force**. If we calibrate above 200—we are a power person. That means if we react in some way with a force person (below 200), we may start a fire and get burned. If however we don't react and stay in our power, we have a better chance of managing the fire and not getting burned. A power person reacting to a force person threatens their sense of survival—which always makes the conflict worse. Is it any wonder that the divorce rate in the United States is between 40 and 50 percent? In every instance of someone I personally know who divorced, one person calibrated above 200 and the other below—including my own parents!

The evolution of consciousness moves very slowly—the average increase for an individual over their entire life is only **five** points. 2,000 years ago, the overall level of consciousness of mankind was 100. It took nearly 2,000 years for consciousness to rise 105 points to 205 in the late 1980's. It increased to the current level of 207 in November of 2003. Advanced states of consciousness above 600 are extremely rare. There are **very** few people on the planet who calibrate above 600—this is the level known as enlightenment. In the history of mankind, only four humans calibrated at the level of 1,000—Krishna, Zoroaster, Buddha, and

Jesus. Reading this book and the *Bhagavad Gita*, which is present-ed in *Warrior Truth* in its entirety, will raise your individual level of consciousness—time and research will tell us just how much.

A great soul is very rare.
Chapter Seven, Verse 19

The most accurate results for measuring consciousness are ob-tained from individuals who calibrate in the **400's**. People who calibrate in the 400's have characteristics of clarity, awareness of context, precision of definition, as well as integrity. Higher levels of consciousness produce more accurate results in measuring con-sciousness due to increased power. Those below 200 will not have enough "juice" to calibrate with any accuracy. Knowing how to calibrate consciousness brings progressive expertise—like any-thing else, the more we do, the better we get. To learn the tech-niques on how consciousness can be measured, I must refer the reader to Dr. Hawkins' books—this book is not concerned with those specific techniques. Every number offered in this book is by my calibration and they have been tested numerous times for the utmost accuracy. Results and numbers will vary depending on the consciousness of the person or persons doing the calibrat-ing. Unless you calibrate in the upper 400's, your measurements will not match mine and will most likely be a lower number.

Dr. Hawkins measured the consciousness of the *Bhagavad Gita* and discovered that it is one of the highest recorded measure-ments of any text existing in the world today. My measurement of the *Bhagavad Gita*, as it was originally written in Sanskrit, is **993**. My calibration is slightly higher than what I've read from Dr. Hawkins. How I framed my question to obtain my measurement is, *as it was originally written in Sanskrit*—which may or may not be the reason my number is higher. Dr. Hawkins measured the *Bhagavad Gita* as a whole—what I have done in *Warrior Truth* is calibrate each of the 18 chapters individually and each verse spoken by Krishna—most being calibrated to a tenth or hundredth of a degree—levels of truth are that sensitive. Of the **700** total verses within the *Bhagavad Gita*, 572 belong to Krishna. Nearly every single verse from Krishna calibrates at 1,000, the level of absolute Truth. The calibration of the combined verses spoken only by Krishna is 999.56. These calibrations are extremely high and indicate pure truth. This fact is not to be taken lightly—we must not dismiss this text due to its age, the language in which it was written, the religion it is associated with, nor that few have any clue what it is telling mankind. The reason the *Bhagavad Gita* is difficult to comprehend is due to its extremely high level of consciousness. Many have struggled to understand the *Bhagavad Gita* due to the wide gap in consciousness between the reader and the text.

To ensure the most accurate calibrations and translation, I have included the verses from Krishna in Sanskrit, rather than an English translation only. Sanskrit means *refined*—it is the sacred language of Hinduism and used mainly for religious discourse. Although I am not a Sanskrit scholar, I did spend a great deal of time with each and every verse, making them readable, easier to understand, and without sacrificing their integrity. I have indicated translated words in **bold**—trying not to offer more than four translated words per verse as it has the potential to be confusing as opposed to interesting.

Translating Sanskrit into English can vary by amazing degrees—we can read one translation of one verse from one person and then read the exact same verse translated by someone else and swear the two verses are different. Sanskrit doesn't translate the same way many languages do—**word order is free**, complicating translations. Because the word order is free, some translations of the *Bhagavad Gita* don't always put the words in the order we expect in English—making the verses awkward to read and understand. When you begin reading Chapter Two, where the verses appear in Sanskrit, you'll understand more clearly how important the syntax becomes. Beginning in Chapter Two, you'll notice I've indicated some verse numbers in **bold**—these are the verses I've referenced elsewhere in the book—there are 104 of these verses. In addition, I did my best to make all the verses gender neutral, using the word *yogin* instead of *yogi* or *yogini*—male and female respectively.

It seems every commentator who has written about the *Bhagavad Gita* has their own perspective. I'm offering a new perspective of consciousness, one which doesn't require you to believe measurable consciousness exists. All I ask is for you to stay open as you read through *Warrior Truth*. If you make it to the end, I'm quite sure you will have a whole new understanding of yourself as well as others in your life. You will also understand the *Bhagavad Gita* as never before. The truths contained within are not only life changing, but lifesaving as well.

The novelist Stephen King wrote a book about writing entitled, *On Writing – A Memoir of the Craft*. Near the very end of this wonderful book, Stephen writes:

> "Writing isn't about making money, getting famous, getting dates, getting laid, or making friends. In the end, it's about enriching the lives of those who will read your work, and enriching your own life, as well."

These are the best two sentences in the book—what I call the gold. My sole intention is to enrich the lives of all the spiritual warriors brave enough to read this book—I can't begin to express how much my life has been enriched by Krishna's teachings. The *Bhagavad Gita* is powerful—it's worth your time to get to know Krishna, because everything He tells us, is *pure gold*.

Introduction

The *Bhagavad Gita* is a discourse on consciousness—arguably the highest level of Truth ever written. It is a conversation between God (Krishna) and man (Arjuna). We can approach this text as an owner's manual on how to live in the world. Our cars come with a manual telling us when to change the oil, how much oil to put in, and what kind of oil to use. Unfortunately we don't arrive into the world with a book telling us how life works. Few, if any of us can remember learning how to walk. We pulled ourselves up, took a step, and fell, sometimes hurting ourselves. Then we got back up and tried again until we finally developed enough strength to figure it out for ourselves. Most of life seems to work the same way—we have to figure it out for ourselves through the painful process of trial and error. Because the human mind cannot distinguish between inherent truth and falsehood, we make mistakes—we fall. If we arrived into the world with an owner's manual telling us how life *really* works, perhaps we wouldn't make so many mistakes, causing ourselves and others to suffer so much. The *Bhagavad Gita* is such a manual for all of humanity—transcending all religious boundaries.

Our hero, **Arjuna**, represents us when we are at our most desperate time of need for answers in our life—when we are brought to our knees and cry out for God. Few of us begin our spiritual journey when we are blissfully happy. We are drawn to the spiritual path because we want help dealing with our problems—and Arjuna has a serious problem. **Krishna** is one of the most beloved gods of the Hindu religion—God in human form—consciousness manifested for us to ask our questions and receive answers back, always ready to help—we only have to ask.

The *Bhagavad Gita (The Song of God)* is one small part within the sixth book of 18 total books comprising the larger work, the **Mahabharata**, meaning, *the great story of the Bharata dynasty.* The calibrated level of consciousness for the *Mahabharata* is

992. The *Mahabharata* is the story of a moral and philosophical struggle between two branches of a single ruling family culminating in an epic battle, the 18 day war of **Kurukshetra**. The *Bhagavad Gita* is usually excerpted and read as an independent sacred work—often referred to as the Hindu Bible. This comparison conveys the importance of these two sacred texts to their corresponding religions, but that's as far as the similarity can extend—the *Bhagavad Gita* is nothing like the Christian Bible. Many are familiar with the Bible, but not everyone knows or has even heard of the *Bhagavad Gita*, let alone how to pronounce it. When we read the verses later in this book, we'll discern for ourselves how vastly different these two texts are.

The *Mahabharata* is the first authentic account of the life of Krishna, written by **Vyasa**, (Vee-YA-sha) believed to be an enlightened man and a contemporary of Krishna. The *Mahabharata* was purportedly written non-stop for two and a half years in secluded retirement in the Himalayas. One of the challenges to reading the *Mahabharata*, besides its incredible length of over 100,000 verses, (at least seven times the length of *The Iliad* and *The Odyssey* combined) is the amount of names and characters in the story. Having a general understanding of the *Mahabharata* takes us deeper into the teachings of the *Bhagavad Gita*.

Vyasa includes himself in the story of the *Mahabharata* as the illegitimate son of Satyavati and the sage, Parasara. Satyavati means truth, making Vyasa, "the son of truth." Vyasa is the father of two important characters in the *Mahabharata*, **Pandu** and **Dhritarashtra**. Pandu is Arjuna's father, representing the intelligence aspect of the human mind—the higher mind or truth revealing consciousness. This quality is called *buddhi*. Pandu's half-brother, Dhritarashtra, represents the quality of the human mind that obscures truth, called *manas*—the ego mind. *Buddhi* reveals truth whereas *manas* obscures truth. Vyasa emphasized this obscuring quality by making Dhritarashtra blind from birth—a clever allegory for how manas obscures truth.

Manas can be understood as the pulling of life and consciousness **outward** toward the material world, whereas *buddhi* is the intelligence that draws life and consciousness **inward** toward the soul and spirituality. *Manas*, the ego mind, and *buddhi*, the higher mind, create two dominant and opposing energy fields of mental function—creating a **duality**, a fundamental principle of creation. Because of these two opposing fields of consciousness—material and spiritual, or individual and Universal—the human mind is unable to discern truth from falsehood. The capacity of our minds to understand and comprehend truth depends on our individual level of consciousness. Each level results in a definition of truth that is in harmony with our specified level. Each and every one of us experiences, perceives, and interprets the world according to our own level of consciousness. The presumption is that whatever we perceive and experience represents Reality.

> *All wrong-doing is involuntary, for man always*
> *chooses what he believes to be for his good.*
> Socrates

Truth brings peace and falsehood brings war—when truth prevails, peace is the result—war is the consequence of falsehood. This dichotomy of truth and falsehood is the basis for our two families about to go to war. The **Kauravas** (below 200) and the **Pandavas** (above 200) are our two related families—they are cousins. The blind king has 100 sons, known collectively as the Kauravas—representing the entire spectrum of negative human characteristics below level 200. Arjuna and his four brothers are known collectively as the Pandavas—chosen by Krishna to direct the course of events in the history of *Bharatavarsha* (India). The Pandava brothers were cheated out of their kingdom by their Kaurava cousin **Duryodhana** and they want their kingdom back. Duryodhana is the blind king's oldest son and antagonist in much of the *Mahabharata*. Arjuna and Krishna were twin avatars of *Vishnu* – *Nara* and

Narayana—taking the incarnations of Arjuna and Krishna respectively. Krishna was born to ensure the spiritual evolution of all humankind and to reestablish the ancient laws of righteousness, the **Sanatana Dharma** (Eternal Truth)—the original name for Hinduism. Krishna's father, *Vasudeva*, was the brother of Arjuna's mother *Kunti*, making Arjuna and Krishna cousins. *Vishnu* is part of the trinity of God in Hinduism—*Brahma-Vishnu-Shiva*. Each of these three primary gods represents the cycle of creation—*Brahma* – 'the creator,' beginning; *Vishnu* – 'the preserver,' middle; and *Shiva* – 'the destroyer,' end. Everything in life has a beginning, middle, and end. This book was purposely written in three distinct parts with the *Bhagavad Gita* in the middle. This triune signifies God not being a definable or limited concept—God is the source of all that exists and is reflected in all that exists—including this book.

King **Kamsa** was the primary reason for *Vishnu* to incarnate Himself as Krishna. It was foretold that the eighth child of *Devaki* (Krishna's mother) will kill Kamsa, Devaki's evil brother. This prophecy was fulfilled when Krishna was 12 years old. Krishna was the eighth *avatar* of *Vishnu*. The *avatar* is a direct descent of God appearing in human form. Only when evil reaches its zenith is such an incarnation called for. A divine incarnation has two purposes; to set things right in a time of evil and to create other God realized souls. The intention of the *Bhagavad Gita* is to align our actions on the side of **dharma**, thereby advancing evolution and consciousness.

> *Whenever virtue declines and vice flourishes, I incarnate*
> *as an Avatar. I appear in visible form from age to age.*
> *Protecting virtue and destroying evil in order to*
> *reestablish righteousness.*
> Chapter Four, Verses 7 and 8

Accepting Krishna as an Incarnation of God in human form can be a big leap of faith for many—we want actual proof, but all we have are ancient writings, like the *Mahabharata*, to validate Krishna's existence. We don't know with any certainty when the *Mahabharata* was written. We know one of the philosophical systems of the *Bhagavad Gita* is **Samkhya** (SUM-kya), the oldest school of Hindu Philosophy, founded by *Kapila*. Very little is known about Kapila, but it's generally believed he lived in the sixth century BCE. Interestingly, Kapila's name is mentioned in Chapter 10, Verse 26: *I am the muni Kapila.* The philosophical foundation of Yoga Philosophy is *Samkhya*—Yoga relates to the **individual** condition of Nature whereas *Samkhya* relates to the **universal** condition of Nature. The *Bhagavad Gita* embodies the universal and individual through Krishna and Arjuna respectively. In Chapter Two, Verse 39, Krishna says: *I have explained the ultimate wisdom of Samkhya to you. Now hear about the knowledge of Yoga.* The word *Samkhya* is used in seven different verses. We could conclude from what little we know about Kapila that the *Mahabharata* was written as early as the sixth century BCE. We know for certain that three of the four **Vedas** were written prior to the *Mahabharata*. The *Vedas* are the most highly revered Hindu scriptures, possibly dating as far back as 5,000 years BCE. The Vedic period is generally accepted as 1,500 to 600 BCE. The *Vedas* are classified as *revealed wisdom*, containing the first philosophical insights and regarded as the final authority. They will be discussed later in the book. There are six primary philosophical systems within Hindu Philosophy—Samkhya, Yoga, and Vedanta represents three of the systems found within the *Bhagavad Gita*. Vedanta is as old as the *Vedas*.

Western historians have colored Indian history as fable and fantasy—British colonial scholars and missionaries didn't want the history of India to conflict with the Christian Bible. Deeply prejudiced views by the British had the intention of destroying the historical importance of Krishna and imposing their Christian religion on India. For Christians, there has been and can only be one savior. True historical facts regarding Jesus are not always agreed upon—how then can we know the true historical facts of Krishna from possibly 600 or more years before Christ? It's distracting to argue over dates—does it really matter? The teachings of Krishna are important and relevant today, they are timeless and true in any age. Nearly every single verse from Krishna in the *Bhagavad Gita* calibrates at 1,000—absolute Truth. These verses wouldn't and couldn't calibrate that high if they did not come from Krishna. Because these teachings exist—Krishna exists.

The more we develop an understanding and relationship with Krishna, the more we connect to His teachings in the *Bhagavad Gita*. Our relationship with Krishna can be anything we want it to be—a character in a story, a myth or legend. He can be our friend, our teacher, or the embodiment of God. We can take a more impersonal approach to Krishna and simply think of Him as another name for consciousness. The whole concept of God can be quite confusing—it seems everyone has a different understanding of what and who God is, which I suspect is related to the vast range of human consciousness. Atheism calibrates at 116. When we define consciousness, we also define God—the all-pervasive universal energy field of infinite power and dimension beyond time—All Present, All Powerful, and encompassing All of Existence.

The relationship Arjuna has with Krishna is as his cousin, his dearest friend, his ally, advisor, messenger, and charioteer. Arjuna takes advantage of Krishna's love, just as we all have a tendency to do—but Krishna gladly plays whatever role we desire of Him. "However a man approaches Me, in the same manner do I go to him" was his creed. Arjuna represents the **individual**, the *Warrior* inside each of us—the model of the struggling human soul—ready to receive the teachings of the Divine in his most desperate time in life. Krishna is *Truth* itself, representing the **universal**—our constant companion, waiting patiently until we cry out for help.

The teachings in the *Bhagavad Gita* were given to Arjuna from Krishna before sunrise on the first day of battle. Arjuna was a great warrior and a man of action—he always knew what to do—but on this morning, moments before war is to begin, Arjuna doesn't know what to do, so he lays down his bow and arrows and sits down in his chariot. It's a powerful human moment in which everyone can relate: *How did this happen? What am I going to do?* Arjuna is us—when we become resistant to life's problems—not wanting to face life as it is. It's only through surrendering to these moments that we become open to the possibility for something new to happen in our lives—when we become humble enough to hear the Truth.

Human catastrophe often becomes God's opportunity—what appears to be a catastrophic event in our life often becomes the gateway to our freedom. Catastrophic events are an opportunity for the evolution of our consciousness and soul. The difficulties we face in life help free us from our attachments to how we want things to be—who we think we are, and what we think our life is about. Arjuna sitting in the middle of the battlefield represents this truth. Arjuna doesn't want this fight—he and his brothers did everything possible to make peace with their Kaurava cousin, but Duryodhana wants war—he wants to kill his cousins. Krishna Himself couldn't stop the war—but this wrong against the Pandavas has to be made right. Arjuna facing the entire Kaurava army in no-man's-land is an allegory for facing our *inner* difficulties. Our search for truth must be an inner search, not an outer search. Sooner or later, we all have to face our inner problems and Kaurava army—which is much easier when we have Krishna by our side.

> *Without real sacrifice (inner transformation),*
> *where comes any better world, any better existence,*
> *or elevated states of consciousness?*
> Chapter Four, Verse 31

Two inherent human powers are **reason** and **feeling**, both are unreliable. We are also endowed with **intuition**—the power of knowing. Intuition is the communication between God and humans—the soul (Universal) cannot be known through the power of reason, only through intuition. Our inborn compass says yes or no—informing us through our intuition what makes us strong or weak. Reason makes us weak, whereas intuition makes us strong. Wisdom is the simple process of avoiding what makes us kinesthetically weak. Our intuition is never wrong, but human reason exhausts itself trying to explain what can never be explained. We cannot use reason in the understanding of God's law.

We *think* we live by virtue of the forces we can control, but in fact, we are governed by power from unrevealed sources (consciousness), power over which we have no control. This is a very important point to understand. We are free to make choices for ourselves, but because of our specific level of consciousness, we don't always make the best choices, causing problems not only for ourselves, but for others as well. Why is Duryodhana being so stubborn? The Pandavas would be happy with five houses in place of their entire kingdom so they can all live in peace, but Duryodhana wants them all dead. His level of consciousness, (around 150) is the real cause of his actions and choices—which will ultimately be the cause of his own death. Because power is effortless, it goes unseen and unsuspected.

I am unseen by men. The confused world does not recognize Me.
Chapter Seven, Verse 25

Prior to the war, the blind king and his personal attendant, Sanjaya, were alone—the king asked Sanjaya what he thought the outcome of the war would be. Sanjaya said: "I have just seen Krishna—covering himself with illusion, he lives as a man, and no one knows him. He is like a worker in a field—we ride by him and forget him. But He is the soul of all creatures, and though our eye is open, it will not see without Him. Arjuna and Krishna hold every life in their hands."

The Twelve Themes of the Bhagavad Gita

The *Bhagavad Gita* is unlike any book we've ever read before—there isn't much of a storyline and Krishna dominates the entire conversation with esoteric teachings. One of the difficulties in understanding the *Bhagavad Gita* is how disorganized the text seems to be. When we read fiction or non-fiction, there is typically a train of thought or plot to follow—but due to the very high level of consciousness of the *Bhagavad Gita*, it's often challenging to follow Krishna's logic. To help us understand Krishna's teachings, I've organized the entire *Bhagavad Gita* into 12 themes. Chapter One is a transition chapter from the storyline of the *Mahabharata*, where the efforts for peace and preparations for war are covered. Krishna begins His sermon, the *Song of God*, in Verse 11 of Chapter Two, discussing **reincarnation** first, one of our 12 themes throughout the *Bhagavad Gita*. After Krishna talks about reincarnation, He then teaches basic elements regarding the human **soul**—moving on to discuss *dharma*, **Yoga**, **karma**, and **enlightenment**—finishing with one final verse in Chapter Two reintroducing reincarnation.

Chapters Two and Three serve as an overview to what I classify as **primary** and **secondary** themes—all 12 themes are presented in these two chapters. There are **four primary themes**—two primary themes are introduced in Chapter Two, **enlightenment** and **consciousness**, and two primary themes are introduced in Chapter Three, **Krishna** and the *gunas*. One half of all the verses from Krishna relate to these four themes. Krishna and consciousness are one-and-the-same—this is an important point that will be made clearer once we begin to read the text itself.

The *gunas* make the list of primary themes due to the amount of verses contained within the *Bhagavad Gita* and also because of their importance in *Samkhya* (SUM-kya) Philosophy. I'm teaching the *gunas* as different levels of consciousness: *sattva* between the levels of 500 and 599; *rajas* between 200 and 499; *tamas* is everything below 200. Enlightenment is 600 and above. The full spectrum of consciousness from 1 to 1,000 is accounted for. **All four primary themes relate to consciousness and the Universal. The eight secondary themes relate to the individual**—our soul, our actions, our selfless acts, our knowledge and wisdom, our relationship to the Universal, our acts of renunciation, our reincarnation, and our Yoga—the methods used to unite the individual with the Universal.

The eight **secondary themes** are divided equally between Chapters Two and Three and relate to consciousness. Chapter Two introduces reincarnation, the soul, Yoga and *karma*. In Chapter Three, renunciation, *bhakti*, *yajna*, and *jnana* (knowledge/wisdom) are introduced. Krishna is teaching Arjuna about enlightenment, and a major element to enlightenment is reincarnation—when we become enlightened, reincarnation ends. **Yogas are all paths to God**—paths to enlightenment. Six of the eight secondary themes are all different paths to enlightenment—they are all different types of Yoga. The two secondary themes not considered as paths to enlightenment are the soul and reincarnation.

Renunciation is introduced in Chapter Three, it means *motiveless action*. Renouncing selfish activities and attachments to personal outcomes is the very foundation of our spiritual progress. **Yajna** is any selfless act we do to benefit others and it has the potential to erase karma. However, if our motive is to erase our karma, yajna won't work—it has to be selfless and with no attachments (ego) or hidden agendas. Karma Yoga is often understood as the path of selfless service, but I don't completely agree with that viewpoint—karma is quite a bit more complicated than what we might think. Karma is all our thoughts, words, and actions. Everything we do with a selfish motive, ego attachment, or desire creates karma for ourselves—no karma is good karma. I'll break down karma and yajna in upcoming sections—perhaps you'll agree with my subtle interpretation.

Most people think of the physical practice when they hear the word *yoga*. The physical aspect of yoga is actually called *hatha-yoga* or *asana*—but is *hatha-yoga* actually a path to enlightenment? No one is ever going to attain enlightenment by doing *hatha-yoga*—enlightenment is mental, not physical. However, *hatha-yoga* can be thought of as a path to the Path. When my wife and I climbed Mt. Wheeler in New Mexico years ago, we drove from Taos to the trailhead before we began our climb. The road to the trailhead could be thought of as *hatha-yoga*, but the real work began once we got out of the car and started our climb on foot. *Hatha-yoga* led me to Yoga Philosophy and the *Bhagavad Gita*—where the real ascent of consciousness and inner transformation begins.

Krishna is the one primary theme above all other themes. About 90% of the entire text of the *Bhagavad Gita* comes from Krishna, and as you'll notice, every verse spoken by Him has been measured—with nearly every verse calibrating at 1,000! God is embodied in the form of Krishna telling humanity how life works through His teachings in the *Bhagavad Gita*. One of our inherent human attributes is freedom, and from freedom comes choice. We are free to make whatever choices we think are best for us—but as we learned earlier, the human mind is inherently defective—we can't always discern truth from falsehood, which is why we sometimes make mistakes and bad choices. Our level of consciousness is our life compass, pointing each of us to our own setting of *true north*—but we are all calibrated differently. The setting on Duryodhana's compass points to anger, hatred, jealousy, and aggression. The setting on Arjuna's compass is aligned with reason, logic, understanding, and wisdom—two very different settings causing this major conflict.

Another reason the text of the *Bhagavad Gita* is so challenging to comprehend is due to many of the verses containing multiple themes. For example, in Verse 50 of Chapter Two, Krishna says:

> *One who is united to cosmic wisdom goes beyond the*
> *effects of both virtue and vice, even here in this life.*
> *Therefore, devote yourself to Yoga, divine union.*
> *Yoga is the art of proper action.*

All four primary themes and six secondary themes are contained within this one verse. *Cosmic wisdom* is consciousness—*united to cosmic wisdom* refers to enlightenment. *Virtue and vice* refers to contrasting levels of consciousness related to the *gunas* that cause us to be reincarnated, *here in this life*. *Devote yourself* is bhakti and *Yoga* is a path to enlightenment or *divine union*. *Proper action* relates to karma, yajna, and renunciation. Nine themes in one single verse—make it ten—Krishna says it. This is only one example that shows the complexity of the *Bhagavad Gita*. When we start to see the primary and secondary themes and how they overlap and relate to each other, we then begin to see the genius and level of consciousness of the text itself. Before we actually read the *Bhagavad Gita*, we'll explore our themes further to better understand them.

Consciousness – Primary Theme

Our journey into exploring the consciousness of the *Bhagavad Gita* begins with this definition:

Consciousness is the invisible field of energy of infinite dimension and potentiality, the substrate of all existence—formless, independent of time, space, and location, yet all-inclusive and all present. (1,000)

Four verses from three different chapters present an almost identical definition of consciousness. These four verses calibrate at the highest level of truth, 1,000. Krishna is telling Arjuna about who He is.

I am unseen by men. Chapter Seven, Verse 25

The whole world does not perceive Me – unchangeable and beyond all qualities. Chapter Seven, Verse 13

The Great Ruler, smaller than the finest atom, the Supporter of all, unimaginable. Chapter Eight, Verse 9

Without all that exists, yet within; inanimate yet animate; so subtle It is imperceptible; so far and yet so near. Chapter 13, Verse 15

Perhaps the most potent truth Krishna reveals is in Chapter 11, Verse 32. He says: *I am the world-destroying Time, annihilating the world.* Time never stands still—nothing can stop it, nothing can bring it back, and nothing can move time forward. Time as we know it, is a linear concept—an invention of the **linear** human mind. Consciousness is **non-linear**, independent of time and space, which is why there are no secrets. Every thought and action that has ever happened is imprinted on consciousness forever.

Consciousness is the cause of the universe. (1,000)

I am the Source of everything—from Me, all creation emerges.
Chapter 10, Verse 8

Consciousness is the only cause—not only is consciousness the maker, but also the material from which it is made. (1,000)

Know that action comes from Brahma (God's Creative Consciousness); this Consciousness derives from the Imperishable Spirit. Therefore, God's all-pervading Creative Consciousness is inherently and inseparably present in Yajna (selfless acts), which in turn is the essence of all creation.
Chapter Three, Verse 15

The intrinsic quality of consciousness is to create. Manifestation is the consequence of the power of the infinite field of consciousness. (1,000)

*Limitless are the **manifestations** of My divine attributes.*
Chapter 10, Verse 40

Consciousness is diverse. The field of consciousness exists independently of mankind, yet is included within. All Existence is inclusive of existence, but not subject to it. Existence is not subject to limitation. (1,000)

Behold My Divine Mystery! I create and sustain all beings,
but I do not depend on them, nor do they depend on Me.
Chapter Nine, Verse 5

Everything is consciousness. (1,000)

Realizing that everything is consciousness during all
activities, such a one goes to Spirit alone. Chapter Four, Verse 24

I, the Unmanifested, pervade the entire universe in My
formless form. Chapter Nine, Verse 4

There are many verses where Krishna says, *I am,* especially in Chapter 10. If we substitute *consciousness is* in place of *I am,* we begin to understand these verses differently. Below are three examples related to the statement that everything is consciousness.

I am the taste in water – the radiance in the sun and moon –
the Aum in all the Vedas – the sound in the silence – and the
heroism in men. Chapter Seven, Verse 8

I am the sweet fragrance from the earth – the luminescence
in the fire – the life in all beings, and the self-discipline in
anchorites (spiritual hermits). Chapter Seven, Verse 9

Among the powerful, I am the power that is free from
longings and attachments. I am the desire which is in
accord with dharma. Chapter Seven, Verse 11

Consciousness knows only truth – only truth has actual existence. (1,000)

Of the unreal (falsehood), there is no existence. Of the real (truth), there is no non-existence. Chapter Two, Verse 16

Any individual increase in consciousness also raises the consciousness of everyone else. (1,000)

Everything is bound to me like a row of pearls on a thread. Chapter 7, Verse 7

All attractor patterns are connected to each other, if only by a single thread. Everything in the universe is connected with everything else. There are no events in the universe that are not detectable by consciousness itself.

Consciousness is omnipresent in the universe. (1,000)
Here are three verses offering a different perspective of the omnipresence of consciousness.

People will reach perfection (enlightenment) by doing their duty as an act of worship to the Lord, whom all beings are evolved and by whom this entire world is permeated. Chapter 18 Verse 46

Dwelling in the world, enveloping all – embracing everything in the universe. Chapter 13, Verse 13

I pervade this entire world with just a single portion of Myself. Chapter 10, Verses 41 and 42

No physical science reveals the beginning or ending of our existence. (1,000)

Creation is an ongoing process without a beginning or end. The source of our existence has no cause – evolution and creation are the same process. This will be explained in more detail when we look at the definition for *Brahman – the causeless cause.*

*The beginningless Spirit – said to be neither
existent nor non-existent.* Chapter 13, Verse 12

*The beginning of all creatures is veiled, the middle is manifested,
and the end again is imperceptible.* Chapter Two, Verse 28

Humans are materialized from the mind of God. (1,000)

Each and every idea that arises within us is a form of pure Consciousness—our perception is Divine Consciousness. We create our own reality with our thoughts. We all think, perceive, and differentiate between one thing and another—**our mind is God**. Through us, God experiences His own creation.

Two verses from two different chapters speaking to this truth.

*The Light of All Lights, said to be beyond darkness. It is
knowledge itself, That which is to be known, the Goal of all
learning, seated in the hearts of all.* Chapter 13, Verse 17

*I am seated in the hearts of all beings – from Me comes
memory, knowledge, and differentiation.* Chapter 15, Verse 15

The Gunas – Primary Theme

The *guna* theory is perhaps the most important contribution of the *Samkhya* tradition. Understanding the *gunas* is fundamental to understanding the *Bhagavad Gita*. I am teaching the *gunas* as varying levels of consciousness, giving them the designation of a Primary Theme. About 10% of all the verses within the *Bhagavad Gita* relate to the *gunas*. **The *gunas* are consciousness in contracted form.** There are three categories of consciousness connected to our actions and or our behaviors—the *gunas* directly relate to these actions. ***Sattva*** represents actions that are the highest levels of ego-consciousness—from 500 to 599. For example, love calibrates at 500 and compassion calibrates at 536. ***Rajas*** are our actions in the middle—from 200 to 499. The lowest level of consciousness is called ***tamas***—actions and behaviors below 200. For example, pride calibrates at 180, jealousy at 160 and anger 150. We all display a combination of the three *gunas*, accounting for the variety found within human behavior. There are many ways in which to understand the *gunas*, but because this book is concerned primarily with consciousness and human behavior, I believe it is easier to understand the *gunas* in this way. The verses to follow help explain the *gunas* further.

> *There is no one on earth who is free from the gunas.*
> Chapter 18, Verse 40

> *Of these, the pure nature sattva gives light and healing.*
> *It binds through attachment to happiness and attachment*
> *to knowledge.*
> Chapter 14, Verse 6

> *Know that rajas is characterized by passion, the source of*
> *desire and attachment – it binds the embodied soul*
> *by attachment to action.*
> Chapter 14, Verse 7

> *Know that tamas arises from ignorance, deluding all*
> *embodied beings. It binds them by heedlessness, laziness,*
> *and sleep.*
> Chapter 14, Verse 8

> *Tamasic intelligence mistakes wrong from right –*
> *looking upon all things in a perverted way.*
> Chapter 18, Verse 32

We are born with our level of consciousness. An individual's level of consciousness is already in effect at birth. (1,000)

One of the more fascinating aspects of consciousness research is the fact that we are born with our level of consciousness. As of now, we don't know why this is, but perhaps what Krishna tells us in Chapters 8 and 14 may give us some insight into this occurrence.

> *The thought with which a dying person leaves their body*
> *determines – through their long persistence in it –*
> *their next state of being.*
> Chapter Eight, Verse 6 (1,000)

> *When rajas prevails at the time of death, a person is reborn*
> *among those attached to activity. Those who die in tamas are*
> *born in the wombs (environment, family) of the deluded.*
> Chapter 14, Verse 15 (1,000)

Our level of consciousness has the freedom to move up or down. Arjuna's brother losing the kingdom is an allegory for the possibility for each of us to also lose our inherent sovereignty—our God given level of consciousness.

> *Those abiding in sattva (500 – 600) go* **upward** *– those in*
> *rajas (200 – 499) stay in the* **middle** *– Those who abide in*
> *tamas, the lowest guna,* **descend** *(below 200).*
> Chapter 14, Verse 18

The effects from extreme loss of consciousness can have devastating results. Timothy McVeigh, the man who bombed the Federal building in Oklahoma City, his level of consciousness at birth was 338, a very healthy number. The day of the bombing, his level of consciousness was a 19. A more recent example is Omar Mateen, who killed 49 people in the Orlando, Florida nightclub in June of 2016. His birth consciousness was 266—on the day of this awful tragedy, his consciousness was 14. Micah Johnson who killed five police officers in Dallas, Texas in July of 2016 calibrated at 13 the day of the massacre. His birth consciousness was 285. The attack in Nice, France by Mohamed Bouhlel—his birth consciousness was 366 and a 12 the night of the mass murders. Catastrophic events that occur time and again that seem to have no apparent cause most often relate to extremely low levels of consciousness. As a society, we search for reasons as to why these events happen—never once considering the *real* cause. Through the work I've done with consciousness, it's stunning how many people lose their birth level. However, I've discovered it is possible to restore birth levels. I'll write more about this phenomenon in an upcoming section – *The Miracle of Krishna*.

Enlightenment – Primary Theme

For those of us who are not enlightened, trying to understand what enlightenment actually is can be challenging. Advanced states of consciousness beginning at 600 are extremely rare—it's unlikely any of us will ever encounter such a person. Enlightenment can be described as being of infinite peace and bliss, characterized by the disappearance of all desires. The **linear** world (form) dissolves into the **non-linear** (formless) where there is no longer **duality**—a *this* creating a *that*, subject and object become one-and-the-same—the *that* is the *this*. In the enlightened state, there is no division—**consciousness doesn't recognize separation.** At these high levels, everything in life is perceived as occurring in slow motion, suspended in time and space—perfect and complete. Our ego gives the illusion of imperfection and separation—but in the enlightened states, when the ego has been transcended, everything is perfect all the time and there are no longer any other people (egos) to contend with. The mind becomes still, because without a subject or an object, there is no longer a *this* doing a *that*. This state is called ***Brahman*** in the *Bhagavad Gita*—the experience of oneness with consciousness.

Brahman is expounded on in Chapter 13, Verses 12 through 17. Here is Verse 12:

I will describe That which is to be known,
the beginningless Spirit (Brahman) –
said to be neither existent nor non-existent.

Brahman is outside the realm of experience—no experience is *Brahman*, because to experience something, we have to be separate from it. By labelling that essence by the name of *Brahman*, we attempt to give form to the formless—and by doing so, it's no longer formless. Yes, it is confusing—many have tried to describe what *Brahman* actually is, but perhaps the best explanation comes from the *Tao Te Ching*, written by Lao Tzu around 600 BCE in China. In Verse 14, Lao Tzu writes:

That which we look at but cannot see is the invisible.
That which we listen to but cannot hear is the inaudible.
That which we reach for but cannot grasp is the intangible.
Beyond reason, these three merge, contradicting experience.
Their rising side isn't bright. Their setting side isn't dark.
Sense-less, unnamable, they return to the realms of
nothingness. Form without form, image without image,
indefinable, ineluctable, elusive. Confronting them,
you see no beginning. Following them, you see no end.

Yet, riding the plow-less plow can seed the timeless Tao,
harvesting the secret transcendence of the Now.

One of my favorite authors and teachers is Ram Dass, whose name used to be Richard Alpert—his guru in India gave him the name Ram Dass, which means *servant of God*. We can't experience Ram Dass without experiencing his guru, Neem Karoli Baba, born in India in 1902. He died September 11, 1973. I calibrate this saint at 981, which is extremely high and extremely rare. His level at birth was 525. Ram Dass and many others have written about this saint and their relationship with him. Reading their writings and recollections of their guru may be the best way for us to begin to understand enlightenment—certainly from a more personal perspective. Enlightened beings have no interest in developing followers or controlling the lives of others. Often, their teachings are very brief and precisely to the point. Neem Karoli Baba exemplifies these truths—his primary teaching was to hold up his index finger and say, *Sub ek! It's all One* —nondual—not two—we are not separate from God. Enlightened beings are not limited by time and space—identification with a personal self is non-existent—there's no ego—there's no difference between self and other. By transcending time and space, we see everything as pure consciousness—everything as the One.

In October of 2014, my wife and I travelled to Taos, New Mexico for a long weekend vacation. For many years the town of Taos has hosted a Wool Festival for all things having to do with fiber arts. Even if you're not into knitting, spinning, and weaving, you'll surely enjoy the fresh mountain air, music, food, and dogs. This wonderful event is held the first weekend in October and the weather is always Chamber of Commerce perfect. Vendor tents are set up around the perimeter of Kit Carson Park on the main street through Taos. Large old cottonwood trees surround the park carpeted with thick green grass makes the perfect setting for any outdoor festival. In the middle of the park are food vendors—tents with tables and chairs for eating—as well as a tent for the many musicians playing throughout the weekend.

Upon entering the park, Martha said, "left or right?" I chose left because of the sun—the morning air was still chilly in the shade. We moved from one tent to another, admiring all the beautiful artistry when about three quarters around the circle of vendors, I decided to sit down under one of the large tents—Martha happily continued shopping without me. I sat down to enjoy the morning—I didn't know I would slip into a state of being I have never experienced.

After settling for a moment, I had the awareness that everything became perfect. Time stopped—there was no past and no future. I had no place to be, nothing I needed to do, and nothing I needed to know. I did not drift off into random thoughts—daydreaming the morning away. I saw everything and everyone without judgment. I remember thinking how beautiful it was that everyone was getting along and cooperating—and if we could do that here at this festival, why couldn't we do the same thing in the world? I was absolutely present, out of my ego, and completely in my soul—pure awareness looking back at itself—a oneness with consciousness. One of my observations during this time was the quality of light, clarity, and color—the shift in beauty I experienced was almost indescribable.

This state of *being* went on for a while, until it was interrupted by a woman asking me if she and her friends could sit at my table. I said, "I wish you would!" My writing isn't remarkable enough to fully describe this event—but it was like a lake that is without motion, clear to the bottom, reflective, and completely still. I crossed over, if only for a few minutes, into enlightenment—and I must say, I hope to experience that state again someday. My level of consciousness during that specific moment was 790. I didn't do anything to cause it—it just happened all on its own. This state of *Brahman* is always right here and right now—the paradox is we are rarely right here and right now—we are in our own way with our thoughts.

Buddha described the journey to enlightenment in the following way. Imagine a mountain of solid rock six miles long, six miles wide, and six miles high. Once every hundred years a crow flies by with a silk scarf in its beak, just barely caressing the top of the mountain with it. The length of time it would take to wear away that mountain is how long it takes to become enlightened.

Below are a few verses from Krishna in the *Bhagavad Gita* speaking to enlightenment or *Brahman*. There are thirty verses within the *Bhagavad Gita* using the word *Brahman*. Remember, the *Mahabharata* is one big poem regarding the process of enlightenment.

Those who have mastered their minds become engrossed in infinite wisdom – they have no further interest in any fruits of actions (outcome). Freed from the chain of rebirth, they attain the state beyond sorrow (Brahman).
Chapter Two, Verse 51

Whoever knows Me to be Unborn and Beginningless, as well as the Supreme Lord of Creation – that person has conquered delusion and attained the sinless state (enlightenment), even while wearing a mortal body.
Chapter 10, Verse 3

Without pride, violence, arrogance, lust, anger, possessions, the "me and mine" consciousness (duality) and peaceful in mind – they are qualified to become one with Brahman.
Chapter 18, Verse 53

Duality

The basic principle of creation is duality, where a **linear** (form, seen) and **non-linear** (formless, unseen) world exists—Individual and Universal. At the levels of consciousness 600 and above, the linear, individual world disappears—duality ceases to be and everything becomes *All One.* If in fact everything is *All One,* then there must be some power making us believe otherwise, creating duality. That power is called *maya*—the **dividing** force in Nature that displays consciousness as a duality, manifesting form out of the formless, finite out of the infinite, the individual from the universal. *Maya* has two functions—to conceal the real and project the unreal. It can be defined as illusion, deceit, and fraud—the real can never be affected by the unreal any more than the earth can be made wet by a mirage. *Maya* is an impersonal force in the consciousness of all unenlightened humans, producing the phenomenon of illusion—

making us believe we are individual and separate from God.

In the laws of Nature, every period of action is followed by a period of rest—sleep always follows action. When Nature goes to sleep after experiencing manifestation, the world of limited experience becomes the cosmic dream of Nature. There are five aspects of limited experience called the **Kanchukas**—Time, *when am I?* Space, *where am I?* Lacking, incomplete, imperfect, *what am I?* Limited Knowledge, *why am I?* And Limited Power, *who am I?* The result of *Maya* and the *Kancukas* is **Purusha** (Spirit) and **Prakriti** (Matter)—Subject and Object are divided and become mutually exclusive. The dual world of Universal and individual becomes permanently established.

> *Only those who surrender to Me (enlightened)*
> *become free from this power of illusion (maya).*
> Chapter Seven, Verse 14

Duality is portrayed in the *Mahabharata* with the Kauravas and the Pandavas—one blood-line, two families. When Arjuna and Krishna are in the middle of the battlefield looking out across at all the men he's about to go to war with; every one of them represents the material, linear world and our *inner* adversaries. In order to become enlightened, Arjuna has to conquer this enormous force, including **Bhishma**, Arjuna's Grandfather—allegorically represented as Arjuna's ego. In order to become enlightened, we have to have God's blessing. Just before battle is to begin, right after Krishna delivers His sermon to Arjuna in the *Bhagavad Gita*, Yudhishthira, Arjuna's oldest brother walks over to Bhishma's chariot and says: *May we have your permission to fight against you?* He then asks: *How will we be able to defeat you? Is it possible?* Bhishma replies: *It is good of you to ask – had you not come to me, I would have cursed you. Death cannot approach me without my permission, and I do not see the man who can even draw close to me in battle.*

In Chapter 10, Krishna says: *God caused man to dream this dream of illusion (maya); it is He alone who can bestow awakening.*

An infinite field of infinite potential organizes all of human behavior. Within this infinite field we call consciousness, smaller fields *(gunas)*, of progressively less power dominate human behavior—everyone embodies consciousness in contracted form. The interactions within these individual fields of consciousness make up the history of civilization. Comprehending life has been through the understanding of a linear model—logical, reasonable, and rational—attempting to make the incomprehensible comprehensible. **Expanding our understanding to a formless, non-linear, intuitive, unseen world, we begin to understand how life and human behavior really works.** The challenge in understanding the linear and non-linear domains is the linear world is observable (form) and the non-linear world is unobservable (formless)—life itself is actually non-linear. Making the shift from our ego (individual) to our soul (universal) and waking up from the *dream of illusion (maya)* of thinking we are who we think we are, we begin to observe the unobservable in all aspects of life—entering into a world where everything becomes possible.

The Power of Allegory and Metaphor

Al-le-gory: A literary, dramatic, or pictorial device in which each character, object, and event symbolically illustrates a moral or religious principle.

Met-a-phor: A figure of speech in which a term is transferred from the object it ordinarily designates to an object in may designate only by implicit comparison or analogy.

The language of Sanskrit is one of the challenges to understanding the *Bhagavad Gita*. **Purusha** and **Prakriti** are two important Sanskrit words that can be understood as **cause** and **effect**. Out of the One *(Brahman)*, in the first glimmer of **duality** comes *Purusha*, Spirit without form—and *Prakriti*, the energy that coalesces into form (matter). It's the Yoga (union) of Spirit and matter that brings creation into manifestation. *Purusha* is the cause and *Prakriti* is the effect. Causality occurs simultaneously rather than as sequence. The cause and the effect are one as neither can exist without the other. This understanding is a fundamental principle called non-dual or **Vedanta**—the most prominent school within the Hindu tradition. Reality is a single homogeneous whole in which all forms are the endless reflection of that One, unborn Spirit *(Brahman)*, who is without beginning and without end.

The major contribution of *Vedanta* philosophy is the additional category of *Brahman*, which causes the initial impulse in Nature—the *Causeless Cause*. Only the existence of an intelligent agent *(Brahman)* can account for the mysterious super-imposition of *Purusa* and *Prakriti*. The primal cause cannot be a modification of *Prakriti*, for then it would be an effect—and an effect cannot affect itself, no more than fire can burn fire. The primal cause **must be separate** and apart from *Purusa* and *Prakriti*.

In the linear world, we believe there are subjects and objects, a knower and a known, setting up models of duality caused by *maya*. In fact, the Maker of all things visible and invisible is beyond both, includes both, and is one with both. This is the essence of enlightenment—awareness is aware of its awareness and of its expression as consciousness. Interestingly, the founder of *Vedanta* philosophy is Badarayana, author of the *Vedantasutra*. Some scholars believe Badarayana is an alias for Vyasa.

The *Bhagavad Gita* combines three main philosophical systems. The *Samkhya* doctrine asserts **two** independent Realities— Spirit and Matter. The *Vedanta* doctrine asserts only **one** Reality that never changes—*Brahman*, but it doesn't reject the *Samkhya* doctrine. The foundation of Yoga philosophy is *Samkhya*, but there is a difference between the two. *Samkhya* relates to the **universal** condition of Nature whereas Yoga relates to the **indi-**

vidual condition of Nature—a single force (Nature) struggling to both separate and reunite. The whole purpose of Yoga is to unite the opposition this force creates. Yoga offers the process on how the individual can know the Universal through direct experience. Arjuna is offered the direct experience of the Universal in Chapter 11. The subtleties of Hindu Philosophy deal with the different perspectives of the relationships between the human soul and *Brahman*, and *Brahman* and the world. The three systems of *Samkhya*, *Yoga*, and *Vedanta* collectively calibrate at 976, which is surprisingly higher than where they calibrate separately. Hinduism in its entirety calibrates at 870.

The Kauravas and Pandavas share one common genealogy, represented in the *Mahabharata* family tree—both families come from one source, one blood-line, going back many generations. It began with Riksha, the son of Samvarana who married Tapati, the daughter of the Sun—their son was named **Kuru**. The Kuru blood-line continued for many generations to Pratipa, who was the father to Shantanu and Bahlika. Duryodhana and Arjuna's Great-Grandfather was Shantanu—Vyasa was their Grandfather. Bhishma was also considered to be their Grandfather, although he had no children of his own. Bhishma and Vyasa were stepbrothers with different mothers and fathers. It's complicated, as many families are.

Bhishma represents ego, and the entire created world is based on this force of individual existence. Bhishma took a vow to never marry and to never take the throne of the kingdom. Bhishma was actually a god—a *Vasu*, incarnated into a human body to fulfill a curse. The curse was to be born on earth as a human and was placed on him by Vyasa's Grandfather, Vasishta, who was *Brahma's* son. *Vasus* are Indra's attendants—Indra is King of the Gods. Bhishma's father was Shantanu, representing Spirit or *Purusha*. Shantanu's first wife was ***Ganga***—she represents consciousness—Nature *(Prakriti)* as **Intelligence**—Bhishma was her son. Ganga is the goddess representing the personification of the Ganges River. After Bhishma was born, Ganga left Shantanu and returned to the river. Her disappearance is an allegory for consciousness being hidden and always flowing.

Shantanu's second wife was *Satyavati*—she represents Nature *(Prakriti)* as **matter**. Vyasa was the illegitimate son of Satyavati and his father was the sage Parasara who raised Vyasa in the forest. Vyasa represents the power of discernment—showing insight, judgment, and the ability to perceive life as separate and distinct— singular Reality must project the idea of duality. Vyasa's two sons, Dhritarashtra and Pandu, cleverly represent the One becoming two. Each son has a different mother (each other's sister). Dhrita-rashtra was blind from birth—his mother, Ambika, closed her eyes while having sex with Vyasa due to his appearance, so he cursed her with a blind son who eventually fathered 100 sons, the Kauravas.

Vyasa's second son from Ambika's sister (Ambalika) was Pandu, which made Dhritarashtra and Pandu half-brothers. Pandu ruled the kingdom for a time due to his brother's blindness, but was killed by a curse. This is when Arjuna, his brothers, their wife Draupadi, and their mother Kunti (Krishna's aunt) moved from the forest back to the kingdom to live with their Kaurava cousins. It's a lot more complicated than what has been offered, which is compli-cated enough. Pandu and Dhritarashtra also had a third brother, Vidura, we'll learn about him later. Hopefully my writing has been clear enough to understand the allegory of a singular Reality *(Brahman)* becoming two *(Purusa – Prakriti)* through distinction. The distinction from one to two happens because of *maya,* **the power of illusion, limiting our perception and ability to discern Truth**. Life is an illusion—believing we are individual and separate from the Universal. The complexity of characters, relationships, behaviors, and storylines within the *Mahabharata* is absolutely fascinating and deepens our understanding of the *Bhagavad Gita*.

Power and Force

My favorite quote summarizing the entire *Bhagavad Gita* comes from Ralph Waldo Emerson:

> *To be yourself in a world that is constantly trying to make you something else is the greatest accomplishment.*

The first two words, **to be**, is part of how Plato defined Power— **to be and to let be**. We stay in our power when we **let things be**, especially with those who calibrate below 200. When we become angry, reactive, judgmental, and not take responsibility for our actions—we step into force. The Emerson quote outlines the duality found in the *Bhagavad Gita*. The first three words, **to be yourself**, relates to Arjuna and his four brothers. The next part of the quote: *in a world that is constantly trying to make you something else* is our opposing family, the Kauravas. *Our greatest accomplishment* is aligning with our **dharma**—our purpose and reason for being here—living our **Warrior Truth**. Most people are afraid **to be** themselves—always seeking validation from the outside world. We don't need anyone or anything outside ourselves to validate our existence. What we've been seeking our entire life is **to be** who we are. My definition of a Warrior is someone who is not afraid **to be** themselves and live their Truth.

To be yourself directly relates to our level of consciousness—it isn't until the level of 250 that we begin to have a healthy self-esteem and inner confidence about ourselves. At the level of 250 and above, people are easy to get along with because they're not interested in conflict, nor are they interested in trying to *make us something else*—all of which comes from a lack of power within, much the same as vanity is an expression of low self-esteem. The freedom experienced at the levels of 250 and above is the result of surrendering opinions and expectations. With nearly four out of five people in the world calibrating below 200, the percentage of people calibrating below 250 is even higher. 91% of the world's population calibrates below 250—61% of Americans. That's a lot of people constantly trying to make us *something else*.

Relationships exist between two people and only two people—we all have unique relationships with others that no one else shares. Often our conflicts reveal themselves through our relationships. What other people believe about us is none of our concern—it has nothing to do with us—it's only a projected image of who others *think* we are. Their projected image of others directly relates to their level of consciousness. When others try to define us and make us *something else*, they do that out of their own fear and survival instincts. We mistakenly buy into these stories when we act and behave in certain ways in order to be accepted. They want to make us *something else* in order to feel safe. They will never feel safe—no matter what we do! It's so much easier **to be** ourselves when we understand this truth about human behavior and consciousness. What others do or say is never about us—it's about them! As long as we have an image about ourselves and perceive the world as separate and different from ourselves, we will forever be hurt and always have conflicts. Measuring ourselves against something or someone is one of the primary causes of conflict. Our lack of self-worth often manifests by hurting other people.

Our *inner* conflicts of doubt, jealousy, and self-worth keep us from knowing ourselves. Our greatest accomplishment is resolving the inner conflict of *I am this* versus *I should be that*—*to be ourselves* or *something else*. The war of Kurukshetra is not only an outer war of learning how to deal with other people, the war of Kurukshetra also represents our *inner* war of who and how **to be** in the world. We create conflict when we deny *what is (I am this)*—which is the state of being where we no longer have conflicts. When we are unable to face life as it is, fear arises—we can't solve the conflicts within ourselves through escape and fear. Arjuna sitting in the middle of the battlefield with Krishna represents this truth—Arjuna isn't going anywhere—he has to overcome his fears and fight, and we do too. **All of our fears are based on falsehoods**

and illusions. Replacing falsehoods with truths, unknowns with knowns, we heal all things seen and unseen. No one can tell us who we are and no one can define us. When we give our power away to others by believing their opinions and projections about who they *think* we are, we've surrendered to Duryodhana and have let him throw us out of our sovereign kingdom.

Our search for truth must be an *inner* search, not an outer search. In Chapter Six, Arjuna expresses his doubts to Krishna—he's not sure about everything Krishna has been teaching him. Instead of looking *within*, Arjuna looks outward. We do this all the time—we look outside ourselves when faced with the smallest of problems. We judge, we blame, we make assumptions, and we accuse others, making them wrong so we can be "right"—creating more conflict in our lives. The truth is—it's us—not something or someone outside of us—our selfishness is the cause. Until we, in our relationships with others, understand ourselves first, we will continue to be the cause of all our future conflicts. How we react to people and situations, especially when we have conflicts, is the best indicator of how well we know ourselves. Reaction equals force—response equals power. Wouldn't it be nice to always be right? As we learned earlier, we can't always be right due to the mind's inability to discern what is true and what is false. Because of that inherent defect in the human mind (the blind King), we make mistakes—sometimes really BIG mistakes.

> *Two types of people exist in this world –*
> *the divine (power) and the demonic (force).*
> Chapter 16, Verse 6

Power is supportive of life and never needs to be justified. Force must always be justified—which results in counter-force, so its effect is limited by definition. Force always moves against something, whereas power doesn't move against anything. Power is compassionate, making us feel positive about ourselves—force is judgmental, which makes us feel poorly about ourselves. Force creates conflict, producing win/lose dichotomies; somebody always loses and enemies are created. Constantly faced with enemies, force needs to be constantly defended. Power makes us strong, while force makes us weak, which is why the Kauravas lost to the Pandavas.

One characteristic of force is arrogance, whereas the characterization of power is humility. Force is pretentious and self-important—it has all the answers—it relies on rhetoric, propaganda, and twisted arguments to gain support and disguise hidden motivations. **Force is a universal substitute for truth**—always distorting truth for its own self-serving purposes. Truth is unassuming and needs no defense. Those who calibrate below 200 must be "right" at whatever cost to themselves or their relationships. Duryodhana was willing to risk his life as well as everyone else's just to fulfill his desire to be king, to always be right, and be in control of everything so he can feel safe. A self-justified attitude (Duryodhana) is the real enemy of peace.

Nothing *out there* has power over us. It isn't life's events, but our attitude and how we choose to react or respond that determines whether such events have a positive or negative effect on our lives— whether they're experienced as opportunities or stress—or whether we choose to give life's events any power. Everything depends on our attitude—the ways in which we think, speak, and hear. A positive person (above 200) will hear what we are saying with a positive attitude and a negative person (below 200) will hear what we are saying with a negative attitude. Our level of consciousness influences how we think—so whatever it is we think of all the time, that is what we will say, hear, and project into the world.

Power Qualities – Above 200

The critical number on the scale of consciousness is **200**— this is the tipping point between weak and strong attractors.

Personal survival is the driving force at levels below 200. All levels below 200 are **destructive** expressions of life whereas levels above 200 are **constructive** expressions of power. Krishna gives us many verses distinguishing those who calibrate above 200—all of them relate to human behavior.

> *Fearlessness, purity of heart, perseverance in acquiring*
> *wisdom and in practicing Yoga, charity, subjugation of*
> *the senses, performance of holy rites, study of the scriptures,*
> *self-discipline, straightforwardness;*
> Chapter 16, Verse 1

> *Non-harming, truthfulness, freedom from anger, spirit of*
> *dedication, peacefulness, non-slanderousness, compassion for*
> *all creatures, absence of greed, gentleness, modesty, reliability;*
> Chapter 16, Verse 2

> *Radiance of character, forgiveness, patience, cleanness, free-*
> *dom from hate, and absence of conceit – these qualities are*
> *the wealth of those born with divine heritage.*
> Chapter 16, Verse 3

> *Discrimination, knowledge, composure, forgiveness, truthful-*
> *ness, control of the senses, peace of mind, joy, sorrow, birth,*
> *death, fear, courage; Harmlessness, equanimity, serenity,*
> *self-discipline, charity, fame, and infamy – these diverse*
> *states as modifications of My nature (Consciousness) are*
> *created by Me alone.*
> Chapter 10, Verses 4 and 5

Force Qualities – Below 200

With nearly 80% of the world's population calibrating below 200 (49% in America), it's rather obvious why we have so much conflict in our lives and in the world. I usually know which side of 200 I may be interacting with—and if I don't know, I can quickly calibrate any individual. Typically, I don't get too involved with people below 200, and if I do, I am very careful about being reactive and stepping into force with them—it's crucial we stay in our power at all times. People below 200 will often dismiss and discredit those who calibrate higher out of fear. Unfortunately, fear runs far too much of the world we live in. One of the subtle ways in which fear shows up is through status quo behavior. Organizations also have collective levels of consciousness that often make safe, status quo decisions. Individuals who never take risks most likely calibrate below 200. A characteristic of someone calibrating in the 400's is the ability to take risks. Notice that the following verses all relate to human behavior as well.

> *Pretentiousness, arrogance, conceit, anger, harshness, and ignorance – these qualities mark the person who is born with a demonic nature.*
> Chapter 16, Verse 4

> *The demonic lack purity, truth, and proper conduct – they say, "The world has no moral foundation, no truth, and no God." They are enemies of the world. All their actions are impurely motivated. Such persons are engrossed in earthly concerns until the moment of death. Bound by selfish hopes and expectations, they are enslaved by anger and passion. "This is my present wealth – however, more shall also be mine. I have killed this enemy. I am successful, strong, and happy. I am rich and well-born – can any others be compared to me?" Harboring bewildering thoughts, they sink into a foul hell. Vain, stubborn and intoxicated by pride in wealth; egotistical and prone to rage, these people despise Me.*
> Chapter 16, Verses 7 through 18

Lacking in insight, their desires, thoughts, and actions are all vain (self-absorbed). These people possess the deluded nature of fiends and demons.
Chapter Nine, Verse 12

We Must All Battle Duryodhana

Not only is the *Mahabharata* a long narrative regarding the process of enlightenment, it is also a book about relationships and human behavior. Every good story has a villain, and the antagonist through much of the first half of the *Mahabharata* is Duryodhana, the oldest of the blind king's 100 sons. Without an understanding of Duryodhana, we might overlook the importance of this character. Metaphorically, Duryodhana is anything in life that punches us in the gut—something happens and we literally don't know what to do next—life comes to a screeching halt. Duryodhana can be a person, an event, a crisis—and most likely he isn't the same for any two people.

As Arjuna sat in the middle of the battlefield with Krishna, he looked over at the opposition and saw his friends, teachers, and relatives—people he knew very well. The conflicts we face in life are often with people we already know. With four out of five people in the world calibrating below 200, we're bound to have conflicts. Many of the people we already know are Kauravas—those we are related to, live with, work with, and interact with on a regular basis.

Duryodhana's level of consciousness is in the range of 150, his is a world of jealousy, vengefulness, antagonism, anger, hatred, and aggression. Arjuna is a *Kshatriya* warrior, calibrating in the 400's—logic dominates at this level, as well as qualities of understanding, reason, and wisdom. Consciousness calibrating in the 400's is potent and people calibrating below 200 sub-consciously sense it. Those who calibrate below 200 are already negative, projecting all sorts of disapproval toward those they don't understand and perceive as a threat. This is a fascinating aspect of consciousness that explains much of human behavior. Survival instincts heighten below the level of 200 and intensify as they lower down the scale. It must be awful to be so fearful that you have to control everyone and everything in order to feel safe—too often in the form of anger and bullying. Living in fear and interacting with someone who doesn't live in fear is no doubt a frightening thing to experience.

Anger is one of the primary emotions for people who calibrate in the 150 range—often expressing itself as resentment and revenge. Anger is connected to desire which often leads to frustration if that desire isn't met. Anger is not the same as violence and aggression—violence is an action—**anger is a form of manipulation used to get what we want**. Few things in life are worse than someone who passes their anger off as self-righteous pride. Angry people are always willing to blame everyone else for what is wrong in their lives, often leading to hatred, which can have devastating consequences. When I state that we must all battle Duryodhana—that means we must look at our anger and how we may be using it to manipulate others. Duryodhana is the metaphor representing anger.

Desire and anger are full of unappeasable craving and
great evil: know this to be the foulest enemy here on earth.
Chapter Three, Verse 37

The distortion of truth (lying) is a symptom of lower levels of consciousness, used to control others and situations as a survival strategy. By distorting truth, it's possible to justify and rationalize any kind of behavior, including anger—making the ends justify the means. Attack, condemnation, revenge, and anger all calibrate at 150. Adolf Hitler said that the bigger the lie the more people will believe it. Hitler calibrated at 141 at the height of his power during World War II. His birth level was 382! Liars mistrust everyone, believing all to be liars, just like themselves.

Duryodhana lives in a world rooted in fear—he has to control everything in order to feel safe. Duryodhana desperately wants to be king—his sense of survival depends on it. Any perceived threat has to be eliminated. Duryodhana was jealous of his Pandava cousins and wanted them destroyed by any means necessary, which is how we come to the famous game of dice in the *Mahabharata*. **Yudhisthira** (Arjuna's older brother) was cheated out of his kingdom gambling. The game of dice was rigged—Duryodhana's uncle, Shakuni, knew how to cheat at dice and the two of them plotted a scheme to cheat the Pandavas out of their entire kingdom. After losing everything they owned in the gambling match, the Pandava brothers and their wife Draupadi were banished from their kingdom for 13 years. Arjuna's brother was the rightful heir to rule the kingdom, and all five Pandavas had to be eliminated in order for Duryodhana to become king.

The Pandava brothers held up their end of the bet, and after being away for 13 years, they returned to reclaim their kingdom. Duryodhana didn't want to give the kingdom back as they agreed, so eventually, war became the only option left. On behalf of Yudhishtira, Krishna went to see Duryodhana to negotiate peace one last time in hopes of preventing war. He asked Duryodhana to restore the Pandavas share of the kingdom—he refused. Krishna then asked for a small portion of territory, then five cities, five villages, and five houses. All efforts to make peace between the two families were declined. Duryodhana exclaimed: "I wouldn't give them the land they could pick up on a needle-point. I dare them to set foot in my kingdom again." Krishna then realized that nothing and no one, not even God Himself could deter Duryodhana from his desire to keep the kingdom—war was the only option left. Krishna Himself authorized the war, saying: *I tried, but war is inevitable, we have to do it.* The *inner* war we all fight is also inevitable—*we have to do it!*

Krishna tried to negotiate a win-win solution, which is how power operates. Force produces win-lose dichotomies—the rights of the accused conflict with rights of the victim. Because of the negative emotions below 200—the rights of others are ignored. The rights of restoring the kingdom back to the Pandava brothers were ignored by Duryodhana. Those who calibrate below 200 are very self-centered, even narcissistic. Having read this far, I doubt you are someone who calibrates below 200 and you probably wouldn't have picked up this book!

Prior to the war, leading up to the *Bhagavad Gita* in the *Mahabharata*, Arjuna and Duryodhana went to Krishna to solicit His support. The two cousins arrived about the same time, but Duryodhana arrived a few seconds before Arjuna. Two seats were placed by Krishna's couch where He pretended to be asleep, one at the foot and one at the head. Duryodhana took his seat at the head of the couch while Arjuna stood patiently at Krishna's feet, showing respect and humility. When Krishna opened His eyes, He saw Arjuna first and gave him the first choice. Krishna promised not to fight in the battle, but one side could have His army and the other could have Him. Without hesitation, Arjuna chose Krishna (Power)—Duryodhana was more than happy to accept Krishna's army (Force).

In Chapter Two, Arjuna has second thoughts about engaging in battle—Krishna warns Arjuna what will happen if he backs down from the fight: *the mighty chariot warriors will assume that you have shunned this war through fear.* Krishna reminds Arjuna that he is a *Kshatriya* warrior and it's his duty to fight—and if he doesn't fight, everyone is going to think he's a coward—which is a fate worse than death for a great warrior like Arjuna. Krishna tells Arjuna that a warrior should seize any opportunity to fight for a noble cause and that it's a sin against our souls to surrender and acknowledge defeat when faced with any kind of challenge. Krishna commands Arjuna to *stand up and fight!* We must all stand strong in our power and fight, no matter how great the challenges we may face in life. The Universe will not give us more than we can handle—whatever life throws at us—we are equal to that challenge.

Arjuna stays in his power when he sits down in his chariot at the end of Chapter One and asks Krishna for guidance. Arjuna doesn't react—he sits and listens, waiting to know what the next right move should be. When we become reactive to life, we move immediately into weakness and force—abandoning our inner strength and power, and thereby surrendering to Duryodhana.

The Complexity of Karma

In Chapter Four, Krishna tells us *the nature of karma is very difficult to understand.* Karma can be very challenging to fully comprehend—yet it's critical in our understanding of the *Bhagavad Gita*. In Chapter One, Arjuna says to Krishna: *Should we not know to avoid sin – we who distinctly perceive the evil, even if these Kauravas understanding is eclipsed?* The word *sin* from this verse means a mistake—a consequence of our mind not being able to discern truth from falsehood (whose understanding is eclipsed). Mistakes have effects or results that create karma.

Karma is the explanation of everything and is often understood as cause and effect—*if this, then that.* This linear definition of karma is the easiest to comprehend since most of us live in the linear world. For example, if we hold our hand over a flame for too long, we get burned—however, *this* causing *that* is not entirely correct. *This* causing *that* is the mental concept of a sequence—which is not cause. A causes B causes C is called deterministic linear sequence. Everything is actually occurring spontaneously (non-linear) as a consequence, and not by some external condition. The flame isn't the cause of our hand being burned. The potential becomes the actual by the power of consciousness when conditions permit, but the conditions (flame) are not the cause. Manifestation is the consequence of consciousness. Why did we hold our hand over a flame? *Should we not know to avoid sin?*

People are always trying to correct effects instead of causes, which is why human consciousness evolves so slowly. **There** are no causes within the observable world—the observable world is a world of effects—cause is a concept that has no actual existence in Reality. Causes are unseen—only the manifestations of effects are observable. Binding karmic actions are not caused by the physical body itself, but by the consciousness that creates those actions. Being an instrument of our ego, we become liable for the karmic consequences of our actions.

Karma-mala

> *Those deluded by the sense of "I" think, I am the doer.*
> Chapter Three, Verse 27

Consciousness becomes **limited** in the human mind through identifying with **separation** *(anava-mala)*, **difference** *(mayiya-mala)*, and **doership** *(karma-mala)*. *Mala* means *impurity* or *to stain*. We mistakenly believe we are the one's doing, thinking, and deciding everything—this is how our linear mind—our ego mind works. We take credit for our success, but when we fail, we tend to use blame, become frustrated, and sometimes get angry from our desires not being met. *Karma-mala* (doership) keeps us ignorant of the one source of all action—**consciousness**. However, *karma-mala* simultaneously enables our souls to fulfill their desires and intentions for experiences. Our belief of *I'm doing this* is the seed for another action we'll be accountable for in the future. Truly selfless actions are very rare—our hidden agendas, motivations, and attachments to our actions create karma in our lives. Vivekananda explains the law of karma in his book, *Practical Vedanta:*

> *Everything that one does leaves mental impressions*
> *(samskaras) that must become experiences, and yet,*
> *given the number of impressions, several bodies (lifetimes)*
> *are required just to experience them all. Inexorably, one is*
> *bound to recurrent cycle of lives.*

Karma is the force that propels our destiny—and our destiny is formed by everything we think, do, and say—creating vast numbers of *samskaras* to be lived out. *Samskaras* are the effects of karma and can apply to both positive and negative actions. One of the men leading the battle for the Kauravas allegorically represents *samskaras*. His name is **Drona** and he is the teacher for both the Kauravas (negative) and Pandavas (positive). We'll learn more about Drona in Chapter One.

Karma means we don't get away with anything. Life is a gamble, inviting us to participate in the probabilities—but the odds of engaging with life can be very high. We can calculate the odds, but we can't always win—but in order to win, we have to participate, because the secrets of life are revealed only by our engagement with life. All of our choices have consequences, but if we are only focused on the results, we probably are not paying attention to our choices. The allegory of the gambling match in the *Mahabharata* is perfect. Yudhisthira wasn't paying attention to his actions when he agreed to gamble with Duryodhana and suffered the consequences of losing his kingdom. Yudhisthira lost due to his ego—he desperately wanted to beat Duryodhana at his own game. This is a powerful teaching of force against force. Yudhisthira is a power person who stepped into force, which often creates a losing situation for the power person. Duryodhana carefully calculated the odds when he lured Yudhisthira into the gambling match (which is why he had to cheat). He also calculated the odds when he waged war against the Pandava brothers—of course, he died and the Pandava's lived. The odds of winning aren't very good when you bet against God—the consciousness of force always causes its own destruction.

In Chapter Two, Verse 47, Krishna tells us to *perform all of our actions without being attached to the outcome*. We must pay attention to our actions and not the results—consequences come second. Our inattention is a type of action—by only focusing on the results, we will never know our inherent worth. We will not create karma when our actions are in authentic alignment with our soul—a perfect definition for **dharma**. Karma Yoga has three elements: alignment with our *dharma*; no attachments to the results; and the understanding that we really aren't *doing* anything—God is doing everything! Or, if the third part is too big of a step to take, consciousness is the cause of our actions, but we still have to pay attention. In Ram Dass's book, *Paths to God*, he explains this in the most beautiful way:

> *If you're going to make a cup of tea right, you can't be busy trying to make the cup of tea right, because while you're busy trying, you're not present with making the tea. You can't be doing both. The right way to make a cup of tea is to start by bringing together everything you need to make the tea, including the knowledge of how to do it. And then you make the tea. While you're making the tea, you're just making the tea – nothing else. You're not worrying about how the tea will turn out, and you're not wondering whether you're good enough to make the tea correctly, and you're not thinking about whether you should serve it with honey. You're just right there, making the tea – being present with every step and acting out of the total harmony of each moment.*

Ram Dass continues:

> *We can't pretend we're right there making the tea when really we're not, when really we're lost in a thought of how well we're making the tea. Until we're no longer attached to our egos in any way, every act we do will have our ego present in it.*

We stand strong in our power when our actions are performed for their own sake, rather than as a means of projecting, enhancing, or conforming to some false image. Our power comes from aligning with our truth and purpose—our *dharma*—not trying to appear greater than we actually are. When we stand steadfast in our power, no matter how strong the negativity directed toward us may be, knowing that whatever is said or done to us doesn't define us, we will never be harmed. If, however, we become reactive (force) from the negativity directed toward us, we have turned our power over to our assailant, giving them permission to hurt us. Yudhisthira losing the gambling match to Duryodhana is a perfect example of this teaching. In contrast, the Pandavas stood strong on the battle-field, even though they were vastly outnumbered—they had Truth on their side (Krishna), and knew their fight was morally right.

> *Consciousness takes no account for anyone's virtue or sin.*
> Chapter Five, Verse 15

Everyone is born under optimal conditions for karmic op-portunities and spiritual evolution (elevation of consciousness). Karma has nothing to do with luck—good or bad. Good karma is no karma. Consciousness (Krishna) is **indifferent**—we are the ones who are solely liable for our actions and choices. Krishna pretending to be asleep when Arjuna and Duryodhana came to ask for His help is an allegory for the indifference of conscious-ness. Arjuna and Duryodhana both made their choices independently of Krishna. Karma is all about the choices we make in life—we have the freedom to align or misalign with Krishna.

> *I remain indifferent and unattached to these actions.*
> Chapter Nine, Verse 9

The war between the Pandavas and Kauravas tells us we don't have a choice about the fight (our participation in life)—but we do have a choice about which side we'll fight for. Krishna doesn't resolve our conflicts, but He does give us the freedom to choose which side to align ourselves with. Krishna gave Arjuna the choice to choose Him or His army—power or force. **Our destiny is not God's to decide, but our choice to decide.** We gamble with our life and destiny when we place our bet on our selfish desires. Arjuna didn't hesitate when he chose Krishna to drive his chariot in the war. Arjuna also calculated the odds, and placed his bet on God.

Duryodhana decided that *the death of my enemy is worth any loss, including my own.* Higher levels of consciousness are better able to discern truth from falsehood, allowing those with higher levels to make better choices. When we know better, we do better. **Consciousness always favors what benefits the whole.** That which supports life is always supported by life. Levels below 200 are egocentric and self-centered. Those below 200 are most likely not going to make choices that benefit the whole, but will instead make choices they think will benefit themselves. Yoga is the participation in something greater than ourselves. Do our choices in life benefit the whole, *something greater,* or do our choices only benefit our selfish desires? There are consequences in making choices that only benefit our selfish desires—Duryodhana learned that lesson with his life.

> *Therefore, perform the work that must be done, without*
> *attachment. By performing all actions (karma) without*
> *self-interest (ego), one obtains the highest good.*
> Chapter Three, Verse 19

Those who calibrate below 200 are problem people—they are self-centered and often challenging to be friends with—relationships are on their terms. When the wheels fall off in life, we soon find out who our true friends are—or who they are not. People we thought were our friends are suddenly nowhere to be found when we're in crisis. Human behavior is rooted in survival—hard-wired into us from the beginning of time. When we are in crisis, that crisis can often be perceived as a threat to the survival of those friends who are now nowhere to be found.

Much of the *Mahabharata* is about relationships—and of course the primary relationship in the *Bhagavad Gita* is between Krishna and Arjuna. One of the aspects the *Bhagavad Gita* addresses is our relationship with God. This is emphasized in Chapter 11 when Arjuna finally realizes who he's been friends with for most of his life—God! As soon as Arjuna figures out that Krishna is God, he begs His forgiveness for all the times he's been so casual with Krishna—not showing Krishna the respect He deserves. Part of the power from Chapter 11 is how it emphasizes our relationship with God and how casual many of us have also been in that relationship. When everything in life is going well, we tend to take God for granted—our respect is casual at best. But when crisis strikes and we cry out for God, what then? Will Krishna be that *indifferent* friend who is suddenly nowhere to be found? The *Bhagavad Gita* offers us the opportunity to clearly define our relationship with God, once and for all. Krishna is always there for us—no matter what—asleep on His couch, waiting patiently for us to wake Him.

There are many reasons why it's important to raise our individual level of consciousness, but perhaps the most important is our happiness. There are sizeable differences in happiness with those calibrating above 200 and those calibrating below. As the levels of consciousness increase, so does the rate of happiness. From level 200 to 300, 60% are happy—life is good. From levels 100 to 200, a dramatic decrease occurs—only 15% of people are happy. From 300 to 400, 70% are happy; from 400 to 500, 79%; from 500 on up, nearly 100% are happy. What's interesting about happiness is that the actual source of happiness isn't outside us. Those calibrating below 200 can be very materialistic, thinking, *the more I have the more I am and the happier I'll be.*

*Everything is bound to me like a
row of pearls on a thread.*
Chapter Seven, Verse 7

When one person elevates their consciousness, everyone's consciousness is also affected. It's in the best interest of everyone on the planet to elevate their own personal level. Not only is our level of happiness affected by our level of consciousness, but also unemployment, poverty, and crime. Above 200, unemployment is 8%; below 200, unemployment is 50%. Poverty above 200 is 1.5%; below 200, poverty is 22%. The rate of crime above 200 is 9%; below 200 the rate is 50%.

The Miracle of Krishna

This section you are now reading created the most internal conflict for me during the writing of this book. Much consideration was given to whether or not I should share this information with anyone who reads *Warrior Truth*. The last thing I want to project is some sort of ego-trip. We just went over cause and effect and how the effect is confused with being the cause. The story to follow is a real-life example of the consequences of misunderstanding the effect for the cause. In this example, I considered the cause and not the effect. Many behavioral disorders could possibly be related to very low levels of consciousness, including depression, which calibrates at about 124; eating disorders, 131; and possibly sexual abuse, 66. The treatment of many behavioral disorders is often treated with low consciousness drugs. The young man in the upcoming story was put on three different medications, all calibrating around 86. Aspirin for example, calibrates at 792 and penicillin calibrates at 947! One of the more popular anti-depressants on the market today calibrates at 84. Marijuana calibrates at 87. Treating low levels of consciousness with low level substances can have devastating results, in my opinion.

In November of 2015, while working on this book, a friend I've known since 1972 contacted me about her son. The last time we communicated, her son was off to college and everything was fine. A few years later, her son was living at home and had been diagnosed with schizophrenia. This is a frightening word and one I know very little about. The first thing I did was calibrate his consciousness—it was 96. I then calibrated his birth consciousness—it was 260. She confided in me that her son tried to take his life, so I measured and found that his lowest level was 52. Had it been 50, he may have completed suicide.

As we learned earlier, Krishna is indifferent—He waits patiently for us to approach Him. My friend's son couldn't go to Krishna to ask for help, so I went on his behalf. Much the same as Arjuna going to Krishna to ask for help—I too asked Krishna to restore this young man's consciousness back to his birth level. In nine days his level rose 164 points! It continued to rise above 300 eight days later. Without telling his mother, he stopped taking his medications without any side effects. At level 266, his "schizophrenic" behavior cleared and my friend got her son back. I believe the cause for his abnormal behavior was a very low level of consciousness—his doctors treated the effects with drugs. It's my belief the medications he was taking held his low level of consciousness in check. I didn't have to see him, talk to him, or have any communication with him, because consciousness is beyond space and time. Everything in the universe is connected with everything else—if only by a *single thread*. There are no events that are not detectable by consciousness itself.

The following is the experience written by the mother for this book.

I am the old friend Ted writes about in this book. My son is the one who was diagnosed with Schizophrenia while in his early 20's. He did, in fact, attempt suicide and was hospitalized a couple of times. There were many psychiatrists who had opinions about what my son's illness was and everyone had their own idea on how to treat him. Because of this, my son was given many medications and different combinations trying to find the "right" one. I contacted Ted to ask if he knew any yoga/spiritual places in our area – my son had expressed an interest in trying a different approach to his "illness". Ted listened to the history and asked if he could intervene on my son's behalf. Of course, we were ready to try anything. The next month was truly miraculous! I am still unsure of what Ted did, but my son continued to improve daily. What he did, worked, and my son is back. I continue to wonder what would have happened if Ted had not come into the picture: more medications – more combination of medications – more psychiatrists unsure of what to do – more hospitalizations? His future would have been bleak. May 3, 2016

We all suffer hardships throughout our lives—at some point we all stand in no-man's-land, wondering how something happened and what should we do next. The choice is ours and ours alone—our best choice is to do what Arjuna did—sit down, get quiet, become humble, and ask Krishna for guidance. We can surrender the kingdom that is rightfully ours or we can stand up and fight for our sovereignty. With some people, something happens that causes them to plummet in consciousness—and due to these very low levels, they exhibit abnormal behavior and start making bad decisions—attempted suicide for example. They may drop to such a level that they show signs of behavior that become labeled as schizophrenic. No longer having enough power to fight for their sovereign level of consciousness—they need someone to ask for help on their behalf. Krishna is always there for us—always ready to help and He will never say no, we only have to ask.

Because we can't see consciousness, some may doubt its existence—or if it does exist, some may believe it exists equally for everyone. We all have different levels of consciousness and because of this variety—we have a wide range of human behavior. Some behaviors we can't explain, so we label it and treat the effects with drugs hoping to get a different effect, often overlooking the cause. This is the reason consciousness evolves so slowly—we can't see it, so we confuse the effects with being the cause. **There are no causes within the observable world—the observable world is a world of effects—cause is a concept that has no actual exis-**

tence in Reality. Causes are unseen—only the manifestations of effects are observable.

My research indicates that those who calibrate at 495 or higher potentially have the ability to raise the consciousness levels of others. But remember, Krishna is actually raising the level, not the individual—I went to Krishna to ask for His help. My internal conflict was, do I share this information, or do I keep this information to myself—only helping those who may come into contact with me? My thoughts go to our veterans who are experiencing an epidemic in suicides. The cure for that epidemic may now have been discovered. The potential and possibilities are mind blowing—but human reason will continue trying to explain what can never be explained. Right now, you may be trying to use reason to explain this occurrence. **We cannot use reason in the understanding of God's law**—we would only be wasting our time trying.

My friend was certainly skeptical, even when I tried to explain what I was doing. Imagine being in her position, not knowing what to do for your child and not finding any answers through modern medicine? Odds are you can think of someone right now who may be suffering from low levels of consciousness. If someone you know has changed from who you used to know—it's possible that's what may be happening with them.

Levels of consciousness can stay the same throughout one's lifetime or move up or down. In the *Mahabharata*, these choices for the movement of consciousness are represented by three different characters. *Vidura* is King Dhritarashtra's and Pandu's half-brother who is insulted by his nephew Duryodhana one too many times and vows not to fight in the war for the Kauravas. He chooses neither side and leaves the kingdom, remaining neutral. *Yuyutsu* is King Dhritarashtra's illegitimate son who crosses over from the Kaurava side to the Pandava side just before battle is to begin, choosing the path of righteousness. He is one of 11 warriors to survive the war and the only surviving Kaurava. He represents an elevation in consciousness. *Karna* learns from Krishna before the war that his mother is Kunti and his father is Surya, the sun god. He is the oldest brother of all the Pandavas, and if the Pandavas win the war, he could take his rightful place as king instead of Yudhisthira. No one knowingly chooses to lower their consciousness, but Karna stays where he is—choosing the Kauravas over his own brothers, representing a lowering of consciousness.

We are ready to begin our discovery into the power of the *Bhagavad Gita*. A lot of material has been covered to fully enjoy this amazing text. I'll keep us on track and guide us every step of the way. When we finish the text itself, I'll outline a practice we can use in our daily life to help elevate our consciousness. My sincerest wish is that my efforts will enrich the lives of everyone who reads this book.

Aum Vaasudevaya Namaha!

The Bhagavad Gita

Many warriors are listed in the first 11 verses of Chapter One—if we haven't read the *Mahabharata* prior to the *Bhagavad Gita*, we don't know who all these people are and how they relate to the text. We are given just enough information to figure out we have good guys and bad guys and Arjuna is stuck in the middle of it all. Arjuna has a history and relationship with everyone listed in these opening verses—he knows all of these people very well and they know him too. Not only are these warriors represented as external relationships, but also our emotional traits we may be all too familiar with—our anger, envy, selfishness, doubts, impatience, jealousy, desire, etc. The *Mahabharata* is a very long and complex narrative regarding the process of enlightenment—in order to become enlightened, we have to conquer and transcend our negative emotional traits. Transcending our ego is the most difficult of all—represented as Arjuna's Grandfather, Bhishma, who Arjuna mortally wounds on the tenth day of battle. The allegory of Arjuna fighting Bhishma is rich with mean-ing. The human ego (Bhishma) cannot be overcome except by an act of will—represented by Arjuna. While Bhishma lay dying, he told Arjuna's brother Karna: *let the war end with me.* After Karna left, Krishna walked unseen beside Bhishma to end his pain, thirst, and hunger, letting Bhishma sleep in peace on the thou-sand points of arrows Arjuna shot into him during their battle.

Vyasa, the author of the *Mahabharata*, gives "heavenly sight" to Sanjaya, King Dhritarashtra's personal attendant. Vyasa tells Sanjaya that he won't be harmed at Kurukshetra and will know everything that happens, day or night, seen and unseen—even the thoughts of those who are there. The king tells Sanjaya to stay in the Kaurava camp and return when the war is finished to tell him everything that happened. When Sanjaya returned to the king, he said he couldn't tell him everything because he didn't have the heart. The entire story of the battle following the *Bhagavad Gita* in the *Mahabharata* is the narration of Sanjaya. As a literary device, Sanjaya serves as an eye witness and narrator.

WHOM MUST I FIGHT?

CHAPTER ONE (993)

47 Verses

Every verse in Chapter One up to Verse 11 in Chapter Two is allegory and metaphor—with most allegories and metaphors—everything is open to interpretation. My intention is to give you some ideas about what is happening in Chapter One, and hopefully you will be able to translate these ideas to your own life. Duality is presented in the first 11 verses with the listing of good guys on one side versus the bad guys on the other. Allegorically this represents, *I am this* versus *I should be that*; the *reality within* versus our *outside reflections*; the *life we've planned* or the *life that is waiting for us*. These three examples all point to **dharma**—our purpose in life and *Warrior Truth*. The Kaurava warriors can be an allegory for others projecting how we're defined. Are the projections others place on us the truth? When the warriors start blowing their conch shells in Verse 12, this is an allegory for all the distractions of life—mostly the negative thoughts and doubts we have about ourselves. It can also be other people's opinions and projections about what we should do, how we should do it, and who we should be. Sometimes it can feel as if a lot of people are blowing their conch shells inside our head. Arjuna then asks Krishna to drive his chariot into the middle of the battlefield so he can see what he's up against. This is no-man's-land, where we don't know what to do next. Times like these can be overwhelmingly lonely. This is where we have a showdown with ourselves, taking a hard look at our personal issues. In truth, I think most people know deep inside what they need to do, but it can be so frightening to make the decision to stand up and fight for our kingdom. Many of us, including Arjuna, make long lists of excuses and reasons not to do what we know we have to do—it can be a radical change in life—starting a new career, ending a relationship, getting a divorce, etc. In the last verse of Chapter One, Arjuna surrenders to Truth—the first step in aligning with our *dharma*.

King Dhritarashtra asked Sanjaya:

Verse 1: *On the holy plain of Kurukshetra, when my offspring and the sons of Pandu had gathered together – eager for battle, what did they, Sanjaya?*

King Dhritarashtra's blindness represents the human mind being incapable of discerning truth from falsehood. He is the father of 100 sons that represent our negative emotional traits below level 200. For example, revenge, anger, greed, hate, jealousy, envy, lust, abuse, stubbornness, dishonesty, meanness, cruelty, the desire to hurt others, harsh speech and thought, impatience, selfishness, arrogance, conceit, pride, sensitive feelings, laziness, cowardice, spiritual indifference, stupidity, impulsiveness, fear of death, worry, superstition, too much sleep, too much eating, pretense of goodness, partiality, doubt, pessimism, etc. This mix of lower levels of consciousness becomes highly defended when confronted with any kind of challenge due to the ego's will to survive.

Sanjaya answers:

Verse 2: *Then King Duryodhana, having seen the armies of the Pandavas in battle array, repaired to his teacher (Drona), and spoke as follows:*

Duryodhana represents anger, hatred, and aggression: *Dur* – "difficult" and *yudh* –"to fight".
Drona (habit, *samskara*) is the teacher to both the Kauravas and the Pandavas – the powerful force of habitual tendencies. *Sams-*

karas are both the negative (Kauravas) and positive (Pandavas) impressions made on the conscious and subconscious mind by past thoughts and actions. Material desires (Duryodhana) supported by habits, (Drona), are all powerful!

Verse 3: Sanjaya continues telling the King that Drupada is aligned with the Pandavas.

Oh teacher, behold this great army of the sons of Pandu, arranged in battle order by the talented disciple, the son of Drupada.

Drupada (dispassion) is the King of Panchala. Drona and Drupada were close friends in childhood. ***The son of Drupada*** is **Dhrishtadyumna**. *Dhrishta* means bold and confident; *dyumna* means glory and strength. Truth-revealing intuition is the only power that can destroy habit. On the 15th day of battle, Dhrishtadyumna cut off Drona's head.

The **Pandavas** listed in Verses 4, 5, and 6 represent the qualities above 200. The Kauravas listed by Duryodhana allegorically represent the specific qualities below 200 that oppose spiritual progress; the soldiers of the ego.

Verse 4: *Here present are mighty heroes, extraordinary bowmen as skillful in battle as Bhima and Arjuna – the veteran warriors, Yuyudhana, Virata, and Drupada;*

Bhima is the second oldest of five Pandava brothers. Bhima will kill Duryodhana by breaking his legs with his mace on the 18th and final day of the war. King Ego (Duryodhana) cannot rule forever.

Arjuna (self-control) is our hero and third Pandava brother.

Yuyudhana (devotion, *shraddha*) is also known as **Satyaki** – who was a close friend to Krishna. Satyaki's grandfather Sini, is the one who battled Bahlika for the right to marry Devaki, Krishna's mother. This is where the generational rivalry within the Kuru bloodline began.

Virata is the King of Matsya, where the Pandava brothers spent their 13th year of exile in in the court of King Virata.

Drupada is King of Panchala and father of Dhrishtadyumna and Draupadi, the wife to all five Pandava brothers.

Verse 5: *The powerful Dhrishtaketu, Chekitana, and Kashiraja; eminent among men, Purujit, Kuntibhoja, and Shaibya;*

Dhrishtaketu is the King of Chedi and a general in the Pandava army. He will be killed by Drona.

Chekitana is a Yadava warrior (Krishna's clan) who fought for the Pandavas.

Kashiraja is the King of Kashi. There was bad blood between his three daughters and Bhishma (Arjuna's Grandfather). Bhishma kidnapped the three sisters to be the wives for his three stepbrothers, Vyasa, Chitrangada, and Vichitravirya. Kashiraja's daughter Amba blamed Bhishma for ruining her life. *Shiva* granted her a wish that enabled her to kill Bhishma in her next life. Amba killed herself to quicken the revenge, taking birth as Drupada's daughter who changed her sex to male becoming ***Shikhandin*** – ultimately helping Arjuna to kill Bhishma.

Purujit is the King of Kuntibhoj and brother of Kunti, the mother of the Pandava princes.

Kuntibhoja is the foster father of Kunti, Arjuna's mother.

Shaibya is also spelled *Shaiva*, relates to *Shiva*.

Verse 6: *The strong Yudhamanyu, the valiant Uttamaujas, the son of Subhadra, and the sons of Draupadi – all lords of great chariots.*

Yudhamanyu was born into the royal Panchala family. His role in the war was to protect Arjuna.

Uttamaujas (of excellent valor) was also a Panchala Prince and along with Yudhamanyu, he was to protect Arjuna, most importantly his chariot wheels.

The son of Subhadra is Krishna's half-sister and Arjuna's wife. Their sons name is *Abhimanyu*, who was 16 during the war and died on the 13th day of battle – killed brutally by his uncle Karna and six other Kaurava men.

The sons of Draupadi: Draupadi is the common wife to all five Pandava brothers and also the daughter of Drupada, who fought for the Kauravas. Draupadi, along with her mother-in-law, Kunti, are two of five virgins in the *Mahabharata*. The *Upapandavas* are the five sons born to Draupadi from each of the five Pandavas. They are Prativindhya, Satanika, Sutasoma, Srutasena, and Srutakarma. They fought in the battle on the side of the Pandavas. All five sons were killed by *Asvattama* on the night of the last day of the war. He survived the war, but was punished and rendered powerless by Krishna to roam the world forever, alone, and without friends. Asvattama is Drona's son.

Verse 7: Duryodhana lists the names of his ego army.

Listen too, about the generals of my army who are prominent among us – I will speak about them now for your information.

Verse 8: *These warriors are thyself (Drona), Bhishma, Karna, and Kripa – victors in battles; Asvattama, Vikarna, the son of Somadatta, and Jayadratha.*

Drona (habit) was the one to advise Arjuna to be devoted to his cousin Krishna.

Bhishma (ego, *asmita*) is Grandfather of the Pandavas and Kauravas – mortally wounded by Arjuna on the tenth day of battle.

Karna (desire, greed, *raga*) is Kunti's illegitimate son by the sun god Surya, the eldest brother of the Pandavas. Karna and Duryodhana were very close friends. Arjuna kills Karna on the 17th day of battle. Self-control kills desire. The evening of Karna's death, Yudhishthira told his brother Arjuna: *I cannot believe the strongest warrior in the entire world is dead. For thirteen years I have not slept without thinking of Karna.*

Kripa (delusion, avidya), Drona's brother-in-law and archery teacher.

Asvatthama (shame), the son of Drona - perhaps the most evil Kuru in the *Mahabharata*.

Vikarna (*dvesha*, greed) is one of the hundred Kaurava sons and Duryodhana's brother.

The son of Somadatta is *Bhurisravas* – he is the first cousin to Dhritarashtra, Pandu, and Vidura. At the Battle of Kurukshetra, he was engaged in a fight with Satyaki (Yuyudhana), killing Satyaki's ten sons. Later on, Arjuna cut off Bhurisrava's hands and was ultimately beheaded by Satyaki. Somadatta's father is Bahlika, Santanu's brother and the oldest warrior to fight in the war – killed by Arjuna's brother Bhima of the 15th day of battle. Somadatta fought for the right to marry Devaki, Krishna's mother. He lost to Sini who fought on behalf of Krishna's father Vasudeva. This is the point in history where the generational rivalry began, culminating in the epic battle at Kurukshetra. Satyaki is Sini's grandson. The war of Kurukshetra goes much deeper in generations than the rivalry between the Kauravas and Pandavas.

Jayadratha (fear of death) is Duryodhana's brother-in-law. Arjuna will avenge the death of his son, Abhimanyu, on the 14th day of battle, severing Jayadratha's head from his body with a razor arrow.

Verse 9: *And numerous other warriors, all well trained for battle and armed with various weapons, are present and ready to give their lives for me.*

Duhshasana is the closest brother to Duryodhana symbolizing anger. Duhshasana is the one who was ordered by his brother Duryodhana to undress Draupadi in front of everyone upon losing the dice game. Krishna famously prevented this from happening by making her sari an endless length of silk.

On the 17th day of the war, Bhima came face-to-face with Duhshasana. Using his bare hands, Bhima broke Duhshasana's right arm and ripped it from his body. He then threw Duhshasana down, jumped on his chest, tore open his ribs, and scooped out his heart.

Verse 10: Duryodhana introduces more warriors

These, our forces, protected by Bhishma are unlimited; whereas their army, defended by Bhima, is limited.

Shakuni represents delusion and is the arch villain of the *Mahabharata*—he is Duryodhana's counselor and uncle. On the 18th day of the war, Pandava brother Sahadeva (resistance to evil) cut off his arms and left Shakuni to die in agony. Shakuni is the one to throw the dice, cheating the Pandava brothers out of their kingdom.

Shalya is the uncle to the twin Pandava brothers, Nakalu and Sahadeva. Shalya represents pride and sided with the Kauravas after being bribed by Duryodhana. The word Shalya means "fault or defect". Pride suppresses qualities over 200 by constricting consciousness.

Kritavarma is the Kaurava warrior representing envy. He was the only Yadava (the clan of Krishna) who fought for the Kauravas. Kritavarma is one of the three villains who planned the murder of the sleeping Pandava brothers, but by misidentification, cut the heads off of the five Pandava children.

Verse 11: *All of you, properly stationed in your places in the divisions of the army, protect Bhishma.*

In the *Mahabharata*, Bhishma counseled Duryodhana against going to war, encouraging him to find a way to make peace with his cousins. Being the Grandfather to the Kaurava brothers and the Pandava brothers, both sides regarded him equally. Duryodhana's existence depends on the support of Bhishma (ego), Drona (habit), and Karna (desire). Ego consciousness is the primary power to delude the positive qualities above 200. Bhishma reveals to the Pandavas the sole way he can be killed in battle by the skill of Arjuna. Bhishma's body was mortally wounded by Arjuna's countless arrows on the tenth day of the war. Even though Bhishma is rendered powerless, he will not die, yet. With the fall of Bhishma, a truce was called and all the warriors from both sides gathered around him. Bhishma said: *if you do not stop the war now, you will all perish.* The war started back up on the 11th day with Drona leading the Kauravas. The ego, represented by Bhishma, cannot be overcome except by an act of the will, represented by Arjuna. Transcending ego and the fear of death is the biggest challenge to enlightenment. Ego says, *without me you will die!* Without an ego, we could not relate to our thoughts, feelings, experiences—and we would not know what we were doing.

Call for Battle – The Noise of Life

These next nine verses are an allegory for everything in life that distracts us—*the noise of life.* We get so caught up in our day-to-day dramas—we can no longer hear our inner voice of intuition. At our yoga studios, we rarely play music during our final resting pose, *savasana.* Even a few minutes of quiet at the end of class can be incredibly powerful. To lie in peace without the noise of life tugging at us and demanding our attention can often be an opening to hear our inner voice of intuition, giving us new insight on life's problems.

Verse 12: *Bhishma, oldest and most powerful of the Kuru blood-line, blew his conch shell with a resounding lion's roar.*

Verse 13: *Then suddenly, a great chorus of conch shells sounded from the Kaurava side.*

Verse 14: *Arjuna and Krishna blew their conch shells.*

Verses 15 through 18: *Krishna, along with the five sons of Pandu, blew their conchs. Following the lead of Krishna and the five Pandu princes, other soldiers blew their conchs.*

Verse 19: *The Kaurava soldiers became worried.*

Verse 20: *Beholding the army of Dhritarashtra ready to begin battle, Arjuna, bearing the banner of Hanuman, lifted his bow and addressed Krishna.*

No-Man's-Land

We all stand in no-man's-land between opposing forces—life is a battlefield of choices. In every moment of our lives, there are choices and consequences that lead us to becoming a victim or a victor. The no-man's-land on the field of Kurukshetra is a metaphor for *I don't know what to do – where do I go from here, and what should I do next?* Crisis can happen to anyone at any time—some catastrophic event happens to us and we are stopped dead in our tracks— having no idea what to do next. No-man's-land is a very lonely place to be when we lose our sense of purpose, just as Arjuna does. For this reason, Krishna stopped Arjuna to give him the teachings of the *Bhagavad Gita*. Whatever battle we are faced with, it must be fought with justice, not desire and anger. When we fight for Truth, we must empty ourselves of wrong intentions and become pure. From this purity comes *dharma*, where we know without a doubt, this is the only thing to do—then, nothing can defeat us.

Verse 21: *Arjuna said to Krishna, please place my chariot between the two armies.*

Verse 22: *On the eve of this war, let me see whom I must fight.*

Verse 23: *Here on this field of Kurukshetra, I wish to see all those who have gathered to fight on the side of Dhritarashtra's wicked son Duryodhana.*

Verses 24 and 25: *Krishna placed Arjuna's chariot between the two armies and said, see Arjuna, this gathering of the entire Kuru bloodline!*

Verse 26: *Arjuna saw members of both armies – grandfathers, fathers, fathers-in-law, uncles, cousins, sons, grandsons, and also comrades, friends, and teachers.*

Verse 27: *With emotional sympathy, Arjuna remembered all the good times.*

Seeing all his kinsmen assembled, Arjuna said:

Verses 28 through 30: *Krishna, my limbs are failing and my mouth is parched. My body trembles – my hair stands on end. I can't remain standing. My mind is rambling – I behold evil omens.*

Arjuna vacillates, and then makes excuses for not wanting to engage in battle.

Verse 31: *Krishna, I do not perceive any worthwhile effect in slaying my own kinsmen in battle.*

Verse 32: *What happiness will it bring to kill them for the sake of a kingdom?*

Verse 33: *The very ones for whose sake we desire empire, enjoyment, pleasure, remain poised here for battle, ready to relinquish wealth and life;*

Verse 34: *Teachers, fathers, sons, grandfathers, uncles, fathers-in-law, grandsons, brothers-in-law, and other kinsmen.*

Verse 35: *Even though these relatives should try to destroy me, still I could not want to destroy them.*

Verse 36: *What happiness could we gain by destroying the clan of Dhritarashtra? Slaying these felons would only put us in the clutches of sin.*

Verse 37: *We are not justified in annihilating our own relatives. How could we attain happiness by killing our own kindred?*

Verses 38 and 39: *They come here without a second thought – but this is not worthy of us. We know better – we must act better.*

Arjuna's logic is based on false reasoning, leading him to the wrong conclusion. He continues adding new arguments to his same line of false reasoning in Verses 40 through 46. These next seven verses are very important—Arjuna is going to have to let go of how he *thinks* he should act in the world—*what should be* versus *what is*—which is the most deceptive way of dealing with life. The moment has come for Arjuna to trust his intuition (Krishna) rather than looking outside himself, behaving the way society dictates, or at least what we *think* society dictates. To go against everything we were taught to believe and way to behave takes the courage of a warrior.

Verse 40: *When the ancient dharma is annihilated, sin (adharma) will overpower the whole family (kula).*

Verse 41: *Krishna, when the women (strisu) become contaminated from lack of dharma, adultery is engendered among the castes (varna).*

Verse 42: *The adulteration of family blood consigns to hell the clan-destroyers, along with the family itself. Their ancestors are degraded.*

Verse 43: *By these misdeeds of family-destroyers, producing admixture of castes, the time-old rites (dharmas) of the caste and clan are annihilated.*

Verse 44: *Krishna, we have often heard men devoid of family religious rites are committed to residing in hell.*

Verse 45: *Motivated by greed for the comfort of possessing a kingdom, we are prepared to kill our own kinsmen – an act surely entangling us in great sin.*

Verse 46: *If, weapons in hand, the sons of Dhritarashtra kill me, wholly resigned and weaponless in battle, that solution will be more welcome and beneficial to me.*

Sanjaya said:

Verse 47: *Arjuna, full of doubt, let go of his bow and arrows and sat down on the seat of his chariot.*

This final verse of Chapter One has great meaning—Arjuna becomes **humble**. Arjuna's bow and arrows represent our human behavioral weapons—our beliefs, our need to know everything, our desire to always be "right", our reactiveness, and all the subtle ways we manipulate others to get what we want, and the not so subtle ways through our anger. Arjuna knows what must be done, but he's resistant to making the choice in front of him—making a list of all the reasons he shouldn't act now. The tough choices we all face are often met with resistance. Only when we become humble can we know the Truth. Krishna is Truth—and through this act of humility, Krishna is now ready to reveal all of life's secrets.

I DO NOT UNDERSTAND!

CHAPTER TWO (996)

72 Verses

Primary, Universal Themes: Enlightenment and Consciousness
Secondary, Individual Themes: Reincarnation, Soul, Yoga, and
Karma

atma – Soul, Self, principle of life and sensation
dharma – code of conduct that sustains the soul, producing virtue
and morality
prajna – wisdom

Here in Chapter Two, Krishna begins His sermon. The imagery presented in Chapter One is potent—Arjuna asks Krishna to drive his chariot into the middle of the battlefield so he can see all the warriors who oppose him. Sunrise is only moments away and both sides are ready to begin battle. As anyone can imagine, Arjuna is having second thoughts about killing his friends, teachers, and relatives. He sits down in his chariot and calls on Krishna to guide him—turning it all over to God. When everything is going well in our lives, we often forget God—our spirituality is random at best. All of us, at some point, are brought to our knees by some catastrophic event—it certainly happened to me. This is when we cry out for help, just as Arjuna does here in the opening of this chapter. Vyasa has brilliantly written a drama that contrasts good against evil—power against force, with God right in the middle of it all, ready to guide us on our personal field of battle. Krishna gave Arjuna the choice to choose Him or His army, and without hesitation, Arjuna chose God. The allegory of Krishna driving Arjuna's chariot is perfect—Arjuna wants God on his side and he wants God to guide him through this intense moment. We are all offered this choice—no one is denied the opportunity to have God drive our chariots and guide our lives. God cannot say no.

Arjuna and his brothers did everything possible to prevent this war from happening. God Himself couldn't stop this war—it has to happen and we often don't understand the big picture of life while it is happening. It usually takes time and patience to see God's plan for each of us. One of my favorite quotes is by Mizuta Masahide, a 17th century Japanese poet. In only nine words, Masahide beautifully sums up these catastrophic moments: *Barns' burnt down, now I can see the moon.* Unimagined gifts can come from every single loss. The events in our lives that bring us to our knees are gifts and opportunities to elevate our consciousness, aligning our lives with our true purpose and creating a stronger connection to the Divine. It's our choice alone as to how we look at these moments. We can look down to see the barn has burned to the ground (negative) or we can look up to finally see the moon (positive).

Sanjaya said to Dhritarashtra:

Verse 1: *Overcome with compassion and sorrow, his eyes filled with tears, Krishna then addressed him.*

Krishna said:

Verses 2: *In such a critical moment, this despondency and behavior is unworthy for an Aryan, it's disgraceful and detrimental to the attainment of heaven.*

Verse 3: *Arjuna, don't surrender to unmanliness, it is unbecoming of you. Rid yourself of this weakness. Arise!*

Arjuna said:

Verse 4: *How can I fight against Bhishma and Drona? They should be worshiped.*

Verse 5: *Being a beggar would be more salutary for me than a life marred by slaying these noble teachers. If I do destroy these mentors, then surely all my happiness will be bloodstained.*

Verse 6: *I can hardly decide which would be better – that they should conquer us, or that we should conquer them? Dhritarashtra's sons stand before us, killing them – we'll have nothing to live for.*

Verse 7: *My inner nature is overshadowed by weakness – my mind bewildered about duty, I pray to You to **advise me** as the best path to follow. I am Your disciple – **teach me**, whose refuge is in You.*

Verse 8: *I don't understand anything. It cannot be done!*

Sanjaya said to Dhritarashtra:

Verse 9: *Arjuna declared to Krishna: I will not fight – then remained silent.*

Verse 10: *Krishna, as if smiling, spoke in the following way.*

Krishna didn't waste His time giving unwanted advice—God waits patiently for us to approach Him and ask for help. When Arjuna and Duryodhana went to see Krishna, He pretended to be asleep on His couch, waiting patiently for the two cousins to approach Him. In Verse 7, Arjuna asks Krishna to advise him and teach him so he can make the best decision.

Almost all social, psychological, and physical fears are an unconscious fear of death. Fear is an anticipation that is focused on the future, which makes all fear an illusion, because the future has yet to happen. Krishna begins his sermon by addressing Arjuna's fears in order to calm him down. **Fear blocks the intelligent understanding of life. Only when we understand ourselves can fear finally end.** The inner battle we all face in life is between our soul and our ego. The ego says, *without me, you will die.* We actually exist and survive in spite of our ego, not because of it. The ego fights to prove death is a reality and God is not. Ego equals survival—it's a product and continuation from the survival of animal evolution—the lower our level of consciousness, the stronger the ego and our need to survive. However, if we lose too much power, we withdraw (level 100), become despondent (level 75), apathetic about life itself (level 50), destructive (level 30), and dangerous (level 20). The root of all fear is ignorance, depriving us of our life, purpose, and *dharma*.

Reincarnation – Secondary Theme

This is the point where Krishna begins His sermon. This is also the point where I include Krishna's verses in Sanskrit and begin to offer calibrations for every verse.

Krishna said:

Verse 11 (999.7) The *Bhagavad Gita* begins

asocyan anvasocas tvam prajnavadams ca bhasase
gatasun agatasums *ca nanuscanti* **panditah**

You lament for those not worth mourning! You justify your sorrow with stories from the past. The truly **wise** mourn neither for the **dead** nor for the **living**.

   Krishna points out to Arjuna that he is thinking one way, speaking in another, and acting in yet another. *You know the truth about the Kauravas – they will commit the worst crimes. You've even said how wicked they are. Then you say something compassionate about them and fail to perform your duty. Your thoughts, words, and actions aren't in agreement.*

Verse 12 (999.9) Non-being can never be

na tvevaham jatu nasam na tvam neme **janadhipah**
na caiva na bhavisyamah sarve vayam atah param

There was never a time when I was not, or you or these **royal ones** – never will any of us cease to exist!

Verse 13 (1,000) Reincarnation

*dehino 'smin yatha dehe **kaumaram** yauvanam jara*
*tatha **deha**ntarapraptir dhiras tatra na **muhayati***

Just as the dweller within this body passes through childhood, **youth**, and old age – so at death is its passage into another **body**; the wise (enlightened) are not **confused** by this.

Verse 14 (999.8) The basic principle of creation is duality.

*matrasparsas tu **kaunteya** sitosna**sukhaduchadah***
agamapayino** 'nityas tams titiksasva **bharata

Arjuna, the ideas of heat and cold, **pleasure and pain**, are produced by contact of the senses with their objects – **they come and they go**. Bear them with patience, **Arjuna**!

Verse 15 (999.8) Enlightenment

yam hi na vyathayantyete purusam purusarsabha
samadukhasukham** dhiram so 'mrtatvaya **kalpate

Those who cannot be disturbed by these contacts, for whom **happiness and unhappiness are the same**, they alone are **worthy** of immortality.

Verse 16 (1,000) Consciousness knows only truth, because only truth has actual existence

*nasato vidyate **bhavo nabhavo** vidyate satah*
ubhayor api drsto 'ntas tvanayos tattvadarsibhih

Of the unreal, there is no **existence**. Of the real, there is no **non-existence**. The final truth of both of these is known by those of wisdom.

Anything that isn't a Reality cannot be calibrated.

Verse 17 (1,000) Consciousness is the cause and only cause

avinasi tu tad viddhi yena sarvam idam tatam
vinasam avyayasyasya na kascit kartum arhati

That Reality which pervades the universe is indestructible.
No one has the power to change the Changeless (consciousness).

Verse 18 (1,000) Transition verse to our next theme, the soul.

antavanta ime **deha nitya***syoktah saririnah*
anasino 'prameyasya tasmad yudhyasva **bharata**

These **bodies** are known to have an end, but the Indwelling Self
(Soul) is **eternal**. It cannot be limited or destroyed.
Therefore **Arjuna**, you must fight!

The Soul – Secondary Theme

Verse 19 (1,000) One Soul cannot kill another Soul

ya enam **vetti hantaram** *yascainam* **manyate hatam**
ubhau tau na vijanito nayam **hanti** *na* **hanyate**

Those who **understand** the Self as the **slayer**; those who **think**
that it can be **slain**: neither of these knows the truth.
The Self does not **kill**, nor is it ever **killed**.

Verse 20 (1,000) *always the same*

na **jayate mriyate** *va kadacin nayam bhutva bhavita va na bhuyah*
ajo **nityah** *sasvato 'yam purano na* **hanyate hanyamane** *sarire*

This Self is never **born** nor does it **ever die**; nor having come into
existence will it ever cease to be. It is birth-less, **eternal**, changeless, and always the same. It is not **slain** when the body is **killed**.

Verse 21 (999.9)

vedavinasinam **nityam** *ya enam* **ajam** *avyayam*
katham sah **purusha partha** *kam* **ghatayati hanti** *kam*

How can someone who truly knows the Self to be imperishable, **eternal, birth-less**, and changeless, possibly think that this **Self** can cause the **destruction** of another? **Arjuna**, who would be **killed**?

Verse 22 (1,000)

vasamsi jirnani yatha **vihaya navani** *grhnati naro 'parani*
tatha sarirani **vihaya** *jirnany anyani samyati* **navani** *dehi*

Just as an individual **casts off** worn-out garments dons **new clothes**, so the body-encased soul *casts off* worn-out bodies and enters others that are **new**.

Verse 23 (1,000)

nainam chindanti sastrani nainam **dahati** *pavakah*
na caiman **kledayantyapo** *na sosayati* **marutah**

No weapon can wound it, **no fire can burn it**, no water can **moisten** it, nor can any **wind** wither it – such is the Soul.

Verse 24 (1,000) Once again

acchedyo 'yam adahyo 'yam **akledyo** *'sosya eve ca*
nityah **sarvagatah** *sthanur* **acalo** *'yam* **sanatanah**

The soul cannot be pierced or cut – it cannot be burnt, **wetted**, or dried. The soul is unchangeable, **all-pervading, eternal**, and **immovable**.

Verse 25 (1,000)

avkakto 'yam **acintyo** *'yam* **avikaryo** *'yam* **ucyate**
tasmad evam viditvainam nanusocitum arhasi

The soul **is said** to be **imponderable**, unmanifested, and **unchangeable**. Therefore, knowing this, you should not grieve!

Verse 26 (1,000) For the sake of argument – in either case

*atha caiman nityajatam nityam va manyase **mrtam***
***tathapi** tvam mahabaho nainam socitum arhasi*

But if you imagine this soul incessantly to be born and to **die**, **even in that case**, you still have no cause to be sorry.

Verse 27 (1,000) Everyone is going to die eventually

***jatasya hi dhruvo mrtyur** dhruvam janma mrtasya ca*
tasmad apariharye 'rthe na tvam socitum arhasi

For that which is born must die, and that which is dead must be born again. Why then grieve about the unavoidable?

Verse 28 (1,000) Beginning, middle, and end

*avyaktadini **bhutani** vyaktamadhyani **bharata***
avyaktanidhananyeva tatra ka paridevana

The beginning of **all creatures** is veiled, the middle is manifested, and the end again is imperceptible, **Arjuna**. Why lament this truth?

Verse 29 (1,000) Behold, describe, and listen

***ascaryavat pasyati** kascid enam **ascaryavad vadati** tathaiva canyah*
***ascaryavaccainam** anyah **srnoti srutvapyenam** veda na caiva kascit*

Some **behold** the soul as a **miracle**. Others **describe** it as **marvelous**. Still others **listen** about the soul as **wondrous**. And there are others, who, even after **hearing** about the soul, do not comprehend it at all.

These three manifestations of beholding, describing, and listening are how the soul reveals itself to human beings. Every person is endowed with two powers of knowing—reason and intuition. **Intuition** is the communication between God and humans. The soul cannot be known through the power of reason, only through intuition. Albert Einstein said: *The intuitive mind is a sacred gift and the rational mind is a faithful servant. We have created a society that honors the servant and has forgotten the gift.* (997)

Verse 30 (1,000) The soul is stronger than the ego

dehi **nityam avadhyo** *'yam dehe sarvasya bharata*
tasmat **sarvani bhutani** *na tvam socitum arhasi*

The One who dwells **in the bodies of all** is **eternal** and **indestructible**, Arjuna. Therefore, you should never grieve for anyone.

Our ego, habits, and desires may affect our consciousness for a while – but they cannot destroy or change our soul. Our God given level of consciousness is our birthright.

Dharma

Krishna now shifts His argument to Arjuna's duty, his *dharma*—which is anything that advances evolution and consciousness. These next eight verses are rather interesting and they bring us back to our Emerson quote – *To be yourself in a world that is constantly trying to make you something else is the greatest accomplishment.* We give our power away when we believe other people's projections of who they *think* we are. Our righteous battle is to live our truth—our *dharma*. No one has the right to tell us who we are. What other people believe about us is none of our concern—it's only a projection of their level of consciousness. Arjuna didn't do anything to Duryodhana—yet, Duryodhana wants to kill Arjuna, his four brothers, and anyone else who he believes threatens his survival. The Pandava brothers are no threat to Duryodhana—it's only a projection coming from his mind. In Verse 32, Krishna uses the word *unprovoked*; all too often people who calibrate below 200 discredit, condemn, and judge others without knowing anything about the other person. Their sense of survival kicks in and all of a sudden someone is trying to make us *something else* in order to feel safe. We must stand strong in our truth and not inwardly waver. When we do so, many will be threatened by our power because they sense our strength and fearlessness. Once we begin to see the subtle ways in which the world is constantly trying to make us *something else*, we increase our power by not believing the projections of who they *think* we are—which most often is something less than who we *truly* are.

Verse 31 (999.9) One's own duty should never be abandoned

svadharmam *api caveksya na* **vikampitum** *arhasi*
dharmyad *dhi yuddhacchreyo 'nyat* **ksatriyasya** *na vidyate*

Even from the point of view of your **own dharma**, you should not inwardly **waver**! There is nothing more auspicious for a *Kshatriya* (level 400 – 499) than a **righteous** battle.

Verse 32 (999.9) An opportunity for the evolution of Arjuna's soul

yadrcchaya copapannam svargadvaram apavrtam
sukhinah ksatriyah partha *labhante yuddham idrsam*

Kshatriyas are **fortunate** when such an *unprovoked* righteous battle has fallen to their lot, **Arjuna** – they find therein an open door to heaven.

Verse 33 (1,000) If you don't fight, you'll be making a big mistake

atha cet tvam imam **dharmyam samgramam** *na karisyasi*
tatah **svadharmam** *kirtim ca* **hitva** *papam avapsyasi*

If you decline to undertake this **righteous combat**, then, having **relinquished** your **own dharma** and glory, you will reap sin (be making a mistake).

The definition of the word *sin* is error. Mistakes are a consequence of the limitations of human consciousness. The human mind and intellect are inherently defective—incapable of discerning truth from falsehood. Socrates said: *All wrong-doing is involuntary, for man always chooses what he believes to be for his good.* (994)

Verse 34 (999.9) Krishna builds His case to get Arjuna to act

akirtim capi bhutani kathayisyanti te 'vyayam
sambhavitasya cakirtir maranad atiricyate

People will always speak of your **disgrace**. For the person with a good reputation, **dishonor** is unquestionably worse than death.

Verse 35 (999.9) more arguments directed at Arjuna's ego

bhayad ranad uparatam mamsyante tvam maharathah
yesam ca tvam bahumato bhutva yasyasi laghavam

The **mighty chariot warriors** will assume that you have shunned this war through fear. Those who once thought so **highly** of you will now think **lightly** of you.

Verse 36 (999.9) and another warning

avacyavadams ca bahun vadisyanti tava hitah
nindantas tava samarthyam tato duhkhataram nu kim

Your foes will speak contemptuously, maligning your **powers.** What could be more **painful** than this?

Verse 37 (1,000) Do your duty and fight this battle

hato va prapsyasi svargam jitva va bhoksyase mahim
tasmad uttistha kaunteya yuddhaya krtaniscayah

If you should die, you will gain **heaven** – if you win, you will inherit the **earth**. Therefore, **Son of Kunti, stand up now** and be determined to fight!

Verse 38 (1,000) Fight!

sukhaduhkhe *same krtva* ***labhalabhau jayajayau***
*tato yuddhaya yujyasva **naivam** papam avapsyasi*

Realize that **happiness and sorrow, profit and loss, victory and defeat** are one and the same – engage in this battle! You will **not** commit sin.

When we fight for what we believe in, regardless of whether we win or lose, it's never a mistake.

Yoga Introduced – Secondary Theme

Verse 39 (1,000) Theory and practice – knowledge into action

*esa te 'bhihita **samkhye buddhir** yoge twimam **srnu***
*buddhya yukto yaya partha **karmabandham** prahasyasi*

I have explained the ultimate **wisdom** of *Samkhya* (theory) to you. Now **hear** about the knowledge of Yoga (practice), understanding both, Arjuna, you shall shatter **the bonds of karma** (become enlightened).

Samkhya (SUM-kya) philosophy is India's oldest philosophical system and has been the single most influential system of thought within Hinduism. *Samkhya* regards the universe as two separate realities—teaching discriminative knowledge *(jnana)*, enabling us to distinguish between Spirit *(purusa)* and Matter *(prakriti)*. Its purpose is to provide knowledge, removing the cause of suffering, and thereby releasing the soul from rebirth. If the soul is indeed free from suffering, misery must then belong to the body. The release from rebirth of the soul is dependent on knowledge and ignorance. *Samkhya* is concerned with the Universal whereas Yoga is concerned with the individual, which is why Krishna tells Arjuna he will now teach him about Yoga.

Verse 40 (1,000) Our efforts are never wasted

nehabhikramanaso 'sti pratyavayo na vidyate
svalpam *apy asya* **dharmasya trayate** *mahato bhayat*

In this practice, no effort for realization (enlightenment) is lost, and what is gained is also never lost. Even a **tiny bit** of this **real religion protects** one from great fear.

Verse 41 (1,000) Inner determination

vyavasayatmika buddhir **ekeha** *kurunandana*
bahusakha hy anantas ca buddhayo 'vyavasayinam

In this Yoga, Arjuna, the inner determination is **single** and one-pointed – whereas the reasoning's of the undecided mind are unending and branch out in many directions.

Kurunandana (Arjuna) – "the pride of the Kuru dynasty"

Verse 42 (999.9)

yam imam **puspitam vacam** *pravadanty avipascitah*
veda*vadaratah partha nanyad astiti vadinah*

The undiscerning rejoices in the **laudatory aphorisms** of the **Vedas**, speaking flowery words and contending there is nothing else;

Verse 43 (999.9) Reincarnation, the consequence of our desires

kamatmanah **svargapara** *janmakarmaphalapradam*
kriyavisesabahulam bhogaisvaryagatim prati

They are filled with desire and have **heaven as their highest goal** (enlightenment), performing numerous sacrificial rites for the purpose of obtaining enjoyment and power; such persons instead embrace the cause of new births, the consequence of these (selfish) desires.

Verse 44 (1,000)

bhogaisvaryaprasaktanam tayapahrtacetasam
*vyavasayatmika buddhih **samadhau** na vidhiyate* (acts for a specific desire)

A discerning state of intellect does not arise in the meditative state of **samadhi** (super-consciousness) in those who cling tenaciously to power and pleasures.

The *Vedas* (to know) in Verses 42, 45, and 46, are the most ancient and highly revered Hindu scriptures. There are four *Vedas* – the *Rig* (998) is the oldest, followed by the *Sama* (984), *Yajur* (999), and *Atharva* (987) *Vedas*. The *Mahabharata* is sometimes referred to as the fifth *Veda*. The *Vedas* are among the highest levels of consciousness ever written, calibrating collectively at 992. The truths declared in the *Vedas* are the exact same truths revealed by Krishna in the *Bhagavad Gita*. The following verses are examples of the over-arching principals of the four *Vedas*.

The **Rig Veda** declares: *The Absolute is Consciousness* (1,000)

Chapter Three, Verse 15: Everything is a manifestation of the Divine.

Know that action comes from *Brahma* (God's Creative Consciousness); this Consciousness derives from the Imperishable Spirit. Therefore, God's all-pervading Creative Consciousness is inherently and inseparably present in *Yajna*, which in turn is the essence of all creation.

The **Sama Veda** declares: *Thou art That* (1,000) The Soul is the same as God.

Chapter 15, Verse 7 (1,000)

A fragment of My eternal Self takes the form of an individual soul within every creature.

The *Yajur Veda* declares: *I am the Absolute* (1,000)

Chapter 10, Verse 8: *I am the Source of everything – from Me all creation emerges.*

Chapter Nine, Verse 4 (1,000)
I, the Unmanifested, pervade the entire universe in My formless form.

The *Atharva Veda* declares: *The Self is the Absolute* (1,000)

Chapter 18, Verse 18 (1,000) Knowledge unites knower with that which is known.

There are three things which motivate actions: knowledge, the knower, and that which is known. There are three constituents of action: the means, the purpose, and the doer.

Krishna continues:

Verse 45 (1,000) The first verse concerning the *gunas*

traigunyavisaya veda nistraigunyo *bhavarjuna*
nirdvandvo nityasattvastho niryogaksema atmavan

The *Vedas* teach us about the **three universal qualities, or *gunas*. Transcend** that domain Arjuna, beyond the pairs of opposites (duality)! Always abiding in purity, harboring no thoughts of receiving and keeping, and be the master of yourself.

Verse 46 (1,000) Those who know *Brahman* know everything

yavan artha udapane sarvatah samplutodake
*tavan sarvesu **vedesu brahmanasya** vijanatah*

To the **enlightened *Brahman*,** the *Vedas* are no more

useful than a reservoir when the entire country is flooded.

Karma – Secondary Theme

The word *karma* was just used for the first time in Verse 39. Krishna now begins to teach Arjuna about this complicated principle.

Our choices are limited only by our perception.

Verse 47 (1,000) We may work if we choose, but the results are entirely God's to give.

*karma**ny evadhikaras te ma **phalesu** kadacana**
*ma **karmaphalahetur** bhur ma te sango 'stv **akarmani***

You have the right to **work**, but never for the **results** (fruits). Never be motivated by **the fruits of action**, but also, don't purposely seek to **avoid acting**.

Yoga – Secondary Theme

Verse 48 (1,000) Krishna's first definition of Yoga given to Arjuna

*yoga**sthah kuru karmani sangam **tyaktva dhanamjaya***
*siddhyasiddhyoh samo bhutva samatvam **yoga ucyate***

Remaining immersed in **Yoga, Arjuna**, perform all action, **renounce** your attachment, and be indifferent to success and failure. This mental evenness **is termed Yoga**.

Verse 49 (1,000) Desire versus Wisdom

*durena hy **avaram karma buddhiyogad** dhanamjaya*
*buddhau saranam anviccha **krpanah** phalahetavah*

Ordinary action performed with desire is **inferior to action united to the guidance of wisdom** – therefore, Arjuna, seek shelter in the ever-directing wisdom. **Miserable** are those who perform actions for personal gain.

Verse 50 (1,000) Ten Themes – a second definition of Yoga

*buddhiyukto jahatiha **ubhe sukritaduskrite***
*tasmad yogaya yujyasva **yogah karmasu kausalam***

One who is **united to cosmic wisdom** (consciousness) goes
beyond the effects of **both virtue and vice**, even here in this life.
Therefore, devote yourself to Yoga, divine union.
Yoga is the art of proper action.

The purpose of Yoga is to unite the individual consciousness with
the Universal Spirit.

Verse 51 (1,000) Enlightenment

*karmajam buddhiyukta hi **phalam** tyaktva manisinah*
*janmabandhavinirmuktah padam **gacchantry** anamayam*

Those who have mastered their minds become engrossed in
infinite wisdom – they have no further interest in any **fruits** of
actions (results). Freed from the chain of rebirth, **they attain**
the state beyond all sorrow (enlightenment).

Krishna says, *those who have mastered their minds:* Earlier I wrote
that *hatha-yoga* is a physical practice and not a path to enlightenment. I also wrote that enlightenment lies in the mind.

Verse 52 (1,000) Impartial – neither right nor wrong

*yada te **mohakalilam buddhir** vyatitarisyati*
*tada gantasi nirvedam **srotavyasya srutasya** ca*

When your **understanding** transcends **beyond the darkness** of
delusion, you will attain indifference regarding matters **that have
been heard** and matters **yet to be heard**.

Verse 53 (1,000) False knowledge keeps us ignorant

*sruti*vipratipanna te yada sthasyati niscala
samadhav acala *buddhis tada yogam avapsyasi*

When your understanding, bewildered by **listening** to the variety of arguments becomes **securely anchored** in the ecstasy of **soul bliss** *(samadhi)*, then you will attain Yoga (enlightenment).

Enlightenment – Primary Theme

Arjuna asked:

Verse 54: *What are the characteristics of an enlightened being?*

Krishna answers:

Verse 55 (1,000) Spiritual comfort versus material happiness

prajahati yada kaman sarvan partha manogatan
atmany evatamana tustah **sthitaprajnas** *tadocyate*

When someone completely relinquishes all desires that rise in the mind, and is entirely contented in the Self, by the Self, Arjuna, they are then considered to be someone **settled in wisdom** (enlightened).

Verse 56 (1,000)

duhkhesv *anudvignamanah* **sukhesu** *vigatasprhah*
*vitaragabhaya***krodhah** *sthitadhir* **munir ucyate**

Those whose consciousness is not shaken by **sorrows**, are free from longings, although surrounded by **pleasures**, or those who are free from worldly desires, fear, and **anger – they are called a muni of steady discrimination.**

A *muni* is an enlightened person – free from desires or emotions.

Verse 57 (1,000) Transcended duality

yah sarvatranabhisnehas tat-tat prapya subhasubham
*nabhinandati na **dvesti** tasya **prajna pratisthita***

Those who have no preference for anything, whether they encounter good or **evil**, and neither welcomes or hates either one, has **established wisdom** (become enlightened).

Verse 58 (1,000) Metaphor

*yada **samharate** cayam **kurmo** 'nganiva sarvasah*
*indriyanindriyarthebhyas tasya **prajna pratisthita***

When the yogi, like a **tortoise withdrawing** its limbs, can fully retire their senses from objects of perception, their **wisdom** manifests **steadiness**.

Verse 59 (1,000) Free from desires

*visaya vinivartante niraharasya **dehinah***
rasavarjam raso 'py asya param drstva nivartate

The **person** who abstains from sense objects finds that the sense objects fall away for a little while, but not the longing for them. But those who behold the Supreme (enlightened) are freed even from longings.

Verse 60 (1,000)

*yatato hy api kaunteya pursasya **vipascitah***
***indriyani pramathini** haranti **prasabham** manah*

Arjuna, even in someone who has a **high degree of enlightenment** (consciousness) and is **striving** for liberation, the **agitating senses** carry the mind off by **force**.

Verse 61 (1,000)

*tani sarvani **samyamya yukta asita** matparah*
*vase hi yasyendriyani tasya **prajna pratisthita***

Those who **control** their senses, **absorbed in contentment, devoted to Me,** are **well established in wisdom.**

Verse 62 (1,000) Downward spiral of consciousness

dhyayato visayan pumsah sangas tesupajayate
*sangat **samjayate** kamah kamat **krodho** 'bhijayate*

Thinking about sense objects causes attachment to them. From attachment, desire is **born**, and desire breeds **anger.**

Verse 63 (1,000) Downward spiral continues

***krodhad** bhavati **sammohah sammohat smrtivibhramah**
smrtibhramasad **buddhinaso buddhinasat** pranasyati*

From **anger** arises **delusion** – **delusion** breeds loss of **memory** – loss of **memory** causes **reasoning** to be ruined. From decay of **discrimination**, annihilation of spiritual life follows.

Verse 64 (1,000) Enlightenment

ragadvesaviyuktais tu visayan indriyais caran
*atmavasyair vidheyatma **prasadam adhigacchati***

Those of self-control, roaming among material objects with control over the senses and devoid of attraction and aversion (like and dislike) – **attains** an unshakable **inner calmness.**

Verse 65 (1,000)

*prasade sarva**duhkha**nam hanir asyopajayate*
*prasannacetaso hy asu **buddhih** paryavatisthate*

In soul bliss (enlightenment), all **grief** is annihilated. Indeed, the **discrimination** of the blissful person soon becomes firmly established.

Verse 66 (1,000)

*nasti buddhir ayuktasya na cayuktasya **bhavana***
*na ca**bhavay**atah **santir asantasya** kutah **sukham***

Those who are undisciplined are without knowledge of one's self or **devotion**. Without **devotion**, there is no **peace** – and **without peace**, how can anyone be **happy**?

Verse 67 (1,000) Metaphor

***indriyanam** hi caratam yan mano 'nuvidhiyate*
*tad asya **harati prajnam vayur navam** ivambhasi*

When the mind succumbs to the wandering **senses**, the individual's **discrimination** is driven from its intended path, just as a **boat** on water is **carried off** course by a **gale**.

Verse 68 (1,000)

tasmad yasya mahabaho nigrhitani sarvasah
*indriyanindriyarthebhyas tasya **prajna pratisthita***

Those whose senses are completely withdrawn in regard to sense objects, their **wisdom** is well **established** (enlightened).

Verse 69 (1,000) Contrasting metaphor of linear and non-linear

*ya **nisa sarvabhutanam** tasyam **jagarti** samyami*
*yasyam **jagrati** bhutani sa **nisa** pasyati **muneh***

That which is **night** *(maya)* for **all creatures** is **wakefulness** to the one of self-mastery. And what is **wakefulness** to an ordinary person – that is **night** to the divinely perceptive **sage**.

Enlightened beings are spiritually awake and materially asleep — whereas most people are materially awake and spiritually asleep. Being spiritually awake determines how well we serve others.

Verse 70 (1,000)

apuryamanam acalapratistham samudram apah pravisanti yadvat
*tadvat kama yam pravisanti sarve sa **santim apnoti** na kamakami*

They are full of **contentment, absorbing** all their desires within,
just as the ocean remains unchanged by waters entering into it –
but not for those who cherish their desires.

Verse 71 (1,000) Transcending duality - enlightenment

*vihaya kaman yah sarvan pumams carati **nihsprhah***
nirmamo** nirahamkarah sa **santim adhigacchati

The person who **relinquishes all their desires** and is unidentified
with the ego and its sense of "me and mine" – **realizes peace**.

Verse 72 (1,000) Summary

*esa **brahmi sthitih** partha nainam prapya vimuhyati*
*sthitvasyam antakale 'pi **brahmanirvanam** rcchati*

This is the "**established in *Brahman***" state (enlightenment)
Arjuna. Those who attain this state are never deluded again.
If one abides in this state, even at the moment of death,
they attain the **freedom of *Brahman***.

HELP ME UNDERSTAND

CHAPTER THREE (999.8)

....

Chapter Three calibrates the highest of all 18 chapters.

43 Verses

Primary, Universal Themes: Krishna and the *gunas*
Secondary, Individual Themes: Renunciation, *yajna, jnana, bhakti*

samnyasa - renunciation

Hidden in the language and ambiguity of the *Bhagavad Gita* is a three-part meaning: physical, mental, and spiritual. The body—the physical aspect—is used for selfless service *(karma Yoga)*; the mind—the mental aspect—is used for awareness, knowledge, and wisdom *(jnana Yoga)*; and the heart—the spiritual aspect—is used for devotion *(bhakti Yoga)*. Each of these three primary yogas found in the *Bhagavad Gita* is a method that takes us to a new understanding about our lives. Awareness and turning inward are the greatest agents for transformation to occur. Perhaps my favorite definition of Yoga is *to understand what we have not understood*. When we know better *(jnana Yoga)*, we do better *(karma Yoga)*. And in doing better—that is, acting without self-interest—our actions of serving others become a form of *bhakti Yoga*. That's the transformation! Both Chapters Two and Three present all 12 themes that will be discussed as Krishna continues teaching to the end of Chapter 18. In Chapter Two, the two primary themes presented were on **enlightenment** and **consciousness**. Here in Chapter Three, our two primary themes are about **Krishna** and the ***gunas***. The four new secondary themes are renunciation, *yajna, bhakti,* and *jnana*.

Arjuna said:

Verse 1: *If you consider knowledge to be better than action,*
why do you keep urging me to engage in this terrible act?

Verse 2: *With these conflicting statements, I'm still confused,*
help me understand. Tell me how I can attain the highest good.

Karma was introduced in Chapter Two—now Krishna goes into more detail concerning the different kinds of actions we perform as humans. Krishna also talks about His actions before telling us how we can free ourselves from karma. ***Yajna*** is any selfless act that benefits others—it's how we can neutralize and erase our karma. A duality develops with these two Sanskrit words—karma adds where *yajna* subtracts.

Krishna said:

Verse 3 (1,000) Knowledge and action – nature of consciousness

*loke 'smin **dvividha** nistha pura prokta mayanagha*
jnanayogena samkhya**nam **karmayogena yoginam

At the beginning of creation, a **two-fold way** of salvation (enlightenment) was given by Me to this world: for the wise, **divine union through knowledge** *(jnana yoga)*; for **yogins,** **divine union through action** *(karma yoga)*.

Renunciation – Secondary Theme

Verse 4 (1,000) Renunciation – *samnyasa*

na karmanam anarambhan naiskarmyam puruso 'snute
*na ca **samnyasa**nad eva **siddhim samadhigacchati***

A person does not avoid incurring karma by simply renouncing actions. **No one reaches perfection** (enlightenment) by **renouncing** work.

Renunciation is a secondary theme and a central teaching throughout the *Bhagavad Gita*. Renouncing our selfishness and attachments to the results of our actions is the foundation for spiritual progress. We renounce things because we want to, not because we think we have to in order to make ourselves look better than others. My favorite definition for renunciation is *dropping the outside reflections for the reality within*. Dropping our *outside reflections* is an action, *karma Yoga*. The *reality within* is our inner truth and inherent wisdom – *jnana Yoga*.

Verse 5 (1,000) *Gunas and Prakriti*

na hi kascit ksanam api jatu tisthaty akarmakrt
*karyate hy avasah karma sarvah **prakrtijair gunaih***

No one can remain inactive for a moment without working – **the qualities** *(gunas)* **born of Nature** *(prakriti)* cause everyone to act.

Verse 6 (1,000) Outward renunciation versus inward renunciation

*karmendriyani **samyamya** ya aste manasa smaran*
*indriyarthan vimudhatma mithyacarah sa **ucyate***

Those who **refrain** from certain acts but not from thinking about them **are said** to be hypocrites.

You may have given up sugar, meat, alcohol, cigarettes, or whatever – but you may still be thinking about what you gave up. It's impossible to abandon mental activity.

Verse 7 (1,000) *Karma Yoga*

*yas tvindriyani manasa **niyam**yarabhate 'rjuna*
*karmendriyaih **karmayogam** asaktah sa visisyate*

But, those who can mentally **control** their senses, staying unattached to their actions, Arjuna, they succeed on **the path of selfless service**.

Verse 8 (1,000) *niyatam* – morally right actions

niyatam *kuru karma tvam karma jyayo hy* **akarmanah**
sarirayatrapi ca te na prasidhyed **akarmanah**

Perform actions that are **morally right** *(niyatam)*, for action is better than **inactivity** – even simple maintenance of the body would be impossible through **inaction**.

Yajna – any selfless act we do to benefit others Secondary Theme

Selfless acts benefitting others are a form of *bhakti-yoga*. When we help those in need, from the goodness of our hearts, we not only serve others, but Krishna as well.

Verse 9 (1,000) *Worldly people* – unenlightened

yajnarthat karmano 'nyatra loko 'yam **karmabandhanah**
tadartham karma kaunteya muktasangah samacara

Worldly people (unenlightened) are karmically **bound by actions** that differ from those performed as *yajna* (selfless acts) – Arjuna, work non-attached **in the spirit of *yajna*** (selflessness).

Verse 10 (1,000) *Prajapati* – the Highest Reality

*saha***yajnah** **prajah** *srstva puro***vaca** **prajapatih**
anena *prasavisyadhvam esa vo 'stva***kamaduk**

Prajapati *(Brahma)*, after **creating** humankind, along with **Yajna**, **said**, in the beginning: "By this shall you propagate – this shall be the cow *(kamaduk)* that yields your desires."

Metaphor – we may feed (raise) our consciousness with the milk of wisdom.

Verse 11 (1,000) *Prajapati* continues

devan bhavayatanena te deva bhavayantu vah
parasparam bhavayantah sreyah param avapsyatha

"With this *yajna* may you **cherish** the *devas* (gods),
and may those *devas* cherish you – thus cherishing **one another**,
may you attain the highest good."

Verse 12 (1,000) *Prajapati* concludes – Contrast

istan bhogan hi vo deva dasyante yajnabhavitah
tair dattan apradayaibhyo yo bhunkte stena eva sah

"Nourished by *yajna* (selfless acts), the *devas* will give you
everything you desire." However, those who enjoy these gifts
without due offerings to them is indeed a **thief**.

Verse 13 (1,000) Contrast: selfish acts – selfless acts

yajnasistasinah santo mucyante sarvakilbisaih
bhunjate te tvagham papa ye pacantyatmakaranat

Those who eat the remnants of *yajna* (selfless) are freed from all
sins – but those who make food only for themselves (selfish)
create more sins.

Verse 14 (1,000) Consciousness is omnipresent

The law of creation is spelled out in Verses 14 and 15.
The intrinsic quality of consciousness is to create.

annad bhavanti bhutani parjanyad annasambhavah
yajnad bhavati parjanyo yajnah karmasamudbhavah

From **food springs all life** – from **rain, food** is begotten. From
yajna, **rain** is the result – and *yajna* (selfless acts) is the result of
action *(karma).*

Verse 15 (1,000) the essence of all creation

*karma brahmodbhavam viddhi **brahmaksarasamudbhavam***
tasmat sarvagatam brahma** nityam **yajne pratisthitam

Know that **action** comes from ***Brahma*** (God's Creative Consciousness); this **Consciousness** derives from the **Imperishable Spirit. Therefore**, God's **all-pervading** Creative Consciousness is **inherently and inseparably** present in ***yajna***, which in turn is **the essence of all creation**.

Not only is consciousness the maker, but also the material from which it is made.

Verse 16 (1,000) A contrast between those who evolve spiritually versus those who do nothing.

*evam pravartitam **cakram** nanuvartayatiha yah*
*aghayurindriyaramo mogham **partha** sa jivati*

That individual, who does not follow the **wheel,** thus set in motion, living in sinfulness and contented in the senses, lives in vain, **Arjuna**!

The metaphor of a wheel in motion represents the cycle of reincarnation. This specific verse also speaks to the evolution of our consciousness, rising up during our life as opposed to being motionless and stuck. Krishna talks about the wheel of life in a beautiful interchange between Himself and Draupadi in the *Mahabharata*. Their conversation takes place after the Pandavas were exiled out of their kingdom to live in the forest. Draupadi says: *How could Duhshasana drag me like an animal? I was born from the fire of Shiva!* Krishna answers: *We are now on the wheel of life that turns and turns, wandering forever from one birth to the next. Here we are kings, there we live out our life on the tip of a blade of grass — but we always live. Nothing can stop the wheel.*

Verse 17 (1,000) Soul

*yas tv**atma**ratir eva syad **atma**trptas ca **manavah***
atma**nyeva ca samtustas tasya **karyam** na **vidyate

But for **those** who rejoice in the **soul** alone and are fully satisfied in the **soul**, finding complete contentment only in the **soul, there are** no further **duties**.

Those who follow their inner wisdom will always do what's right and treat everyone with respect.

Verse 18 (1,000) Enlightenment

***naiva** tasya krtenartho nakrteneha kascana*
*na casya sarvabhutesu **kascid** arthavyapasrayah*

Such a person has **no** reason to do anything or not do anything. They are not dependent on **anyone** for anything.

Karma – Secondary Theme

Verse 19 (1,000) Any action performed with desire creates *karma*

*tasmad asaktah satatam **karyam karma samacara***
*asakto hyacaran **karma** param **apnoti** purusah*

Therefore, **perform** the **work** that **must be done**, without attachment. By performing **all actions** *(karma)* without self-interest (ego), one **obtains** the highest good.

Verse 20 (1,000) *lokasamgraham* – what holds the world together

***karma**naiva hi **samsiddhim** asthita **janaka**dayah*
lokasamgraham evapi sampasyan kartum arhasi

By **right action** alone, ***Janaka*** and others like him reached **enlightenment.** You too should follow this path of action, simply for the purpose of rightly guiding mortals.

Verse 21 (1,000) Examples speak louder than words

yadyad acarati sresthas tattad evetaro janah
sa yat **pramanam** *kurute lokas tad* **anuvartate**

Whatever a great being does is **imitated** by others – their actions set a **standard** for everyone.

At the opening of this chapter, I wrote, when we know better, we do better—and when we do better, our actions become a form of *bhakti-yoga*.

Krishna – Primary Theme

Verse 22 (1,000) Consciousness is the cause of our actions

na me parthasti kartavyam trisu lokesu kimcana
nanavaptam avaptavyam varta eva ca **karmani**

There is no compelling duty I have to perform, there is nothing to obtain that I don't already have. Yet, I am consciously present in the performance of **all actions**.

The power of causes is unseen and only the manifestation of effects is observable. Human beings are a product of a visible Nature and an invisible God—a paradox.

Verse 23 (1,000) Krishna

yadi hyaham na varteyam jatu **karma***nyatandritah*
mama vartmanuvartante manusyah **partha** *sarvasah*

If at any time I did not continue to perform **actions**, without pause, everyone would imitate My way, **Arjuna**.

Verse 24 (1,000) Krishna

utsideyur ime loka na kuryam **karma** *ced aham*
samkarasya ca carta syam upahanyam imah prajah

If I did not perform **actions**, the universe would be annihilated.
I would be the cause of dire confusion and total destruction.

Karma – Secondary Theme

Verse 25 (1,000) Contrast of attachment and non-attachment

saktah **karma***nyavidvamso yatha kuruvanti* **bharata**
kuryad vidvams tathasaktas cikirsur lokasamgraham

As the unenlightened perform **actions** with attachment and hope
of reward, **Arjuna**, so the wise should act with dispassionate
non-attachment, to gladly serve as an example for others.

Verse 26 (1,000) *inspire others*

na buddhibhedam janayed **ajnanam karmasanginam**
josayet sarvakarmani vidvan yuktah samacaran

Under no circumstances should the wise disturb the
understanding of the **ignorant** that are **attached to their actions**.
Instead, the wise, should inspire others to conscientiously perform
all dutiful actions.

Gunas – Primary Theme

Verse 27 (1,000) *karma-mala*

prakrteh *kriyamanani* **gunaih karma***ni sarvasah*
ahamkaravimudhatma kartaham iti **manyate**

All **actions** are performed by the **attributes** *(gunas)* of **Nature**
(Prakriti). Those deluded by the sense of "I" **think,** *I am the*
doer.

Krishna gives us three steps on how to end our *karma*. Step one
is to align with our *dharma*—our purpose in life. We act because
it's our *dharma* to act. Step two is to act as purely as we can without thinking about the results of our actions. Here in this verse,

Krishna gives us step three—act without thinking of ourselves as being the *doer*. These three steps make our lives into a living prayer.

Verse 28 (1,000) The knower of truth remains unattached

*tattvavit tu mahabaho **gunakarmavibhagayoh***
***guna gunesu** vartanta iti matva na sajjate*

The knower of truth (an enlightened being) regarding the various ***gunas** (tamas, rajas, sattva)* and their **actions** (behaviors) – remains unattached, knowing that it is the ***gunas*** as sense attributes that are attached to the ***gunas*** as sense objects.

Verse 29 (1,000) We are on our own path of awakening

prakrter guna**sammudhah sajjante **gunakarmasu
tan akrtsnavido mandan krtsnavin na vicalayet

Deluded by the ***gunas*** of ***prakriti***, the ignorant become attached to the **activities of those *gunas***. Those who know the truth should not confuse the minds of those who have imperfect understanding.

Contrast of those who are enlightened and those who are not.

Verse 30 (1,000) Stop acting under the influence of ego

*mayi sarvani **karmani samnyasadhyatma**cetasa*
*nirasir nirmamo bhutva yudhyasava **vigatajvarah***

Dedicate all your **actions** to Me! **Devoid** of egotism and expectation, with your attention concentrated on the **soul, free from worry**, be engaged in the battle of activity and fight!

Verse 31 (1,000) Right Attitude – the first quality of spiritual progress – stop complaining.

*ye me **matam** idam **nityam** anutisthanti manavah*
*sraddhavanto 'nasuyanto mucyante te 'pi **karmabhih***

Those of faith who **ceaselessly** practice *(anutisthanti)* **My commands** *(matam)*, without complaining, they too become free from all ***karma***.

The cause of our problems is not everyone else – it's us! We must stop judging others and judge ourselves instead!

Verse 32 (1,000) *anutisthanti* – regularly perform; *matam* – injunctions (see Verse 31)

*ye tvetad abhyasuyanto **anutisthanti** me **matam**
sarva**jnana**vimudhams tan viddhi nastan acetasah*

But those who denounce this **teaching** of Mine and do not **live according** to it, wholly deluded in regard to true **knowledge** *(jnana)*, know them to be doomed.

Verse 33 (1,000) Levels of consciousness

*sadrsam cestate **svasyah prakrter** jnanavan api
prakrtim yanti **bhutani** nigrahah kim karisyati*

Even the wise (enlightened) act according to the tendencies of **their own nature** (level of consciousness) as **all living creatures** live according to their own Nature – why try to change anything?

Verse 34 (1,000) The soul is always content – the ego is never satisfied.

*indriyasyendriyasya rthe ragadvesau vyavasthitau
tayor na vasam agacchet tau hyasya paripanthinau*

Attraction and repulsion of the senses for their specific objects is completely natural. Beware of the influence of this duality. These two psychological qualities are one's own enemies!

Verse 35 (1,000) Each one of us is here for the divine purpose of the universe to unfold.

sreyan **svadharma** *vigunah* **paradharamat** *svanusthitat*
svadharme *nidhanam sreyah* **paradharmo** *bhayavahah*

One's own duty, though imperfect, is superior to **duty other than one's own**, though perfect. It is better to die in *svadharma* than *paradharma* which brings prosperity.

Never compare yourself to someone else.

Jnana/Knowledge – Secondary Theme

Arjuna asked:

Verse 36: *Krishna, why are people compelled to perform evil, even against their will – compelled it seems, by force?*

Krishna answers:

Verse 37 (1,000)

kama esa **krodha** *esa* **rajoguna**samudbhavah
mahasano mahapapma viddhyenam iha vairinam

It is desire and **anger**, born of the *guna*, *rajas*. It is the impelling force – full of unappeasable craving and great evil: know this to be the foulest enemy here on earth.

Desire calibrates at 125 and anger 150. At these low levels of consciousness, our actions and behaviors are deeply rooted in personal survival—people will act from very selfish motives at these levels, distorting the truth so that they are never wrong. I don't mean to contradict Krishna, but for the sake of consistency in this book, I categorize this *guna* as *tamas* rather than *rajas*, because both desire and anger calibrate in the mid-100's. However, *rajas* is indeed the impelling force causing us to act. There are editions of the *Bhagavad Gita* that have five extra verses at this point.

Desire – Verses 38 through 43 – new subject

Verse 38 (1,000) Metaphors

dhumenavriyate vahnir yathadarso malena ca
*yatholbenavrto **garbhas** tatha tenedam **avrtam***

As fire is obscured by smoke, a mirror by dust, and an **embryo** is enveloped by the womb, so is knowledge **covered** by desire.

Verse 39 (1,000) Desire

avrtam jnana**m etena jnanino **nityavairina
***kamarupena kaunteya** duspurenanalena ca*

Arjuna, knowledge is **concealed** by **anger**, the **eternal enemy** of the wise, in the form of desire, the insatiable fire.

Verse 40 (1,000) Desire

indriyani mano buddhir** asyadhisthanam **ucyate
*etair vimohayatyesa **jnanam** avrtya **dehinam***

The senses, mind, and intellect are said to be the stronghold of this eternal enemy. **Knowledge** is eclipsed by desire, which deludes the **embodied soul**.

Verse 41 (1,000) *niyamya* – take control

*tasmat tvam **indriya**nyadau **niyamya** bharatarsabha*
*papmanam prajahi hyenam **jnana**vijnananasanam*

Therefore, Arjuna, **take control of the senses**, and then destroy desire, the annihilator of **knowledge** and discrimination.

Verse 42 (1,000) The wisdom of the Soul is unmatched

indriyani** paranyahur **indriye**bhyah pram **manah
***manasas** tu para **buddhir** yo **buddhih** paratas tu sah*

The senses are stronger than the body – the **mind** is stronger than **the senses** – **intelligence i**s stronger than the **mind** – but the Self is stronger than **intelligence**.

Verse 43 (1,000) The Soul is superior to intelligence

evam buddhih param buddhva samstabhyatmanam atmana
*jahi **satrum** mahabaho **kamarupam durasadam***

Now that you know the Self is superior to intelligence,
and disciplining the self (ego) by the Self (soul), annihilate
the **enemy in the form of desire, difficult to conquer.**

Wisdom never lies – Only Truth is recognized by consciousness.

HOW CAN THIS BE?

CHAPTER FOUR (996)

42 Verses

Primary Themes: Krishna, *gunas*, and Enlightenment
Secondary Themes: Yoga, Reincarnation, *karma, jnana, yajna,* and *bhakti*

tattva – that-ness, essence, truth
pranayama – life control
shraddha and *ashraddha* – faith and doubt

Krishna reveals more about Himself in the first 15 verses of this chapter before discussing enlightenment and His actions. He continues talking about how to free ourselves from *karma* by reintroducing *yajna* (selfless actions) from Chapter Three. Krishna explains the different ways of expressing devotion—*bhakti Yoga*—as well as teachings on knowledge and wisdom, before concluding the chapter discussing faith, *(sraddha)*, and doubt *(asraddah)*. *Jnana Yoga* develops the kind of discriminating wisdom that can differentiate the real from the unreal. Remember, *maya* has two functions, one is to conceal the real and the other is to project the unreal. Wisdom is different from knowledge—knowing something isn't wisdom—its knowledge. The assumption with *jnana Yoga* is that all spiritual wisdom lies hidden within each of us—we only have to discover it. We discover our inner wisdom with faith. Real faith develops when we question spiritual truths *(how can this be?)*—the spiritual truths Krishna offers throughout the *Bhagavad Gita*.

Krishna – Primary Theme

Verse 1 (1,000) The embodiment of consciousness

*imam **vivasvate yogam** proktavan aham avyayam*
*vivasvan manave praha **manur iksvakave** 'bravit*

I taught this imperishable **Yoga to *Vivasvat*** (the sun god) –
Vivasvat passed on this knowledge to *Manu* –
and ***Manu*** told it to ***Ikshvaku*.**

Consciousness descends downward from God to man,
represented by *Manu*. *Ikshvaku* is the son of *Manu* and the first
king of *Kshatriyas*.

Verse 2 (1,000) Universal to individual

*evam paramparapraptam imam **rajasayo** viduh*
*sa **kaleneha mahata** yogo nastah paramtapa (Arjuna)*

Handed down in succession, the **royal sages** knew it. Through
the **long passage of time**, this Yoga was lost sight of on earth,
tormentor of foes.

The first two verses reveal more about Krishna, describing how
consciousness manifests into human embodiment. *Ikshvaku* is the
first king of the *Kshatriyas*, and as we've already learned, *Kshatri-*
yas calibrate in the 400's. *Handed down* implies consciousness descending to those below 400. Because of our many incarnations
through time, we forgot this Yoga. However, in spite of our for-
getfulness, we still have within us the knowledge on how to unite
with God (to become enlightened).

Verse 3 (1,000) Yoga

*sa evayam maya te 'dya **yogah** proktah **puratanah***
***bhakto** 'si me **sakha** ceti **rahasyam** hyetad uttamam*

Today I have informed you about that same **ancient Yoga**,
for you are My **devotee** and **friend**. This sacred **mystery** is indeed
the producer of supreme benefit to all.

Arjuna asked:

Verse 4: *Vivasvat was born first, and your birth occurred later –
how then can I understand when you say you communicated this
Yoga in the beginning, before your birth?*

Krishna responds:

Verse 5 (1,000)

*bahuni me vyatitani janmani tava **carjuna**
tanyaham veda sarvani na tvam vettha **paramtapa***

You and I have experienced many births, **Arjuna**.
I am acquainted with all of them, whereas you
remember none of them, **Arjuna**.

Toward the end of the *Mahabharata*, Krishna and Arjuna are sitting under a tree in the rain—Krishna is telling Arjuna about
their past lives together. No one knows what lives those were and
it is unknown what was said between them.

Verse 6 (1,000) *Born as a man, I must act as a man*

*ajo 'pi sannavyayatma **bhutanam** isvaro 'pi san
prakrtim svam adhisthaya **sambhavamyatmamayaya***

Though unborn and of changeless Essence – yet, being the Lord
of **all creation**, abiding in **My own Nature, I embody Myself
by Self-evolved maya-delusion.**

Verse 7 (1,000) *I incarnate as an Avatar*

*yadayada hi **dharmasya** glanir bhavati bharata
abhyutthanam **adharmasya** tadatmanam srjamyaham*

Whenever **virtue** declines and **vice** flourishes, Arjuna,
I incarnate as an Avatar.

Verse 8 (1,000) Krishna

*paritranaya sadhunam vinasaya ca **duskrtam***
dharma**samsthapanarthaya sambhavami **yuge yuge

I appear in visible form from **age to age**. Protecting virtue
and destroying **evil** in order to reestablish **righteousness**.

Verse 9 (1,000) *punarjanma* – rebirth

*janma **karma** ca me **divyam** evam yo vetti **tattvatah***
*tyaktva deham **punarjanma** naiti mam eti so 'rjuna*

Those who know the **secret** (truth) of My **divine** birth and **actions** are not **reborn** after death – they come to me, Arjuna!

The word **tattvatah** in Verse 9 means *that-ness,* essence, truth, reality, principle, and category. *Samkhya* attempts to comprehend the universe as a sum of twenty-five categories, the *tattvas* are a type of map for the various states of human consciousness, organized as five groups of five, beginning with the five elements: earth, water, fire, air, and space. The second groups of five are the five senses: smell, taste, sight, touch, and hearing; followed by the five powers of action: mouth, hands, feet, genitals, and bowels; followed in turn by the five sense organs: nose, tongue, eyes, skin, and ears. The remaining five are *manas* – mind and mental functions; *ahamkara* – ego; *buddhi* – intelligence; *prakriti* – nature; and finally, *purusa* – the unchanging experience of always being ourselves – which makes *purusa* different than the other 24 *tattvas*.

Verse 10 (1,000) Enlightenment – *many have attained My nature*

*vitaraga**bhayakrodhah** manmaya mam upasritah*
*bahavo **jnanatapasa** puta **madbhavam** agatah*

Purified by the **asceticism of knowledge**, freed from attachment, **fear**, and **anger** – absorbed and sheltered in Me, many have attained **My nature**.

Verse 11 (1,000) God responds in whatever aspect we hold dear.

ye yatha mam prapadyante tams tathaiva bhajamyaham
*mama **vartmanuvartante** manusyah partha sarvasah*

In whatever way people are devoted to Me, in that measure I manifest Myself to them. Everyone, in every manner of seeking Me, Arjuna, **pursues a path to Me**.

However a man approaches Me, in that same manner do I go to him was Krishna's creed.

Verse 12 (1,000)

*kanksantah karmanam siddhim **yajanta** iha **devatah***
ksipram hi manuse loke siddhir bhavati karmajam

Desiring success for their actions here on earth, people **worship the gods**, because achievement accruing from activity is readily attained in the world of people.

Success in a material world is easy when the material world is designed specifically for that purpose.

Verse 13 (1,000) *gunas and castes* – four levels of consciousness

caturvarnyam** maya srstam **gunakarmavibhagasah
tasya kartaram api mam viddhyakartaram avyayam

I am the Creator of a system based on **four castes** *(varnas)* according to the division of ***gunas** and **actions** of each.

Though I am its Creator, being changeless, I am not the Creator.

Four Levels of Consciousness:

Below 200 – *tamas* – *Sudra*;
200 – 399 – *tamas-rajas* – *Vaishya*;
400 – 499 – *rajas-sattva* – *Kshatriya*;
500 – 599 – *sattva* – *Brahmin*.

I'm offering a different understanding of the caste system than what is commonly accepted. Consider what Krishna is telling us in this verse. He says, *according to the division of the gunas and actions*. The understanding I'm offering of *gunas and actions* is levels of consciousness and human behavior. He isn't saying, according to family tradition or heredity—which is what most people believe the caste system to be based on. The caste system will be discussed further in Chapter 18.

Verse 14 (1,000) Indifference of Krishna

na mam karmani limpanti *na me karmaphale* **sprha**
iti mam yo 'bhijanati karmabhir na sa badhyate

Actions do not affect Me, nor have I **longings** for their fruits. Those who understand Me in this way are also free from their actions.

Verse 15 (1,000) *dutiful actions* are in alignment with our *dharma*

evam **jnatva** *krtam karma purvair api mumuksubhih*
kuru karmaiva tasmat tvam purvaih **purvataram** *krtam*

Knowing this, even the **wise** have sought salvation since pristine times, performing dutiful actions. Therefore, act dutifully, as the ancients of **bygone** days.

Karma – Secondary Theme

Verse 16 (1,000) *true action*

*kim **karma** kim **akarmeti** kavayo 'py atra mohitah*
*tat te karma pravaksyami yaj **jnatva moksyase 'subhat***

Even the wise are confused about **action** and **inaction**.
Therefore, I will explain what constitutes true action –
knowledge that will **free you from evil**.

Verse 17 (1,000) Contrast of human action – selfish and selfless

karma**no hyapi boddhavyam boddhavyam ca **vikarmanah
***akarma**nasca boddhavyam gahana **karma**no gatih*

The nature of *karma* is very difficult to know. In order to fully
understand the nature of **proper action**, one must understand the
nature of **forbidden action** (selfish) and the nature of **inaction**
(selfless – free from *karma*).

Verse 18 (1,000) Krishna clarifies action and inaction.

***karmanyakarma** yah **pasyed akarmani** ca **karma** yah*
sa buddhiman manusyesu sa yuktah krtsnakarmakrt

Discriminative among all, those who **behold inactivity** in **action**
and **action in inaction** – they have attained the goal of all
actions and are free (from *karma*).

One practical approach to *karma* is through asking ourselves,
what can we do today to make tomorrow better? If we take care of
business today, doing what needs to be done, without attachment,
we set our life up for having a better tomorrow.

Enlightenment and Karma

Verse 19 (1,000)

yasya sarve samarambhah kamasamkalpavarjitah
jnanagnidagdhakarmanam *tam ahuh* **panditam budhah**

Those **whose actions are purified by the fire of wisdom**, whose actions are all without selfish desires or longings for results, the **wise**, call this person, a *pandita*.

Verse 20 (1,000)

tyaktva karmaphalasangam nityatrpto *nirasrayah*
karmany **abhipravrtto** *'pi naiva kimcit karoti sah*

Relinquishing attachment to the fruits of work, always content, and independent of material rewards, the wise never perform any binding actions, **even in the midst of activities**.

Verse 21 (1,000)

nirasir **yatacittatma tyaktasarvaparigrahah**
sariram kevalam karma kurvan napnoti kilbisam

They incur no sin *(karma)* performing mere bodily actions, having **renounced all sense of possession**, free from hopes, and whose heart is **controlled by the soul**.

Binding karmic actions are caused by consciousness, not by the physical body itself. We can be inactive physically, but we are never inactive mentally.

Verse 22 (1,000) Contentment

yadrcchalabhasamtusto dvandvatito vimatsarah
samah siddhav **asiddhau** *ca krtvapi na* **nibadhyate**

Those who receive with contentment whatever befalls them, **unaffected by dualities** (likes and dislikes), devoid of jealousy, envy, or enmity, looking equally on success and failure, that person is **free from** *karma*.

Yajna – Secondary Theme

The next six verses are highly esoteric and not easily understood. These secret teachings are meant to be revealed through an oral tradition, handed down from teacher to student. Most of my comments with the verses only point the way. We obviously aren't sitting with each other as we go through each verse, so I can't answer any questions that may come up for you. Sanskrit words like *yajna* are challenging—but even words such as offering, sacrifice, oblations, and fire can be challenging as well. It helps to isolate these six verses and study them together.

Verse 23 (1,000) *true yajna* are actions that are purely selfless.

*gatasangasya muktasya **jnanavasthitacetasah***
***yajna**yacaratah karma samagram praviliyate*

All *karma*, or effects of actions, completely melts away from an enlightened being that is free from attachments, **their mind enveloped in wisdom**, and performing true *yajna*.

Verse 24 (1,000) Everything is consciousness – it's all God.

***brahma**rpanam **brahma** havir **brahma**gnau **brahma**na hutam*
***brahma**iva tena gantavyam **brahma**karma**samadhi**na*

The process of offering and the offering itself are both Spirit (consciousness). The fire and the one making the offering into it are other forms of Spirit (consciousness). Realizing that **everything is consciousness** during all activities, **such a one goes to** Spirit alone.

The personal soul is no different from the Universal Soul—each individual embodies consciousness in contracted form (which can be measured). The word *samadhi* found in the final Sanskrit word

of this verse means *oneness with God*—which is the realization
that everything is consciousness and that we ourselves are part of
the Universal Soul. *Samkhya* philosophy asserts two independent
realities, Spirit and Matter. *Vedanta* asserts one reality which never
changes—the world of matter *(prakriti)* is merely another form of
consciousness.

Verse 25 (1,000) Krishna explains different types of *yajna*

daivam *evapare* **yajnam yoginah** *paryupasate*
brahmagnav *apare* **yajnam yajne**naivopa**juhvati**

In truth, there are those **yogins** who sacrifice to the *devas* –
others offer the self as a **sacrifice** made by the self, in the
fire of Spirit alone.

Verse 26 (1,000) Transcending the senses

srotradinindriyany **anye** *samyam***agnisu juhvati**
sabdadin visayan **anya** *indriy***agnisu juhvati**

Certain devotees offer as **oblations** in the **fire** of inner control,
their powers of hearing and **other** senses. Others offer as **sacrifice**
in the **fire** of the senses, sound and **other** sense objects.

We don't have a choice about the war, but we do have a
choice to which side we'll fight for—Pandavas or Kauravas.
The Pandavas are the spiritual aspect and the Kauravas are
the material aspect of life. Do we choose God or God's gifts?

Verse 27 (1,000) All spiritual wisdom lies hidden within –
we only have to discover it!

sarvanindriyakarmani **prana***karmani capare*
atmasamyamayogagnau juhvati jnana*dipite*

Others following the path of *jnana Yoga* offer all their activities
of the senses, and the **life force** as **oblations** in the **yogic fire of**

self-control, kindled by **knowledge**.

Verse 28 (1,000) There are many ways to express devotion

*dravyayajnas **tapo**yajna **yoga**yajnas tathapare*
***svadhyayajnanayajnasca** yatayah samsitavratah*

Other devotees offer wealth, **self-discipline**, and the methods of **Yoga** – while other individuals offer self-control, keeping strict vows, still others offer as sacrifices **self-study and the acquirement of scriptural wisdom**.

Reading the *Bhagavad Gita* is the acquirement of scriptural wisdom.

Pranayama – New Subject

Verse 29 (1,000) *arresting the cause of inhalation and exhalation*

***apane juhvati pranam** prane 'panam tathapare*
***pranapana**gati ruddhva **pranayama**parayanah*

Others **offer** the incoming breath of ***prana*** into the outgoing breath of ***apana*** – and the outgoing breath of ***apana*** into the incoming breath of ***prana*** – thus arresting the cause of inhalation and exhalation.

Below are two verses from Chapter Five that also discuss *pranayama*. Combining and commenting on these verses together may help our understanding of what *pranayama* actually is. *Pranayama* is a combination of two Sanskrit words—*prana*—life, and *yama*—control. *Pranayama* is life control, not only breath control. The human breath ties the soul to the body. *Pranayama* is a method to release the soul from the bondage of the breath. When the heart becomes quiet, exhalation and inhalation are no longer needed – thus arresting the cause of inhalation and exhalation and releasing the soul back to God.

Chapter Five, Verse 27 (1,000) The breath ties the Soul to the body.

sparsan krtva bahir bahyams caksus caivantare bhruvoh
pranapanau *samau krtva nasabhyantaracarinau*

Our souls descend into our bodies and become identified with our senses. Our souls may be withdrawn from our senses through **pranayama** and be reunited with God.

Chapter Five, Verse 28 (1,000) Reverse process

atendriyamanobuddhir munir *moksaparayanah*
vigatecchabhayakrodho yah **sada mukta** *eva sah*

Controlling their senses, mind, and intellect, the *muni*, wholly devoted to enlightenment *(moksaparayanah)* – with no trace left of desire, fear, and anger, is **always free.**

A **muni** can withdraw consciousness from external objects at will. Our souls descend into our bodies and become identified with our senses.

The idea is to dissolve breath into mind—mind into intuition—intuition into perception of the soul—and soul into Spirit. Our souls may be withdrawn from our senses through *pranayama* and be reunited with God. In the *Mahabharata*, Krishna's brother *Balarama* ended his life in this way. He went into a trance and a stream of light came out of his forehead like a silver serpent and coiled its way up to the sky. *Balarama* was the incarnation of *Adishesha*, the name of the serpent on which Lord *Vishnu* reclines.

In my book *Warrior Self,* I included the following passage from *Health, Healing, and Beyond,* by Krishnamacharya's son, T.K.V. Desikachar. I calibrate Krishnamacharya's level of consciousness at 732— he was an enlightened man, a legendary healer, and Yoga teacher. His consciousness at birth measured 386. Desikachar writes about his father and his ability to stop his breath and heartbeat.

I had heard about my father's control over his heartbeat all my life. As a science student, I was frankly skeptical. I would ask him, "Father, is this really possible?" One day in 1965, after I already had been studying with him for several years, he closed his eyes and told me to feel his pulse. I did, and it began to fade until it disappeared. There was no pulse at wrist or neck, and absolutely no breath. This went on for at least a couple of minutes, and then started up again.

Krishnamacharya never taught this technique to anyone, including his own son, believing that it wasn't useful to society and that it was only an achievement, or ego trip.

Prana is the greatest of all forces, which God uses to create and sustain the universe. Every atom of our bodies has elements of *prana*. Verse 29 speaks to two specific functions of life force—*prana* and *apana*. From the opposite pulsations of *prana* and *apana*, inhalations and exhalations of the breath are born. These two currents either bind or release the soul. The *Bhagavad Gita* teaches us about *pranayama* so that we can understand that the body isn't made of tissues and bones, but of life force—*prana*—consciousness, condensed from the consciousness of God.

Yajna – Secondary Theme Continued

Verse 30 (1,000) *prana*

*apare niyataharah **prana**n pranesu **juhvati**
sarve 'pyete **yajna**vido **yajna**ksapitakalmasah*

Others offer different kinds of ***prana*** and their functions as **offerings** into the fire of the one common prana. These devotees are knowers of the true fire ceremony of wisdom that consumes their karmic sins (errors).

Verse 31 (1,000) *kurusattama* – best of the Kurus (Arjuna)

***yajna**sist**amrta**bhujo yanti **brahma** sanatanam
nayam loko 'sty **ayajnasya** kuto 'nyah kurusattama*

By partaking of the **nectar**-remnant of any of these spiritual fire ceremonies, they (yogins) go to the **Infinite Spirit**. But this realization of Spirit belongs not to ordinary people of this world who are **non-performers of the true spiritual rites**, Arjuna. Without real sacrifice, where comes any better world, any better existence, or elevated states of consciousness?

Without inner transformation, which can elevate our consciousness, we remain identified with our ego. Our level of consciousness directly relates to our level of happiness.

Verse 32 (1,000) Enlightenment through *yajna* – selfless actions

evam bahuvidha **yajna** *vitata* **brahmana** *mukhe*
karmajam *viddhi tan sarvan evam jnatva vimoksyase*

Various spiritual **yajna** are thus found as ways to attain **Brahman**. Know them all to be **born of action** – and understanding this, you will find salvation.

Studying various forms of liberating actions described in the *Vedas*, learned from yogins or realized by intuition, devotees adopt the most suitable forms of worship.

Verse 33 (1,000) Contrasting spiritual and material

sreyan dravyamayad yajnaj **jnanayajnah paramtapa**
sarvam karmakhilam **partha** *jnane parisamapyate*

Knowledge sacrifice is superior to material sacrifice, **Arjuna**. All action which does not bind, **Arjuna**, is consummated in wisdom.

All spiritual actions are effective, dissolving *karmic* effects from past and present actions.

Jnana Yoga – Secondary Theme

Verse 34 (1,000) Three ways to learn – humility, questioning, and service.

*tad viddhi pranipatena pariprasnena **sevaya***
*upadeksyanti te **jnanam** jnaninas **tattvadarsinah***

The sages who have **realized Truth** will teach you this
knowledge. Learn it through humility, questioning,
and by **service**.

Arjuna surrendered his knowing and resistance at the end of
Chapter One—he became **humble**. Throughout the *Bhagavad
Gita*, Arjuna asks Krishna questions. When Krishna's teachings
are completed at the end of Chapter 18, Arjuna will serve Krishna
by acting as he has been taught.

Verse 35 (1,000) With enlightenment, you attain everything

*yaj jnatva na punar **moham** evam yasyasi **pandava***
*yena bhutani **asesena** draksyasy atmany atho mayi*

Knowing this knowledge, you will not fall into **delusion** again,
Arjuna. By that knowledge, you will behold the **entire** creation
in yourself, and then in Me.

Verse 36 (1,000) Some crimes are sins, but not all sins are crimes

*api ced asi **papebhyah** sarvebhyah papakrttamah*
*sarvam **jnana**plavenaiva vrjinam samtarisyasi*

Even if you were the **most sinful** of all sinners, you would safely
cross the sea of sin by the sole raft of **knowledge**.

Rid yourself of sin (mistakes) by knowledge.

Verse 37 (1,000) Metaphor – knowledge and action

*yathaidhamsi samiddho '**gnir bhasmasat** kurute '**rjuna***
jnanagnih sarvakarmani bhasmasat kurute tatha

As a burning **flame** turns firewood **into ashes, Arjuna**, so does
the *fire of knowledge* turn all *karma* to ashes.

Verse 38 (1,000) *In due course of time* – step by step – patience

*na hi jnanena sadrsam **pavitram** iha vidyate*
*tat svayam **yogasamsiddhah kalena**tmani vindati*

Nothing else in this world is as **purifying** as knowledge.
In due course of time, the devotee who is **successful in Yoga**
will spontaneously realize this within their Soul.

Faith and Doubt

Verse 39 (1,000) *sraddha* – faith

*sraddhavam **labhate jnanam tatparah** samyatendriyah*
***jnanam labdhva param santim** acirenadhigacchati*

The person of **faith, engrossed** in the Infinite, who gains
knowledge and has control over their senses, **having obtained
knowledge**, they immediately attain **supreme peace**
(enlightenment).

Verse 40 (1,000) *asraddah* – doubt – a contrast from Verse 39

ajnascasraddadha**nasca samsayatma **vinasyati
*nayam loko 'sti na paro na **sukham** samsayatmanah*

Those **without knowledge** *(ajnas)*, **without faith** *(asraddah)* and
full of doubt are **lost**. The unsettled individual has neither this
world nor the next, nor the supreme **happiness** of God.

Verse 41 (1,000) Enlightenment

***yogasamnyastakarmanam jnana**samc**hinna**samsayam*
*atmavantam na karmani **nibadhnanti** dhanamjaya*

Those who have **renounced actions by Yoga** and who have **torn**
apart their doubts by **knowledge**, becomes poised in the Self (enlightened) – no actions **bind** them, Arjuna.

Verse 42 (1,000) Stand up!

*tasmad **ajnana**sambhutam **hrtstham jnana**sinatmanah*
chittvainam samsayam yogam atisthottistha bharata

Stand up, **Arjuna**! Take shelter in Yoga, slashing with the sword of **knowledge** this doubt born of **ignorance existing in your heart** about yourself.

ONLY THE WISE

CHAPTER FIVE (996)

29 Verses

Primary Themes: Enlightenment and Consciousness
Secondary Themes: Renunciation, *karma*, Soul, and *jnana*

Vyasa has been very clever in presenting the teachings of Krishna into a conversation between God and man. Arjuna keeps asking questions in Chapters Two through Four and then here at the opening of Chapter Five. Personally speaking, if God was sitting in my truck, I'm sure I would have a lot of questions! In Chapter Two, Arjuna asked Krishna what an enlightened being actually is. Here in Chapter Five, Krishna spends this entire chapter talking about **enlightenment** and higher levels of **consciousness**—primary themes introduced in Chapter Two.

Renunciation *(sannyasa)* is indispensable for our spiritual practice. By looking closely at our attachments, we begin to understand how much we may be defining ourselves through all our *outside reflections*. No thing has anything to do with who we are! No *outside reflection* has anything to do with our reality within. By surrendering who we are not, we begin to see the reality of who we *truly* are.

Arjuna asked:

Verse 1: *Which is better, serving in the world or seeking wisdom* in *seclusion?*

Krishna answers:

Verse 2 (1,000) *sannyasa*

samnyasah *karmayogasca nihsreyasakarav ubhau*
tayos tu **karmasamnyasat karmayogo** *visisyate*

Enlightenment is found by **renunciation** and performance of action. But of these two, the **Yoga of action** is superior to the **renunciation of action**.

Verse 3 (1,000)

*jneyah sa **nityasamnyasi** yo na **dvesti** na kanksati*
*nirdvandvo hi mahabaho **sukham** bandhat **pramucyate***

A **constant *sannyasi*** (renunciant) has neither **likes** nor **dislikes** and is **not bound** by duality.

A major shift in consciousness occurs at level 500. Many geniuses calibrate at 499, but making the jump to 500 is a rare occurrence. Isaac Newton, Albert Einstein, Sigmund Freud, Stephen Hawking; composers Arnold Schoenberg, Richard Strauss, and Giuseppe Verdi, as well as many others, all calibrate at 499. At the level of 500, the emotional, conceptual linear mind moves to a non-linear context. Meaning, significance, and value are reprioritized. The mind shifts from 'objective' to experiential subjectivity. This shift profoundly influences our decisions and choices. Love becomes the guiding principle—love serves above 499 whereas the ego seeks to be served below 500. Our understanding of duality concerning likes and dislikes shifts to something far different than what most of us can comprehend below 500.

Samkhya and Yoga

Verse 4 (1,000) Two sides of the same coin

***samkhyayogau** prthagbalah pravadanty na panditah*
ekam** apy asthitah samyag ubhayor **vindati phalam

Only fools speak of the differences between ***samkhya*** and **Yoga**. Those truly established in **one, receives** the **benefits** of both.

The philosophical basis of Yoga is *Samkhya*. There is no knowledge equal to the *Samkhya* and no power equal to Yoga.

Verse 5 (1,000) There is no knowledge without Yoga and no Yoga without knowledge.

*yat **samkhyaih** prapyate sthanam tad yogair api gamyate*
ekam samkhyam** ca yogam ca yah **pasyati** sa **pasyati

This state attained by the followers of **Samkhya** is also attained by those who practice Yoga. Those who **see Samkhya** and Yoga to be **one**, truly **see**.

Enlightenment – Primary Theme

Verse 6 (1,000)

***samnyasas** tu mahabaho **duhkham** aptum ayogatah*
yogayukto** munir brahma **nacirenadhigacchati

True **renunciation** is **difficult** to achieve without God-uniting actions (Yoga). By the **practice of Yoga**, the ***muni* quickly obtains** the Infinite (enlightenment).

Verse 7 (1,000) Enlightenment

yogayukto visuddhatma** vijitatma **jitendriyah
***sarvabhutatmabhutatma** kurvan api na lipyate*

No taint *(na lipyate)* touches the **sanctified person of action** who is engaged in **Divine communion** (Yoga), who has conquered ego consciousness, who is victorious over their senses, and who feels **their self as the Self existing in all beings**.

From levels of 500 to 539, love is still subject to conditions. At level 540 and up, love becomes unconditional.

Verse 8 (1,000) *I myself do nothing*, is *conscious recognition of Truth*.

*naiva kimcit karomiti yukto manyeta **tattvavit***
***pasyan** srnvan sprsan jighrann asnan gacchan svapan svasan*

Those who have **conscious recognition of Truth**, who are united to God, automatically **perceives**, *I myself do nothing*, even while engaged in seeing, hearing, touching, smelling, eating, walking, breathing, or sleeping.

God is the *Doer* of all actions—which can be a challenging truth to fully comprehend. Going back to our discussion regarding *karma*, we saw how cause and effect are actually occurring simultaneously and that the cause of our actions comes from consciousness—related to our specific level of consciousness. Our misidentification with the effect as the cause is what slows our evolution of consciousness. *Conscious recognition of truth* is the true understanding of cause and effect.

Verse 9 (1,000)

pralapan visrjan grhnann unmisan nimisann api
indriyanin*driyarthesu vartanta iti dharayan*

Even though they see, hear, touch, smell, eat, move, sleep, breathe, speak, reject, hold, and open or close their eyes – realize it is only the **senses** working among sense objects.

Verse 10 (1,000) another metaphor

brahmany *adhaya* ***karmani*** *sangam* ***tyaktva karoti*** *yah*
lipyate na sa ***papena padmapatram*** *ivambhasa*

Dedicating **all actions** to **Brahma** and performing them **without attachment**, they are no more stained by **evil** than a **lotus leaf** by muddy water.

Verse 11 (1,000)

kayena ***manasa buddhya*** *kevalair* ***indriyair*** *api*
yoginah karma kurvanti sangam ***tyaktva****tmasuddhaye*

For self-purification, yogins perform actions solely with the body, **mind**, **intellect**, and even the **senses** – **abandoning** any interest in the acts themselves *(kevalair)*.

Verse 12 (1,000) Contrast of those who are enlightened and those who are not.

*yuktah karmaphalam **tyaktva santim** apnoti naisthikim*
***ayuktah** kamakarena phale **sakto** nibadhyate*

Those united to God obtain **lasting peace** by **abandoning** attachments to the outcome. Those who are **not united** to God (not enlightened) are ruled by their desires – through such **attachments**, they remain in bondage.

Bondage refers to reincarnation – it's our delusion which causes us to reincarnate. When a person becomes enlightened, delusion and rebirth ends.

The Soul – Secondary Theme

Verse 13 (1,000) There are nine openings in the human body

*sarvakarmani manasa **samnyasyaste sukham** vasi*
***navadvare pure** dehi **naiva** kurvan na karayan*

Having mentally **renounced** all activities, the soul rests **blissfully** in the **city of nine gates** – **neither** doing nor causing actions.

The city of nine gates is a reference to the body.

Verse 14 (1,000) Consciousness is the cause and only cause

na kartrtvam na karmani lokasya srjati prabhuh
*na **karmaphala**samyogam svabhavas tu pravartate*

God does not create in humans the consciousness of being doers of action, nor does God cause actions by them nor entangle them with the **fruits of actions**. Consciousness is the originator of all of these.

Jnana – Secondary Theme

Verse 15 (1,000) Consciousness is indifferent

nadatte kasyacit papam na caiva sukrtam vibhuh
ajnanenavrtam *jnanam* **tena muhyanti** *jantavah*

Consciousness takes no account for anyone's virtue or sin. **Ignorance obscures insight** – mankind is **thereby bewildered** *(muhyanti)*.

Ignorance obscures insight – mankind is thereby bewildered. This verse is exactly what I was discussing in *The Miracle of Krishna*— we confuse the effect as being the cause. Trying to treat the effects of low levels of consciousness with pharmaceuticals that are themselves low levels of consciousness makes zero sense—*mankind is thereby bewildered.*

Verse 16 (1,000) The fire of suffering becomes the light of consciousness

jnanena tu td **ajnanam** *yesam nasitam atmanah*
tesam *adityavaj* **jnanam prakasayati** *tat* **param**

But those who have banished **ignorance** by Self-knowledge, **this knowledge**, like the **illuminating** sun, reveals the **Supreme**.

Enlightenment – Primary Theme

Verse 17 (1,000) Reincarnation ends when we become enlightened

*tadbuddhayas tadat***manas** *tannisthas* **tatparayanah**
gacchantyapunaravrttim **jnananirdhutakalmasah**

Their **mind** and intellect immersed in Spirit, their soul one with Spirit, **solely devoted to Spirit, erase their sins with knowledge** – only the wise reach this state of non-return.

Verse 18 (1,000) All One

vidyavinayasampanne **brahmane gavi hastini**
suni *caiva svapake ca* **panditah** *samadarsinah*

Enlightened beings see no difference between a **learned**, humble **Brahmin**, a **cow,** an **elephant,** a **dog**, or even a dog-eater.

Verse 19 (1,000) *Brahman*

*ihaiva tair **jitah** sargo yesam samye **sthitam manah***
*nirdosam hi samam **brahma** tasmad **brahmani** te sthitah*

In this very world they have **conquered** the round of birth and death, whose **mind is anchored** in sameness; for *Brahman* is without flaws, therefore in *Brahman* they rest.

Verse 20 (1,000) Enlightenment described

na prahrsyet priyam prapya nodvijet prapya capriyam
***sthirabuddhir asammudho brahmavid** brahmani sthitah*

The knower of Spirit, abiding in *Brahma*, with **unswerving discrimination** and **free from delusion**, is neither jubilant at pleasant experiences nor downcast by unpleasant experiences.

Verse 21 (1,000) Joy, a God-given quality of our Soul

*bahyasparsesvasaktatma vindatyatmani yat **sukham***
*sa **brahmayogayuktatma** sukham **aksayam asnute***

Unattracted to the **outside world** (external objects), yogins experience the **joy** inherent in the Self. **Engaged in divine union of the soul with Spirit**, they **obtain eternal** bliss.

Perhaps my favorite personon the planet is the Dalai Lama, Buddhist monk and the spiritual leader of Tibet. This verse always makes me think of the Dalai Lama because he is always laughing and happy. The Dalai Lama calibrates at the very high level of 573, joy and unconditional love *(ananda)*.

Verse 22 (1,000)

*ye hi **samsparsaja** bhoga **duhka**yonaya eva te*
adyantavantah kaunteya na tesu ramate budhah

Because sense pleasures **produced from outward contacts** have a
beginning and an end, they only bring **misery**, Arjuna.
No sage seeks happiness from them.

Verse 23 (1,000) *Yogin* equals an enlightened being

saknotihaiva yah sodhum prak sariravimoksanat
*kama**krodho**bhavam **vegam** sa yuktah sa **sukhi** narah*

They are true yogins who, on this earth, even up to the very
moment of death, have conquered every **impulse** of desire and
wrath. They are truly **happy**!

If we can conquer our desires, we can conquer our anger and
achieve happiness.

Verse 24 (1,000) Enlightenment – *brahmanirvanam*

yo 'ntahsukho 'ntararamas tathantarjyotir eva yah
*sa **yogi brahmanirvanam brahmabhuto** 'dhigacchati*

The one who finds happiness within, joy within, light within –
that **yogin becomes one with Spirit**. They attain **complete
liberation in Spirit**.

Verse 25 (1,000) *Rishis – seers –* the rarest of all humans (900's)

*labhante **brahmanirvanam** rsayah ksinakalmasah*
*chinnadvaidha **yatatmanah** sarvabhutahite ratah*

They attain **liberation in Spirit**, the *rishis*, whose **sins are
obliterated**, doubts destroyed, **self-restrained**, and dedicated
to the **welfare of mankind**.

Verse 26 (1,000) *brahmanirvanam* – used in this verse and the previous two.

kamakrodha*viyuktanam yatinam* **yatacetasam**
abhito **brahmanirvanam** *vartate* **viditatmanam**

Renunciants who are without **desire** and **anger**, who have **controlled their mind** and **know themselves**, are **completely free**, both in this world and beyond.

Verse 27 (1,000) A *muni* can withdraw consciousness from external objects at will.

sparsan krtva bahir bahyams *caksus caiv****antare** bhruvoh*
pranapanau *samau krtva* **nasabhyantaracarinau**

The yogin **does not accept impressions from external contacts from the outside world**. With inner gaze fixed on the spot **between** the eyebrows and having balanced both **inward and outward breathing** through the **nose**;

See Chapter Eight, Verse 10, regarding the *Shiva-netra*.

Verse 28 (1,000) Continuing
atendriyamanobuddhir munir *moksaparayanah*
vigatecchabhayakrodho yah **sada mukta** *eva sah*

Controlling their senses, mind, and intellect, the *muni*, wholly devoted to enlightenment – with no trace left of desire, fear, and anger, is **always free**.

Verse 29 (1,000)

bhoktaram **yajnatapasam** *sarvalokamahesvaram*
suhrdam **sarvabhutanam** *jnatva mam* **santim** *rcchati*

Knowing Me as the Enjoyer of **holy rites** and **austerities**, the Lord of Creation and Friend to **all creatures**, attains **peace**.

FOREVER IN ME

CHAPTER SIX (997)

....

47 verses

Primary Themes: Enlightenment
Secondary Themes: Renunciation, Yoga, and the Soul

dukham – suffering, an impediment that hinders the progress of the soul.
sukham – pleasure, agreeable, comfortable, happy, prosperous.
nirvana – the end of our unfulfilled desires.

We are exploring the *Bhagavad Gita* with a new understanding of consciousness—it's helpful to think of Yoga as the practices that guide us to these higher levels. Verse 23 in this chapter offers us the true definition of Yoga—the absolute union with Spirit—**enlightenment**, when duality ends. Chapter Six continues discussing enlightenment by contrasting those who calibrate above 600 and those below. Our two Sanskrit words *dukham* and *sukham* emphasize this contrast of consciousness—suffering and pleasure. We learned in Chapter Two that the basic principle of creation is duality—subject and object. In Chapter Three, Krishna told us to *beware of the influence of duality*—our Souls are always content while our egos are never satisfied. The first verse in this chapter relates to attachments—we have attachments because of our likes and dislikes. Although levels of consciousness in the 500's are quite rare, these levels are still attached to happiness. We know that levels below 200 are selfish and levels above 200 are more selfless, higher levels still have the understanding of *mine* and *yours* (duality)—so a sense of selfishness still exists. There is a contrast in this chapter as well as the entire *Bhagavad Gita* between the Soul (Self) and ego (self)—Universal and individual—Pandavas and Kauravas—wisdom and ignorance—war and peace—duality!

Verse 1 (1,000) Contrast

*anasritah karma**phalam karyam** karma karoti yah*
*sa **samnyasi** ca yogi ca na **niragnir** na cakriyah*

True **renunciants** and yogins perform **dutiful** and spiritual actions without desiring their **fruits** – unlike those who live without sacrifice *(niragnir)* or those who abandon actions.

Verse 2 (1,000) Renunciation is the same as Yoga

*yam **samnyasam** iti prahur yogam tam **viddhi** pandava*
*na hy **asamnyastasamkalpo** yogi bhavati kascana*

Understand, what is spoken of in the scriptures as **renunciation** is the same as Yoga, Arjuna – those who **have not renounced their selfish desires** *(samkalpo)* cannot be a yogin.

These first two verses summarize the previous four chapters.

Verse 3 (1,000) Yoga

*aruruksor muner yogam **karma** karmanam **ucyat**e*
yoga**rudhasya tasyaiva **samah** karmanam **ucyate

For the *muni* (meditator) **desiring ascension** (rising of consciousness), **action** is called *their way* – when they have mastered this **Yoga, serenity** is called *their way.*

Verse 4 (1,000) Enlightenment

*yada hi **nendriyarthesu** na **karmasv** anusajjate*
sarvasamkalpasamnyasi yogarudhas tadocyate

Those who have overcome attachments to both **sense objects** and **actions**, and are **free from all selfish motives** – that person is said to have attained firm union of the soul with the Spirit (Enlightenment).

Crossing Over – Ego to Soul

Verse 5 (1,000) Friend or enemy – *I am* or *I should be*

uddhared *atmanatmanam natmanam* **avasadayet**
atmaiva hy atmano bandhur atmaiva **ripur** *atmanah*

Uplift the self (ego) by the Self (Soul); let the self never be
self-degraded – for each person is their own friend or **enemy**.

Verse 6 (1,000) Transform the self (ego) into the Self (soul)

bandhur atmatmanas tasya yenatmaivatmana **jitah**
anatmanas tu **satrutve** *vartetatmaiva* **satruvat**

The person whose self (ego) has been **conquered** by the Self
(soul), the Self is the friend of the self; but, the self (ego)
behaves **inimically** (hostile), **as an enemy** toward the self (ego)
that is not controlled.

Verse 7 (1,000) Transcending duality

jiatmanah prasantasya paramatma samahitah
*sitosna***sukhaduhkhesu** *tatha* **manapamanayoh**

Victorious over the ego (above 600) and always one with Spirit, a
sage remains serene, regardless of cold or heat, **pleasure** or **pain**,
in **honor or dishonor**.

Verse 8 (1,000) Enlightenment

jnanavijnanatrptatma kutastho **vijitendriyah**
yukta ity ucyate yogi samalostasmakancanah

Yogins who have **conquered their senses**, absorbed in truth and
Self-realization – look with an equal eye on earth, stone, or gold.

Verse 9 (1,000) All One - Unconditional love – Level 540 and up

*suhrnmitra***r***yudasinamadhyastha***dvesya***bandhusu (43 letters)*
sadhusv **api** *ca* **papesu** *samabuddhir* **visisyate**

Great yogins are impartial to all: **patrons, friends,** enemies, strangers, mediators, **hateful people,** relatives, the **virtuous** and the **ungodly.**

*** In some editions of this text, an extra verse is included after Verse 9.

Meditation – new subject

Verses 10 through 14: Krishna teaches meditation. (984)

Verse 10: Choose a quiet place to meditate alone.

Verse 11: It should be clean and the seat should be firm, neither too high, nor too low.

Verse 12: Concentrate the mind on one point, practicing Yoga for self-purification.

Verse 13: The word *nasikagram* found in Verse 13 means *origin* of the nose, not tip of the nose. The origin of the nose is the spot between the two eyebrows, the seat of spiritual vision.

Verse 14: Meditating on God should be the final goal.

Verse 15 (1,000) *nirvana* – extinction of the flame of life

yunjann evam sadatmanam **yogi niyatamanasah**
santim nirvana*paramam matsamstham adhigacchati*

When yoked continuously, the **yogin of restrained thought** attains the **peace** of My being, the final *nirvana.*

Earlier a quote from Vivekananda was offered, speaking to our unfulfilled desires *(samskaras)* being the cause of rebirth—*nirvana*

signifies the end of our unfulfilled desires. By entering this highest
state of restrained thought, the yogin becomes liberated from rebirth. They can retain this state while conscious, subconscious, or
in super-conscious states. The yogin can watch their body in this
state of ecstasy while it is working or inactive. The inactive state is
called *savikalpa samadhi*. Properly instructed yogins learn to enter
and leave these active and inactive states (suspended animation,
trance) at will. In Chapter Four, I included the story of Krishnamacharya's ability to stop his heart and breath. It is my belief
that this is what Krishnamacharya was demonstrating to his son.
In our previous chapter, the word *brahmanirvanam* was used in
Verses, 24, 25, and 26, translated as *liberation in Spirit*. Verse 18
is a continuation of this verse.

Verse 16 (1,000) Commitment

natyasnatas tu yogo 'sti na caikantam anasnatah
na catisvapnasilasya jagrato naiva carjuna

Arjuna, the gourmand, the scanty eater, the person who
habitually oversleeps, the one who sleeps too little –
none of these people finds success in Yoga.

Verse 17 (1,000) Contrast – *yukta*; proper, sensible, skillful

yuktaharaviharasya yuktacestasya **karmasu**
yuktasvapnavabodhasya yogo bhavati **dukkhaha**

Those who eat a regular proper diet, relaxes, **works**, sleeps, and
remains awake (aware) will find Yoga the destroyer of **suffering**.

Verse 18 (1,000) Continuation from Verse 15

yada viniyatam **cittam atmany** *evavatisthate*
nihsprhah *sarvakamebhyo* **yukta** *ity* **ucyate** *tada*

One **is called "yoked"** when their **mind** (*citta*, feelings) is
restrained *(viniyatam)* and comes to rest upon their **Self** alone,

without craving for any object of **desire.**

Verse 19 (1,000) Unshaken by the outside world

*yatha **dipo** nivatastho nengate **sopama smrta***
***yogino yatacittasya** yunjato yogam atmanah*

Just as a candle **flame** does not flicker in a windless place – that is
the **well-known metaphor** of **a yogin** of **restrained mind** who
yokes themselves to the yoga of the Self.

Yoga – Secondary Theme

The purpose of Yoga is to provide a practical method for uniting
the ego with the Soul. Every system of religion and school of philosophy in India acknowledges Yoga as the most scientific means
for realizing philosophical truths.

Verse 20 (1,000) The ego perceives itself as the Soul

yatroparamate** cittam **niruddham yogasevaya
*yatra caivatmanatmanam **pasyan** atmani **tusyati***

In that state, the **restrained** mind, stilled through the **practice of
Yoga**, the ego **perceives** itself as the Soul and is content in
the Soul;

Verse 21 (1,000) Once enlightened, always enlightened

sukham atyantikam** yat tad **buddhigrahyam atindriyam
***vetti** yatra na caivayam **sthitas calati** tattvatah*

When a yogin **experiences infinite happiness beyond the
senses**, which can be grasped by **awakened intelligence**,
they become **established** there, never **removed** from Truth.

Verse 22 (1,000) *immune to the greatest grief*

*yam **labdhva** caparam labham **manyate** nadhikam tatah*
*yasmin **sthito** na **duhkhena** gurunapi **vicalyate***

Once that state is **found** (enlightenment), the yogin **considers** it the treasure beyond all treasures – **established** therein – they are **immune** to even the **greatest grief**.

Verse 23 (1,000) A third definition of Yoga from Krishna

*tam vidyad **duhkhasam**yogaviyogam yogasamjnitam*
*sa **niscayena yoktavyo** yogo 'nirvinnacetasa*

This state is known as Yoga – the **pain-free** state (enlightenment). This Yoga should **certainly** be **practiced** with firm resolve and a stout heart – **disregarding matters of the world**.

Verse 24 (1,000) Be present

*samkalpaprabhavan kamams **tyaktva** sarvan asesatah*
*manasaivendriyagramam **viniyamya samantatah***

Abandoning all desires born of selfish purposes, **restricting** the senses **from all sides** with the mind itself;

Verse 25 (1,000) Don't give up

*sanaih sanair uparamed buddhya **dhrtigrhitaya***
atma**samstham manah krtva **na kimcid api cintayet

With the intellect held **securely with determination**, the mind absorbed in the **Soul, thinking of nothing at all**, step by step, you will attain tranquility (enlightenment).

Verse 26 (1,000)

*yato yato niscarati **manas** cancalam asthiram*
*tatas tato **niyamya**itad atmany eva vasam nayet*

Whenever the **mind** wanders away – whatever the reason – withdraw it from those distractions and return it to the sole **control** of the Self.

Verse 27 (1,000) Enlightened – *brahmabhutam* – one with Spirit

prasantamanasam hy enam yoginam **sukham uttamam**
upaiti santarajasam **brahmabhutam akalmasam**

Supreme happiness comes to the yogin who has completely **calmed** their **mind** and controlled their passions – free from **impurities**, they become **one with Spirit**.

Verse 28 (1,000) Yogic practice does not mean *hatha-yoga*

yunjann evam sadatmanam yogi **vigatakalmasah**
sukhena **brahmasamsparsam** *atyantam* **sukham** *asnute*

The yogin, **free from all impurities**, ceaselessly engaging in yogic practice, easily attains the **endless bliss of continuous mergence with Spirit** *(Brahman)*.

Verse 29 (1,000) The *atman* exists equally in all beings *(sarvabhutani atmanam)*

sarvabhutastham *atmanam* **sarvabhutani** *catmani*
iksate yogayuktatma *sarvatra samadarsanah*

With the **soul united to Spirit by Yoga**, seeing equality for all things, the yogin **beholds** their Self in **all creatures and all creatures in Spirit**.

Verse 30 (1,000) Grace always finds us worthy

yo mam **pasyati sarvatra** *sarvam ca mayi* **pasyati**
tasyaham na pranasyami sa ca me na **pranasyati**

Those who **see** Me **everywhere** and **beholds** everything in Me, **never lose sight** of Me, nor do I **ever lose sight** of them.

We see others in ourselves when we see ourselves and others in God.

Verse 31 (1,000) Unconditional love, regardless of the conditions we may live.

sarvabhutasthitam *yo mam bhajaty ekatvam asthitah*
sarvatah vartamano 'pi sa yogi mayi vartate

The yogin who is established in Divine unity, realizing Me as **pervading all beings**, stays forever in Me, however they may live.

Verse 32 (1,000) Unconditional Love

atmaupamyena sarvatra samam pasyati yo 'rjuna
sukham *va yadi va* **duhkham** *sa yogi paramo matah*

Those who feel for others even as they feel for themselves, whether in **grief or pleasure**, are the best types of yogins, Arjuna.

atmaupamyena – an analogy to one's self

Arjuna said:

In these two verses, Arjuna is expressing doubt and resistance

Verse 33: *Krishna, owing to my restlessness, I do not see the permanent effects of the equanimity of Yoga you have described to me.*

Verse 34: *The mind is unsteady, tumultuous, powerful, and obstinate! Krishna, I consider the mind as difficult to control as the wind!*

Krishna said:

Verse 35 (1,000) Krishna explains how the mind can be controlled.

asamsayam mahabaho mano **durnigraham** *calam*
abhyasena *tu kaunteya* **vairagyena** *ca grhyate*

Undoubtedly the mind is restless and **difficult to control** – but with steady **practice** and **non-attachment**, Arjuna, the mind can be controlled.

Verse 36 (1,000) God's Promise

asamyatatmana yogo **dusprapa** *iti me matih*
vasyatmana tu yatata sakyo 'vaptum upayatah

This is my word – Yoga (enlightenment) is **difficult to attain** by the undisciplined individual, but it can be achieved through self-control and proper methods.

Arjuna asked:

Verses 37 – 39: *What happens to someone who is unsuccessful in Yoga? Don't they perish like a sundered cloud if they do not find their way to Brahma? Please remove my doubts forever – no one can resolve my doubts but you.*

Krishna answers:

Verse 40 (1,000) Krishna clearly answers Arjuna's questions

partha naiveha namutra vinasas tasya vidyate
na hi **kalyanakrt** *kascid* **durgatim** *tata gacchati*

Arjuna, those who perform **virtuous** actions never meets destruction. Whether in this world or the next, they never fall into **evil** situations!

Verse 41 (1,000)

prapya punyakrtam lokan **usitva** *sasvatih samah*
sucinam srimatam **gehe yogabhrasto** *'bhijayate*

A yogin who has not yet reached the enlightened state, gains entry to the world of the virtuous, **where they remain** for many years – afterward, they are reborn on earth in a good and prosperous **home.**

Verse 42 (1,000) *kule* – Noble birth

athava *yoginam eva kule bhavati dhimatam*
etad dhi **durlabhataram** *loke* **janma** *yad* **idrsam**

Or they may reincarnate into a family of enlightened yogins –
this type of noble **birth** is **rare** in this world!

Verse 43 (1,000)

*tatra tam **buddhisamyogam labhate paurvadehikam***
*yatate ca tato bhuyah **samsiddhau** kurunandana*

There, Arjuna, they **recover the Yoga discrimination** (previous
level of consciousness?) **attained** in their **former existence** (previous life), trying more earnestly for spiritual success.

Verse 44 (1,000) *sabdabrahma* – study of the *Vedas* is not the
highest reality attained.

*purvabhyasena tenaiva hriyate hy **avaso** 'pi sah*
*jijnasur api yogasya **sabdabrahma**tivartate*

The yogin is sustained, **involuntarily**, by their previous practice
of Yoga; their desire to practice yoga again transcends the **study
of the *Vedas***.

Verse 45 (1,000) *yogabramhsah* – enlightenment reached during
one lifetime

prayatnad** yatamanas tu yogi **samsuddhakilbisah
*anekajanmasamsiddhas tato yati **param gatim***

By diligently following their path, the yogin, **purified of sin** by
their **efforts** over many lifetimes, finally enters the **Supreme
Refuge** (enlightenment).

Verse 46 (1,000) Krishna proclaims the excellence of Yoga

***tapas**vibhyo 'dhiko yogi **jnanibhyo** 'pi mato 'dhikah*
***karmibhyas** cadhiko yogi tasmad yogi bhavarjuna*

The yogin is deemed greater than **body-disciplined** ascetics, even
greater than the followers of the **path of wisdom** or of the **path
of action** – therefore, be a yogi Arjuna!

Verse 47 (1,000) Knowledge of God is superior to all other types of knowledge.

yoginam api sarvesam madgatenantaratmana
***sraddha**van bhajate yo mam sa me **yuktatamo** matah*

Those with **devotion** absorb themselves in Me, with their souls immersed in Me, I regard as **the very best** among all yogins.

This last verse and entire chapter supports my earlier statement regarding *hatha-yoga* not being a path to God, enlightenment, or self-realization. *Hatha-yoga* is a physical practice – enlightenment lies in the mind.

COME TO ME

CHAPTER SEVEN (999.2)

....

30 Verses

Primary Themes: Krishna, Consciousness, Enlightenment, and the *gunas*
Secondary Themes: Yoga, and *bhakti*

jiva – consciousness of the Soul, the principle of life.
maya – illusion, deceit, fraud, displaying consciousness as duality.
shraddha – devotion, faithfulness, trust, confidence.

Chapter Seven is about how we approach God, why we approach God, and at what level we approach God. In Chapter Two, only one verse was offered telling us who Krishna really is. In Chapter Three, two verses. The opening 15 verses of Chapter Four tell us more about the powers of Krishna. The final verse of Chapter Five reveals even more about Krishna and only three verses in Chapter Six. This entire chapter is about Krishna—which makes this chapter quite different from the previous five. Verse Five gives us a new Sanskrit word to learn and comprehend—*jiva*. This word will be explained when we get to that specific verse. The ground work has been prepared with all twelve primary and secondary themes presented in the previous five chapters. Krishna carefully keeps us from making assumptions and drawing conclusions about His message—going to great lengths to make everything perfectly clear for us. Chapter Seven now takes us deeper into the teachings of the *Bhagavad Gita* as well as Krishna Himself.

Verse 1 (1,000) Krishna

mayy asaktamanah partha *yogam yunjann madasrayah*
asamsayam *samagram mam yatha jnasyasi tac* **chrnu**

Absorb your mind in Me, Arjuna, take shelter in Me, and follow the path of Yoga. **Hear** how you shall know Me **beyond all doubts**, with all My attributes and powers.

Verse 2 (1,000) Everything that is to be known is based on knowledge and action *(vijnanam)*

jnanam te 'ham savijnanam idam vaksyamy asesatah
yaj jnatva neha bhuyo 'nyaj jnatavyam avasisyate

I **will teach** you **in detail**, both **theoretical knowledge** and the **knowledge** which can be known only by direct spiritual experience – knowing both – nothing in this world **remains to be known**.

Verse 3 (1,000) Enlightenment is very rare

manusyanam sahasresu kascid yatati siddhaye
yatatam api siddhanam kascin mam vetti tattvatah

Among many **thousands, perhaps one strives** for spiritual **attainment** – and among the blessed true seekers that diligently try to reach Me, **perhaps one** knows Me in **truth** as I am.

Krishna – Primary Theme

Verse 4 (1,000) 8 *tattvas* – manifested nature – Krishna's lower nature

bhumir apo 'nalo vayuh kham mano buddhir eva ca
ahamkara itiyam me bhinna prakrtir asadha

My **manifested nature** (Form – *Prakriti*) has **eight** aspects: **earth, water, fire, air, ether**, mind *(manas)*, intelligence *(buddhi)* and ego *(ahamkara)*.

Verse 5 (1,000) *jiva* is the consciousness of the soul

apareyam itas tv anyam prakrtim viddhi me param
jivabhutam mahabaho yayedam dharyate jagat

My different and **higher nature** is the *jiva*, Arjuna, the self-consciousness and life-principles that sustains the universe.

Jiva is the same consciousness that recognizes its oneness with God, but operates as an individual entity—the individual soul. *Jiva* works as a sort of "middle man." As *Para-Prakriti* (Pure Nature – Krishna's higher nature), it's attuned to consciousness, and as the ego, it's attuned to the soul. The *jivatman* (individual) connects us *(yoga)* to the Universal Soul.

Verse 6 (1,000) *It all begins and ends with Me*

etadyoni*ni* **bhutani sarvani***ty* **upadharaya**
aham *krtsnasya jagatah* **prabhavah pralayas** *tatha*

Realize all beings originate from **these two energies** of Mine *(prakriti and paraprakriti)*, the **womb of all beings.**
I Create and Dissolve the entire universe.

Verse 7 (1,000) *Pearls on a thread*

matah **parataram** *nanyat kimcid asti dhanamjaya*
mayi sarvam idam **protam sutre manigana** *iva*

There is nothing at all that **transcends** Me Arjuna.
Everything is **bound** to me like a row of **pearls** on a **thread.**

Verse 8 (1,000) Everything is consciousness

raso 'ham apsu *kaunteya* **prabha** *'smi* **sasisuryayoh**
pranavah **sarvavedesu sabdah** *khe* **paurusam nrsu**

I am the **taste in water** O son of Kunti – the **radiance in the sun and moon** – the *Aum **in all the Vedas*** – the **sound** in the silence – and the **heroism in men.**

Verse 9 (1,000) Consciousness

punyo **gandhah** *prthivyam ca* **tejas** *casmi vibhavasau*
jivanam **sarvabhutesu tapas** *casmi tapasvisu*

I am the sweet **fragrance** from the earth – the **luminescence** in the fire – the life in **all beings**, and the **self-discipline** in anchorites (spiritual hermits).

Verse 10 (1,000) Consciousness

*bijam mam **sarvabhutanam** viddhi partha sanatanam*
***buddhir** buddhimatam asmi **tejas tejasvinam** aham*

Know Me to be the eternal source of **all creatures**, Arjuna. I am the **intelligence** of the wise and the **radiance** of **vital beings**.

Verse 11 (1,000) *kamo* – Nature of Consciousness – the desire to end all suffering.

balam balavatam caham kamaragavivarjitam
***dharmaviruddho** bhutesu kamo 'smi bharatarsabha*

Among the powerful, I am the power that is free from longings and attachments. I am the desire which is **in accord with dharma**, O Best of the Bharatas.

Gunas – Primary Theme

Verse 12 (1,000) The *gunas* do not affect consciousness – consciousness affects the *gunas*.

*ye caiva **sattvika bhava rajas** as **tamasas** ca ye*
matta eveti tan viddhi na tv aham tesu te mayi

Know that all **qualities** of *sattva*, *rajas*, and *tamas* emanate from Me. Though they are in Me, I am not in them.

Verse 13 (1,000) Consciousness is unchangeable and beyond the *gunas*.

***tribhir gunamayair** bhavair ebhih sarvam idam jagat*
*mohitam **nabhijanati** mam **ebhyah** param avyayam*

Because they are **deluded by the three qualities of Nature,** the whole world **does not perceive** Me – unchangeable and **beyond** all qualities.

Verse 14 (1,000) *Gunas, maya,* and enlightenment

*daivi hy esa **gunamayi** mama **maya** duratyaya*
*mam eva ye **prapadyante mayam etam** taranti te*

It is difficult to go beyond the influence of My divine **hypnosis,** saturated with these **three qualities** *(gunas)*. Only those who surrender to Me (become enlightened) **become** free from this **power of illusion** *(maya)*.

Maya limits our perception of Truth.

Verse 15 (1,000) delusion: *mudhah* – dominated by *tamas*

*na mam duskrtino **mudhah prapadyante naradhamah***
***mayayapahrtajnana asuram** bhavam asritah*

The lowest of humans, whose discrimination has been stolen by *maya*, perpetrators of evil and misguided **fools,** follow the path of **demonic** beings, failing to surrender to Me.

Verse 16 (1,000) Four different levels of consciousness

caturvidha bhajante mam janah sukrtino 'rjuna
arto jijnasur artharthi jnani ca bharatarsabha

There are **four kinds** of **people** who worship Me Arjuna; those who want relief from suffering, those who seek wisdom, the cravers for power here and in the hereafter, and the **wise,** Arjuna.

Krishna lists *four kinds of people* that could align with our four caste classifications. *The wise* would be the *Brahmin's; those who seek wisdom* would be *Kshatriya's; those who want relief from suffering* would be *Vaishya's;* and *Sudra's* would be *those who crave power here and in the hereafter.*

Verse 17 (1,000) *jnani* – enlightened being

*tesam **jnani nityayukta ekabhaktir visisyate***
*priyo hi **jnanino** 'tyartham aham sa ca **mama priyah***

Best among them are the **enlightened, always attached** in **single-minded devotion**. I am exceedingly dear to the ***jnanis***, and they are exceedingly **dear to Me**.

Verse 18 (1,000) *jnani* – enlightened being

***udarah** sarva evaite **jnani** tv atmaiva me matam*
asthitah** sa hi yuktatma mam **evanuttamam gatim

All are **noble**, but the ***jnani*** I consider as My own Self. Unwaveringly **settled** in Me alone as **their highest goal**.

Verse 19 (1,000) Enlightened levels are extremely rare.

***bahunam janmanam ante** jnanavan mam prapadyante*
vasudevah sarvam** iti sa **mahatma sudurlabhah

After many lifetimes, the *jnani* attains Me (becomes enlightened), realizing, *"The Lord is everywhere!"* A **great soul** is very **rare**.

Verse 20 (1,000) Human behavior

*kamais tais tair **hrtajnanah** prapadyante 'nyadevatah*
*tam tam **niyamam asthaya** prakrtya niyatah svaya*

Led by their own **inclinations** (levels of consciousness), their **discrimination** stolen by this or that craving, **pursuing** this or that obsessive desire, many seek lesser gods.

Bhakti – Secondary Theme

Verse 21 (1,000) *bhakti – sraddha*

*yo yo yam **tanum bhaktah sraddhaya**rcitum **icchati***
*tasya tasy**acalam sraddham** tam eva vidadhamy aham*

Whatever **deity** (form) a **devotee faithfully desires** to worship, it is I who makes their **devotion** strong and **steady**.

Verse 22 (1,000) No sincere worship is ignored by God

*sa taya **sraddhaya yuktas** tasyaradhanam ihate*
***labhate** ca tatah **kaman** mayaiva **vihitan** hi tan*

Absorbed in **devotion**, intent on the **worship** of embodiment, the devotee thus **receives** the fruits of their longings – yet those **desires** are **granted** by Me alone.

Verse 23 (1,000) Limited understanding equals limited results

antavat** tu **phalam** tesam tad bhavaty **alpamedhasam
devan devayajo yanti madbhakta yanti mam api

Those of **limited understanding** receive **limited results**. The devotees of those deities go to them – My devotees come to Me.

Krishna – Primary Theme

Verse 24 (1,000) Contrast of form and formless

*avyaktam vyaktim apannam **manyante** mam **abuddhayah***
*param bhavam **ajananto mamavyayam** anuttamam*

Those **lacking wisdom think** of Me as taking a finite form, like a human being – **not understanding** that **I am infinite** (formless) in Nature.

Verse 25 (1,000) *I am unseen by men* (formless)

*naham prakasah sarvasya **yogamayasamavrtah***
mudho** yam nabhijanati loko mam **ajam avyayam

Seemingly **eclipsed** by My own *Yoga-Maya* (creative power), **I am unseen by men**. The confused world does not recognize Me as the **Unborn** and **Eternal**.

Verse 26 (1,000) *No one knows Me*

vedaham *sam*atitani **vartamanani** *carjuna*
bhavisyani *ca bhutani mam tu* **veda** *na kascana*

I know about every creature of the **past**, **present**, and **future**, Arjuna – but no one **knows** Me.

Einstein said: *Know that the distinction between past, present, and future is only a stubbornly persistent illusion (maya).* (997)

Verse 27 (1,000) Duality

icchadvesasamutthena dvandvamohena bharata
sarvabhutani sammoham *sarge yanti paramtapa*

Descendant of Bharata, at birth, **all creatures** are born into **delusive ignorance**, caused by the dualities generated from likes and dislikes.

Verse 28 (1,000) Enlightened

yesam tv **antagatam papam** *jananam punyakarmanam*
te **dvandvamoha**nirmukta *bhajante* **mam drdhavratah**

But righteous people, **free from sin**, are liberated from the **delusion of duality** and are **devoted to Me**.

Verse 29 (1,000)

jaramaranamoksaya *mam asritya yatanti ye*
te **brahma** *tad viduh krtsnam* **adhyatmam karma** *cakhilam*

Those who seek deliverance from the cycle of birth, **old age, and death**, by taking refuge in Me – will know *Brahman*, the **highest self**, and all the secrets of *karma*.

Verse 30 (1,000)

sadhibhutadhidaivam mam *sadhiyajnam* ca ye viduh
prayanakale 'pi ca mam te vidur yuktacetasah

Those who know Me in the **physical**, the **astral**, and the **spiritual**, with heart united to the soul, continue to know Me, even **at the time of death.**

PATH OF LIGHT

CHAPTER EIGHT (995)

....

28 Verses

Primary Themes: Krishna and Enlightenment
Secondary Themes: Reincarnation, Yoga, Soul, and *bhakti*

punarjanma – rebirth
yuga – a particular span of time, one of four ages of the world
anusmara – remembrance

Chapter Eight may contain the most esoteric teachings of any chapter in the entire *Bhagavad Gita*. My intention is to keep you on track with the bigger picture of what Krishna is teaching Arjuna. Once you have finished the entire book, come back again and again to revisit these teachings—they will reveal themselves more fully with time. The level of consciousness in which the *Bhagavad Gita* was written is extremely high—it can be a tough nut to crack with one reading.

Arjuna asks eight questions at the opening of this chapter: *What is Spirit? What is Spirit's intelligence as the individual Soul? What is Karma? What are the physical body and physical universe? What are the astral body and astral universe? How is Spirit present in the body as the Soul? How at the hour of death can I be with you?* Arjuna's last question about death is his most important question. Understanding death is more important than understanding life, because whether or not we understand life, it generally remains the same. The whole quality of our life changes the moment we understand death—even a little understanding of death is enough to transform our entire way of thinking. We are constantly moving toward death without ever stopping to think about it. Understanding that each day is truly a gift helps make each and every day count. What we've created in our current life will be waiting for us to face in our next life, just as the consequences and conflicts we create today will be waiting for us tomorrow. Reincarnation is a compassionate way of learning about responsibility—what we do in this life and how we do it determines how we're reborn.

Arjuna asked:

Verse 1:

kim tad ***brahma*** kim ***adhyatmam*** kim ***karma*** *purusottama* ***adhibhutam*** *ca kim proktam* ***adhidaivam*** *kim ucyate*

Krishna, please tell me, **what** is **Brahman**? What is **Adhyatmam**? What is **Karma**? What is **Adhibhutam**? And what is **Adhidaivam**?

Verse 2:

adhiyajnah *katham ko 'tra dehe 'smin madhusudana* ***prayanakale*** *ca* ***katham jneyo 'si niyatat mabhih***

O Slayer of the Demon Madhu (Krishna), what is **Adhiyajnah**, and what manner is **Adhiyajnah** present as the soul in this body? **How at the time of death** are you to **be known** by the **self-disciplined**?

Krishna answers:

Verse 3 (1,000) *svabhavo* – the second, higher *prakriti* of God

aksaram brahma *paramam svabhavo 'dhyatmam ucyate* ***bhuta****bhavodbhavakaro visargah* ***karma****samjnitah*

The **Indestructible** and Supreme Spirit **is called Brahman** (consciousness). **Adhyatmam can be explained** as the continuous flow of consciousness *(svabhavo)*. **Karma** is the name for the creative force *(visargah)* that brings the variety of **beings** into existence.

Verse 4 (1,000) Everything is *Brahman* and an expression of *Brahman*

adhibhutam ksaro *bhavah* **purusas** *cadhidaivatam*
adhiyajno *'ham evatra* **dehe** *dehabhrtam vara*

Adhibhutam is the basis of **perishable**, physical existence (form).
Adhidaivam is *Purusa*. I, the Spirit within the **body** am
Adhiyajnah, the Origin and Maker of all.

Verse 5 (1,000) *smaran* - remembering

antakale *ca mam eva* **smaran** *muktva* **kalevaram**
yah prayati sa madbhavam yati nasty **samsayah**

Lastly, those who only **remember** Me enter my Being
at the hour of their passing, when **the body** is abandoned.
This is truth beyond doubt.

Verse 6 (1,000) Perhaps this is the reason we are born with our
specific level of consciousness.

yam yam **smaran** *bhavam* **tyajaty** *ante kalevaram*
*tam tam evaite kaunteya sada tad***bhava***bhavitah*

The **thought** with which a dying person **leaves** their body
determines – through their long persistence in it, Arjuna –
their next **state of being**.

Verse 7 (1,000) *It's your life – fight! I can't live your life for you.*

tasmat sarvesu *kalesu mam* **anusmara yudhya** *ca*
mayy arpitamanobuddhir mam evaisyasy **asamsayah**

Therefore, always remember Me and **fight**! Surrender your
mind and understanding to Me! **Without a doubt** you will
come to Me.

Verse 8 (1,000) Again, this verse does not mean *hatha-yoga*.

abhyasayogayuktena **cetasa** *nanyagamina*
paramam purusam divyam *yati parthanucintayan*

Arjuna, they attain the **Supreme Effulgent Lord** *(purusam)* whose **mind**, disciplined by constant Yoga practice, is immovably fixed on the thought of Him.

Verse 9 (1,000) Higgs boson particle

kavim puranam *anusasitaram* **anor** (atom) **aniyamsam anusmared** *yah*
sarvasya dhataram acintyarupam **adityavarnam** *tamasah parastat*

Meditating on the **eternal** and **omniscient**, the Great Ruler, **smaller than the finest atom**, the Supporter of all, unimaginable, always **remembering** the Being who **shines like the sun.**

The Higgs boson particle was detected in July of 2012. It is the subatomic particle that gives other particles their mass. Without the Higgs boson, mass fundamentally doesn't exist. For better or worse, the Higgs boson has become synonymous with the term, "God particle." It seems Krishna knew about this particle all along—after all, He's the one who created it.

Verse 10 (1,000) *Shiva-netra*

prayanakale *manasacalena* **bhaktya** *yukto yogabalena caiva*
bhruvor madhye **pranam** *avesya samyak sa tam param* **purusam upaiti** *divyam*

At the time of death, endowed with **devotion**, placing their **prana** in between their two eyebrows through the power of Yoga, and with an unshaken mind, **attains** this supreme, divine **Purusa**.

The *Shiva-netra* is located between the two eyebrows. It is commonly referred to as the third eye or the eye of intuition and is believed to be the doorway to heaven. When the third eye opens, all illusion ends. Back in Chapter Five, Verse 27 also spoke about the *Shiva-netra*; as well as Verse 13 in Chapter Six: *nasikagram*, meaning origin of the nose, the spot between the two eyebrows, the seat of spiritual vision.

Chapter Five, Verse 27: *The yogin does not accept impressions from external contacts from the outside world. With inner gaze fixed on the spot between the eyebrows and having balanced both inward and outward breathing through the nose;*

Enlightenment – Primary Theme

Verse 11 (1,000) *Brahmacaryam* – a life of self-discipline

*yad aksaram **vedavido vadanti** visanti yad yatayo vitaragah*
*yad icchanto **brahmacaryam caranti tat** te padam **samgrahena***
pravaksye

That abode, which the **knowers of the *Veda* declare** as
Unchanging, in which renunciants free from attachments
lead a life of self-discipline – the method for attaining *That*,
I will explain to you **in brief**.

Krishna assures Arjuna that enlightenment is attainable through certain practices *(caranti)* described in the following verses.

Verses 12 and 13 (1,000) Our souls can enter or leave any of the nine openings in our bodies.

***sarvadvarani** samyamya **mano hrdi** nirudhya ca*
*murdhny adhayatmanah **pranam** asthito yogadharanam*

om** ity ekaksaram **brahma** vyaharan **mam anusmaran
***yah prayati** tyajan **deham** sa yati paramam gatim*

Closing the nine gates of the body, confining the **mind** within the **heart**, the full **life force** fixed in the head – those who engage in the steady practice of Yoga, uttering the single syllable *Aum*, the Holy Word of *Brahman*, and **remembering Me** at the time of their **final exit** from **the body**, reaches the Highest Goal (enlightenment).

Verse 14 (1,000) Krishna tells us to make our lives a prayer.

*ananyacetah satatam yo **mam smarati** nityasah*
*tasyaham **sulabhah** partha nityayuktasya **yoginah***

Arjuna, for the *yogin* (devotee) who constantly **remembers Me**, with their mind intensely focused on Me, I am **easily reached**.

Verse 15 (1,000) Enlightened beings do not need to be reborn.

*mam upetya **punarjanma** duhkhalayam asasvatam*
*napnuvanti **mahatmanah samsiddhim paramam gatah***

Having attained Me, having **achieved the highest perfection** – **the great souls** incur no further **rebirths** in this world of misery.

Verse 16 (1,000) Yogins not yet enlightened are reborn

***abrahmabhuvanal** lokah **punaravartino** 'rjuna*
*mam upetya tu kaunteya **punarjanma na** vidyate*

Those who are not yet free from the world (enlightened) **return back again** Arjuna, even from **the high sphere of *Brahma*** (between 500 and 599). One who reaches Me (above 599) O son of Kunti, is **never reborn**.

Brahma – My Highest Abode

Verse 17 (1,000)

***sahasrayuga**paryantam ahar yad **brahmano** viduh*
ratrim yugasahasrantam te 'horatravido janah

They are true knowers of "**day**" and "**night**" who understand the
Day of *Brahma*, which endures for **a thousand cycles,** and the
Night of *Brahma*, which also endures for **a thousand cycles**.

The word *yuga* is a general term for designating an age or particular span of time. Depending on the formula, various figures
determine the length of *yugas*. There are four *yugas*: *Kali, Dvapara,
Tetra,* and *Satya*. According to the *Bhagavata Purana*, the *Dvapara*
lasts 864,000 years – this is the *yuga* we are currently in. The four
yugas comprise an aggregate of 4,320,000 years.

Verse 18 (1,000) *emerges from – sinks into* – rebirth and death

avyaktad *vyaktayah sarvah prabhavanty* ***aharagame***
ratryagame *praliyante tatraiva****vyakta****samjnake*

At the dawn of *Brahma's* Day, **all creation**, reborn,
emerges from the state of **non-manifestation** (formless) –
at the dusk of *Brahma's* Night, all creation sinks into (dissolves)
the sleep of **non-manifestation**.

Verse 19 (1,000) Reincarnation

bhutagramah sa evayam ***bhutva bhutva*** *praliyante*
ratryagame *'vasah partha prabhavanty* ***aharagame***

Again and again Arjuna, the same multitudes of people helplessly
take rebirth. Their series of incarnations ceases at **the coming of
Night**, and then reappears at **the dawn of Day**.

Verse 20 (1,000) *Brahman* never perishes, everything else does.

paras *tasmat tu bhavo 'nyo '****vyakto*** *'vyaktat* ***sanatanah*** (eternal)
yah sa sarvesu bhutesu ***nasyatsu*** *na vinasyati*

Higher than the unmanifested, the true **Unmanifested** exists
(Brahman), the **Eternal,** and the Absolute – which remains un-
touched when all existence **perishes**.

Verse 21 (1,000) Enlightenment

*avyakto 'ksara ity uktas tam ahuh **paramam gatim***
*yam prapya **na nivartante** tad dhama paramam mama*

The **Unmanifested**, the Unchanging Absolute, is thus called
the **Supreme Goal**. Those who attain My highest abode,
never comes back.

Verse 22 (1,000) Free from birth and death

*purusah sa **parah** partha **bhaktya labhyas** tv ananyaya*
yasyantahsthani bhutani yena sarvam idam tatam

By **unwavering devotion** *(bhakti)* Arjuna, the highest ***Purusa***
is **reached**. God alone, the Omnipresent, is the Abode of all
creatures.

The Two Paths

Mysterious and highly esoteric, Verses 23 through 26 explain how
our souls become free from **rebirth**. This contrast of light and
dark is often used as a metaphor for knowledge and ignorance.
The *two paths* are used here as a metaphor for enlightenment and
reincarnation.

Verse 23 (1,000) The path of freedom and the path of rebirth

*yatra **kale** tv anavrttim avrttim caiva yoginah*
*prayati yanti tam kalam **vaksyamy bharatarsabha***

I will now **explain** to you, the **Best of the Bharatas**,
the path which at the **time** of death, yogins attain freedom –
and also the path where there is rebirth.

There are two paths for the soul at the time of death. The path
where there is no further rebirth is *anavrttim*—and the path re-
turning back to life is *avrttim*.

Verse 24 (1,000) The *path of light* leads to enlightenment

agnir jyotir ahah suklah sanmasa uttarayanam
tatra prayati gacchanti *brahma brahmavido* janah

Fire, light, daytime, the **bright** half of the lunar month, and the six months of the northern course of the sun – pursuing this path at the time of departure, **the knowers of God** go to **God**;

Verse 25 (1,000) The *dark path* leads to rebirth

dhumo ratris tatha krsnah **sanmasa** daksinayanam
tatra **candramasam jyotir** yogi prapya **nivartate**

Smoke, nighttime, the dark half of the lunar month, and the **six months** of the southern course of the sun – those who follow this path reach the **lunar light** and **return again**.

Verse 26 (1,000) These *two paths* of light and dark (enlightenment and rebirth) will always exist.

suklakrsne **gati** hy ete *jagatah* sasvate mate (according to the *Veda*s)
ekaya yaty **anavrttim** anyayavartate punah

These two paths for **exiting the world** are to be understood as eternal. The way of light (knowledge) leads to **release** (enlightenment), the way of darkness (ignorance) leads to rebirth.

Verse 27 (1,000) Never deluded into following darkness

naite **srti** partha janam **yogi muhyati** kascana
tasmat sarvesu kalesu **yogayukto** bhavarjuna

The **devotee**, who understands these **two paths** Arjuna, is never **deluded** into following darkness. Therefore, Arjuna, at all times, remain **steadfast in Yoga**.

Verse 28 (1,000) Enlightenment

*vedesu **yajnesu tapahsu** ca 'va **danesu** yat punyaphalam pradistam*
***atyeti** tat sarvam idam viditva **yogi param sthanam** upaiti cadyam*

Those who know the truth about the two paths gains merit
far beyond any implicit study of the scriptures (the *Vedas*),
sacrifices, **penances**, or **charity.** That **devotee reaches** the
Supreme Abode (enlightenment).

BECAUSE OF ME

CHAPTER NINE (999.3)

34 Verses

Primary Themes: Krishna, Consciousness, and Enlightenment
Secondary Themes: *bhakti* and *karma*

samsara – the passage of the soul in the cycle of births and deaths

Arjuna doesn't speak at all in this chapter, nor did he speak in Chapter Seven—he listens. Both chapters are similar—Krishna is explaining what and who He really is—telling Arjuna that everything we do, see, feel, think, and know is because of Him. Chapters Two through Eight are mostly intellectual knowledge—discussing our 12 themes. Chapter Nine is more intimate knowledge, beginning with the very first verse—*I shall now reveal the secret wisdom*. Krishna is going to reveal the greatest of all secrets – the one about Him. Verse 22 of this chapter is perhaps my favorite verse, it's the central teaching of the secrets revealed in this chapter. *When you reside in My consciousness, whatever you lack, I give—and whatever you have, I protect.* When we are thinking of the Divine, we become the Divine. The Divine always takes care of us and the Divine always protects us. This is the secret Krishna reveals to Arjuna here in Chapter Nine.

Verse 1 (999) Knowledge *(jnanam)* and Action *(vijnanam)*

*idam tu te **guhyatamam** pravaksyamy anasuyave*
*jnanam vijnanasahitam yaj jnatva **moksyase** 'subhat*

I shall now reveal, you who are **free from disbelief**,
the ***secret*** knowledge. Possessing intuitive realization
of this knowledge, you shall **escape** the miseries of
material existence (an unenlightened life).

Verse 2 (998) *The most secret of all secrets*

rajavidya rajaguhyam *pavitram idam uttamam*
pratyaksavagamam dharmyam *susukham kartum avyayam*

This intuitive realization is the **king of sciences, the royal secret**,
the purest knowledge, and the **essence of *dharma* –
easily understandable**. It is the direct perception of truth –
the imperishable enlightenment – attained through ways
(of Yoga) very easy to perform.

Verse 3 (1,000) *nivartante* – the cycle of birth and death.

asraddadhanah *purusa* **dharma***syasya paramtapa*
aprapya mam nivartante **mrtyusamsaravartmani**

Those without faith in this ***dharma*** cannot attain Me, Arjuna.
Again and again they tread the **death-darkened path of
*samsara*** (material existence).

A reference to the dark path from Chapter Eight.

Krishna and Consciousness – Primary Themes

Verse 4 (1,000) *sarvabhutani* – all that is created

maya tatam idam sarvam jagad **avyaktamurtina**
matsthani **sarvabhutani** *na caham tesv avasthitah*

I, the **Unmanifested**, pervade the entire universe in My formless
form (consciousness). **All that is created** abides in Me, but I do
not abide in them.

avyakta – Beyond the unmanifested: See Verse 20, Chapter 8

Verse 5 (1,000) One of many paradoxes of God

na ca matsthani **bhutani pasya** *me yogam aisvaram*
bhutabhrn na ca bhustastho mamatma bhutabhavanah

Behold My Divine Mystery! I create and sustain **all beings**, but I do not depend on them, nor do they depend on Me.

Verse 6 (1,000) Reason becomes limited in describing Truth.

yathakasasthito nityam ***vayuh*** *sarvatrago mahan*
tatha ***sarvani bhutani*** *matsthanity upadharaya*

As **wind** moves freely in the **infinitudes of space**, and has its being in space, so do **all creatures** have their being in Me.

matsthani – they exist in Me: used in the last three verses.

*** There are some editions of the *Bhagavad Gita* that have an extra verse at this point.

Verse 7 (1,000) *kalpa* – cycle of time

sarvabhutani *kaunteya prakrtim yanti* ***mamikam***
kalpaksaye *punas tani* ***kalpadau*** *visrjamy aham*

Arjuna, **at the end of one cycle, all beings** merge **into Me.**
At the beginning of the next cycle, I create them again.

Verse 8 (1,000)

prakrtim *svam avastabhya visrjamy* ***punah punah***
bhutagramam *imam krstsnam avasam* ***prakrter*** *vasat*

By My own **material nature**, I produce **again and again** this **host of creatures**, all subject to the finite laws of **Nature**.

Verse 9 (1,000) Consciousness is indifferent (asleep on the couch)

na ca mam tani ***karmani nibadhnanti*** *dhanamjaya*
udasinavad asanam asaktam tesu ***karmasu***

But all these **actions** don't **restrict** Me, Arjuna, for I remain indifferent and unattached to these **actions**.

Verse 10 (1,000) The act of creation is not dependent on anything

mayadhyaksena prakrtih suyate sacaracaram
hetunanena kaunteya jagad viparivartate

It is solely My direction that causes **material nature** to produce the animate and inanimate beings. Because of Me (consciousness), Arjuna, the world is created and annihilated again and again.

Verse 11 (1,000) *manusim* – in human form

*avajananti mam **mudha manusim** tanum asritam*
param bhavam** ajananto mama **bhutamahesvaram

Fools, oblivious to My **transcendental nature** as the **Maker of all that is**, disregards Me when I descend in human form.

Duryodhana didn't know who he was dealing with.

Verse 12 (1,000) Below 200 – *mogha* – in vain

moghasa moghakarmano moghajnana vicetasah
***raksasim asuram** caiva **prakrtim** mohinim sritah*

Lacking in insight, their desires, thoughts, and actions are all vain (proud, self-absorbed). These people possess the deluded **nature** of the **atheistic** (level 116) and the **demonic**.

Verse 13 (1,000) Contrast from previous verse.

***mahatmanas** tu mam partha daivim prakrtim asritah*
*bhajanty ananyamanaso **jnatva bhutadim** avyayam*

But **great souls** Arjuna, expressing their natural divine qualities *(sattva)*, **know** Me as the imperishable **source of life**.

Verse 14 (1,000) *bhakti*

***satatam kirtayanto** mam yatantas ca drdhavratah*
*namasyantas ca mam **bhaktya** nityayukta **upasate***

Always absorbed in Me, firm and resolute in their **worship** and **devotion**, they **sing** My glories and always praise My name.

Verse 15 (1,000) Internal worship contrasted with external worship *(yajanta)*

jnanayajnena ca 'py anye yajanta mam upasate
ekatvena prthaktvena bahudha visvatomukham

Others worship Me by performing *yajna* **of knowledge** (internal), also in various ways *(yajanta)* – first **as the Many**, and **then as the One**.

Verse 16 (1,000) Forms of Consciousness – *aham* – I am

aham kratur aham yajnah svadhaham aham ausadham
mantro 'ham aham eva ajyam aham agnir aham hutam

I am the ritual, I am the **sacrifice**, the **oblation** to ancestors, the **medicinal herb**, I am the **holy chant**, I am the **clarified butter**, I am the sacred **fire**, and I am the **offering**.

Verse 17 (1,000) More forms of Consciousness

pitaham asya jagato mata dhata pitamahah
vedyam pavitram omkara rk sama yajur eva ca

I am the Father of this world, the Mother, the Ancestor, the **Preserver**, the **Purifier** – I am what is to be known, **the sacred *Aum***, and also the *Rig*, *Sama*, and *Yajur Vedas*.

If you'll recall earlier comments regarding the *Vedas*, four were listed. Here in Verse 17, only three *Vedas* are listed. Missing from this list is the *Atharva Veda*, thought to be at least several centuries younger than the oldest *Veda*. For a long time, the *Atharva Veda* was not included or granted the same status as the other three *Vedas*. I find it interesting that this *Veda* is not included with this verse, or anywhere else in the *Bhagavad Gita*. I believe the *Atharva Veda* was written after the *Bhagavad Gita*, which is why it's omitted in this verse. It may not be included because it was during the time when it didn't share the same status as the other three *Vedas*. Either way, it may shed more light on when the *Bhagavad Gita* was actually written—a truth we may never confirm. There is no absolute dating for any of the *Vedas*. The *Rig Veda* is the world's oldest religious text in continuous use— believed to have been written between 1,500 and 1,200 BCE. However, as I stated earlier, it may be as old as 5,000 BCE.

Verse 18 (1,000) More forms of Consciousness

*gatir bharta prabhuh saksi nivasah saranam suhrt
prabhavah pralayah sthanam nidhanam bijam avyayam*

I am the Ultimate **Goal,** the **Upholder,** the **Master,** the **Witness,**
the Shelter, the Refuge, and the **most intimate Friend.**
I am the Origin and the Dissolution, the Foundation,
the Cosmic Storehouse, and **the Seed Indestructible**.

Verse 19 (1,000) Consciousness

*tapamy aham aham varsam nigrhnamy utsrjami ca
amrtam caiva mrtyus ca sad asac caham arjuna*

I bestow heat and I give and withhold the **rain.**
I am Immortality and also **Death.** I am **Being** (*sat* - form)
as well as **Non-Being** (*asat* - formless), Arjuna.

Verse 20 (1,000)

*traividya mam somapah putapapa yajnair istva svargatim
prarthayante
te punyam asadya surendralokam asnanti divyan divi
devabhogan*

Those who know the three *Vedas*, purified of sin by *soma* rites, worships Me by *yajna* (selfless acts), and thus win their desires of entry into heaven. There, in the **sacred kingdom of *Indra*,** devotees enjoy the celestial pleasures of the gods.

This verse confirms that Vyasa didn't somehow omit the *Atharva Veda* from Verse 17.

Verse 21 (1,000)

*te tam **bhuktva** svargalokam visalam ksine **punye** martyalokam visanti*
*evam trayidharmam anuprapanna **gatagatam** kamakama labhante*

But after **enjoying** the glorious world of heaven, they return at the expiration of their good **merit**. Thus abiding by the scriptural regulations, desiring the enjoyments, they travel the **cyclic path** (birth and death) between heaven and earth.

Materialistic people spend their lives in search of materialistic gains, which can't be taken with them at death. Spiritual people work to find God.

Verse 22 (1,000) That which supports life is supported by life

ananyas cintayanto mam ye janah paryupasate
tesam nityabhiyuktanam yogaksemam vahamy aham

When you reside in my Consciousness, whatever you lack, I give. And whatever you have, I protect.

Verse 23 (1,000)

*ye 'py anyadevatabhakta **yajante sraddhayanvitah***
*te 'pi mam eva kaunteya **yajanty avidhipurvakam***

Even devotees of other gods, who **worship** them **with faith**, they also worship Me, Arjuna, but **without true understanding**.

Verse 24 (1,000)

*aham hi **sarvayajnanam bhokta** ca prabhur eva ca*
*na tu mam **abhijananti** tattvenatas cyavanti te*

I am the only **Enjoyer** and object **of all sacrifices**. But those
(the worshipers of My lesser forms) who do not **recognize** Me
in My true nature – are born again and again.

Verse 25 (1,000) Devotees can rise only as high as the objects and
the objectives of their worship.

*yanti **devavrata devan pitrin** yanti pitrvratah*
***bhutani** yanti bhutejya yanti **madyajino** 'pi mam*

Devotees of the gods go to them – and **to ancestor** worshipers
go their devotees – to the **nature spirits** go those who seek them
– but **My devotees** come to Me.

Verse 26 (1,000) Heartfelt love is the only sacrifice God desires

***patram puspam phalam toyam** yo me bhaktya prayacchati*
*tad aham bhaktyupahrtam **asnami** prayatatmanah*

The **reverent** present to Me a **leaf,** a **flower**, a fruit or **water,**
given with pure intention as a devotional offering, I will **accept**.

Verse 27 (1,000)

*yat **karosi** yad **asnasi** yaj juhosi dadasi yat*
*yat **tapasyasi** kaunteya tat kurusva **madarpanam***

Whatever actions **you perform**, whether **eating**, observing
spiritual rites, offering gifts, or in **self-disciplines**, Arjuna –
dedicate all of them as **offerings to Me.**

Verse 28 (1,000) No sin is unforgiveable

***subhasubhaphalair** evam moksyase karmabandhanaih*
***samnyasayogayuktatma** vimukto mam upaisyasi*

No action can enchain you with **good or evil actions. With your Self steadfastly anchored in Me by Yoga and renunciation**, you shall win freedom (enlightenment) and come to Me.

Who we are today is not who we were yesterday.
I once was blind, but now I see.

Verse 29 (1,000) Consciousness is *impartial*

*samo 'ham **sarvabhutesu** na me **dvesyo** 'sti na **priyah***
*ye bhajanti tu mam **bhaktya** mayi te tesu capy aham*

I am impartial toward **all beings**. To Me, none are **hateful** and none are **dear**. But those who give Me their **heart's love** are in Me, as I am in them.

Verse 30 (1,000) We can change the direction of our life at any time.

*api cet **suduracaro** bhajate mam ananyabhak*
***sadhur** eva sa **mantavyah** samyag vyavasito hi sah*

Even a consummate **wicked person** who turns away from all else to worship Me exclusively, **may be counted** among the **good**, because of righteous resolve.

Verse 31 (1,000) *I give you My promise*

*ksipram bhavati dharmatma sasvacchantim **nigacchati***
*kaunteya **pratijanihi** na me **bhaktah pranasyati***

They quickly become righteous and **attain** unending peace. Arjuna, **I give you my promise** – My **devotees** never **perish!**

Verse 32 (1,000) Everyone can become enlightened.

mam hi partha vyapasritya ye 'pi syuh papayonayah
striyo vaisyas** tatha **sudras** te 'pi yanti **param gatim

Anyone who takes shelter in Me, Arjuna, women, *vaishyas*, *sudras* or even sinners – all beings can achieve the Supreme Destination (enlightenment).

sudras – below 200 and *vaishyas*, 200 to 399.

Verse 33 (1,000) *Bhakti Yoga*

*kim punar **brahmanah punya** bhakta **rajarsayas** tatha*
*anityam **asukham lokam** imam prapya **bhajasva** mam*

How easily may I be attained by **sainted *Brahmins*** (500 +) and pious **royal sages**. Those who have entered this impermanent and **unhappy world adore** only Me.

Verse 34 (1,000) Summary
manmana** bhava **madbhakta** madyaji mam **namaskuru
*mam evaisyasy yuktvaivam atmanam **matparayanah***

Always thinking of Me, devoted to Me, worshiping Me, and **bowing to Me**,Having obtained Me and remaining **devoted to Me**, they shall truly be Mine own.

MY DIVINE SPLENDOR

CHAPTER TEN (996)

....

42 Verses

Primary Themes: Krishna, Consciousness, and Enlightenment
Secondary Theme: *bhakti*

The *Bhagavad Gita* is indeed a sacred scripture—Chapter 10 leaves no doubt about that truth. There are three ways to perceive the soul: listening, describing, and beholding. Beginning in Chapter Two up until now, Arjuna has been **listening** to Krishna. Now, Krishna is going to **describe** in great detail who He is. In Chapter 11, Arjuna **beholds** the entire universe. In Chapter Nine, Krishna tells Arjuna that consciousness is our friend, not our enemy—consciousness responds to our thoughts, feelings, and interpretations. In this chapter, Krishna says He is the same consciousness and teaches Arjuna how to connect to Him. Nothing stands between us and the compassionate intelligence of the universe, except our understanding.

Verse 1 (999.3) *Once more* – summary of previous chapters.

bhuya eva **mahabaho srnu me paramam vacah**
yat te 'ham priyamanaya **vaksyamy hitakamyaya**

Listen once more to My **supreme word**.
I will **speak further for your benefit**.

Verse 2 (999.3) God is both beyond creation and in creation

na me viduh suraganah **prabhavam** *na* **maharsayah**
aham **adir** *hi devanam* **maharsinam** *ca sarvasah*

Neither the hosts of angels nor the **great sages** know My **glories**. Even the angels and sages are **created beings** that have their **origin** in Me.

Verse 3 (1,000) Enlightenment

*yo mam **ajam anadim** ca vetti lokamahesvaram*
*asammudhah sa **martyesu sarvapapaih** pramucyate*

Whoever knows Me to be **Unborn** and **Beginningless**, as well as the Supreme Lord of Creation – that person has conquered delusion and attained the **sinless state** (enlightenment), even while wearing a **mortal** body.

Diversity of Consciousness – Primary Theme

Verses 4 and 5 (1,000)

*buddhir **jnanam asammohah** ksama **satyam** damah samah*
***sukham duhkham** bhavo 'bhavo bhayam cabhayam eva ca*

***ahimsa** samata tustis **tapo** danam yaso 'yasah*
bhavanti bhava bhutanam matta eva prthagvidhah

Discrimination, **knowledge**, **composure**, forgiveness, **truthfulness**, control of the senses, peace of mind, **joy, sorrow**, birth, death, fear, courage;

Harmlessness, equanimity, serenity, **self-discipline**, charity, fame, and infamy – these diverse states are modifications of My nature (consciousness), created by Me alone.

Verse 6 (1,000) Seven levels of consciousness in creation

***maharsayah sapta** purve **catvaro manavas** tatha*
*madbhavam **manasa** jata yesam loka imah **prajah***

The seven Great *Rishis*, before them the **four** great *manus*, endowed with My power, and born from My **mind**. From these progenitors come all **living creatures** on earth.

The seven *Great Rishis* are the divine beings to whom the *Vedas* were revealed, representing seven levels of consciousness in creation. The highest levels are the gods or *devas*. The human level is next, followed by the animals, birds (38), and reptiles (17). The sixth level is aquatic creatures (fish, 6) and the seventh level is everything that is inanimate, stationary, and immobile. *The Primeval Four (Manus)* are the mind-born sons of *Brahma*, the Creator— the first differentiation of Spirit from which creation evolves. The *Manus* are the fathers of mankind. *Manu* means law-giver—giving order to the different levels of creation. Each *Manu* is associated with a particular creative manifestation and dissolution. The *Manu, Vaivasvata*, is defined as the father of human beings.

Krishna – Primary Theme

Verse 7 (1,000) *United to Me*

etam **vibhutim yogam** *ca mama yo* **vetti tattvatah**
so 'vikampena yogena **yujyate** *natra* **samsayah**

Those who **know** the **truth** of My **glory** and **powers**, are unshakably **united** to Me. This is beyond **doubt**.

Verse 8 (1,000) *sarvasya prabhavo – The source of everything*

aham **sarvasya prabhavo mattah** *sarvam* **pravartate**
iti matva bhajante mam **budha** *bhavasamanvitah*

I am the **Source of everything – from Me** all creation **emerges**. With this realization, the **wise** adore Me.

Verse 9 (1,000)

maccitta *madgataprana* **bodhayantah** *parasparam*
kathayantas ca mam nityam **tusyanti** *ca* **ramanti** *ca*

Their thoughts fully on Me, their beings surrendered to Me, **enlightening** one another, proclaiming Me always, My devotees are **content** and **joyful**.

Verse 10 (1,000) *buddhiyogam* - enlightenment

*tesam **satatayuktanam** bhajatam **pritipurvakam**
dadami buddhiyogam tam yena mam upayanti te*

To those who are **always devoted** to Me, and who worship Me **with love**, **I impart enlightenment** by which they come to Me.

Verse 11 (1,000) Keep the lamp burning

*tesam ev**anukampartham** aham ajnanajam **tamah**
nasayamy atmabhavastho **jnanadipena bhasvata***

From pure **compassion**, I remove the **darkness** that is born out of their ignorance with the **radiant lamp of wisdom**.

God caused man to dream this dream of illusion –
it is He alone who can bestow awakening.

Arjuna said:

Verses 12 through 18: (937) *You are indeed the very One the illumined sages of all lands and all epochs have testified. Neither do the gods nor demons know You. Surely, You alone know Yourself through Yourself alone. Please describe in detail Your divine glories by which You pervade the universe. In what aspects and forms may I know You? Tell me in detail of Your powers and glories, as I can never hear enough.*

Krishna said:

Verse 19 (977)

***hanta** te **kathayisyami** divya hy atmavibhutayah
pradhanyatah kurusrestha nasty **anto** vistarasya me*

Very well, **I will tell you** of My divine glories –
but only the most **outstanding** ones, Arjuna,
for there is no **end** to My variety.

Verses 20 through 38 (1,000)

In nearly every one of these verses, Krishna states, *I am*. By sub-
stituting *consciousness is* we get a clearer picture of what Krishna
is telling us. In my book, *Warrior Self*, I go into greater detail explaining all the Sanskrit words. I am presenting these verses here
without interruption. These 19 verses thoroughly describe all seven
forms of consciousness and beyond—but Krishna gives one last
beautiful verse just to make sure everything about consciousness
is understood when He says: *I am the silence in all hidden things.*

*I am the Spirit in the heart of all living beings. I am the Origin,
Existence, and End of all beings.*

*Among the Adityas, I am Vishnu; among the luminaries,
I am the bright sun; among the Maruts, I am Marichi;
among all the stars, I am the moon.*

*Of the Vedas, I am the Samaveda; among the gods, I am Vasava;
among the senses, I am mind;* **in living beings, I am consciousness***.*

*Of the Rudras, I am Shankara and of the Yakshas and Rakshasas,
I am Kubera, god of Wealth.*

Of the Vasus, I am Pavaka; and of mountain peaks, I am Meru.

*Know Me to be the chief among priests, Brihaspati; among warriors,
I am Skanda. Of the expanses of water, I am the ocean.*

*Of the great Rishis, I am Bhrigu; among words,
I am the single syllable Aum; of sacrifices,*

*I am the silent repetition of mantra; of the immovable objects,
I am the Himalayas.*

*Of all the trees, I am the Ashvattha; among the divine Rishis,
I am Narada; of the Gandharvas, I am Chitraratha;
among the siddhas, I am the muni* **Kapila.**

*Of stallions, know Me to be Uchchaihshravas, born from nectar
generated from the churning of the ocean; among elephants,
Indra's white elephant, Airavata; and among men, the king.*

*Of weapons, I am the thunderbolt; of cows, I am Kamadhuk.
I am Kandarpa, the god of love, the cause of childbirths;
and I am Vasuki among serpents.*

*I am Anata among the Naga serpents; I am Varuna among water
deities; I am Aryaman among ancestors; I am Yama among all those
who maintain law and order.*

Of the Daityas, I am Prahlada; among measurers, **I am time**;
*among the animals, I am the king of beasts; and among birds,
I am Garuda.*

*Of purifiers, I am the wind; among the warriors, I am Rama; of the
aquatic creatures, I am Makara; among rivers, I am the Ganga.*

*Of all creations Arjuna, I am the beginning, middle, and end.
Of all knowledge, I am the wisdom of the Self; of all arguments,
I am logic itself.*

Among all letters, I am the letter A; Of the dual words, I am the compounds. I am Imperishable Time; and I am the Creator who sees everything.

*I am all-devouring Death; and the origin of things that are yet to be.
Of the feminine, I am fame, fortune, speech, memory, wisdom,
faithfulness, and patience.*

*Of hymns, I am Brihat-Saman; among poetic meters, I am Gayatri; of the
months, I am Margasirsha; of the seasons, I am Kusumakara, the spring.*

Of all cheating, I am gambling; I am the radiance of the radiant; I am victory and resolution; I am the goodness of the good.

Of the descendants of Vrishnis, I am Vasudeva; of the Pandavas, I am Arjuna; among the sages, I am also Vyasa; I am the poet Ushanas.

I am the rod of discipliners; I am the wise policy of those who seek victory; **I am also the silence of all hidden things***, and wisdom of all knowers.*

Verse 39 (1,000) *nothing can exist without Me*

yac capi sarvabhutanam **bijam** *tad* **aham** *arjuna*
na tad asti vina yat **syan** *maya bhutam caracaram*

Furthermore – whatever being exists, **I am** the **seed** (origin). There is nothing Arjuna, moving or motionless, that can **exist** without Me.

Verse 40 (1,000)

nanto 'sti mama **divyanam** *vibhutinam paramtapa*
esa tuddesatah prokto **vibhuter vistaro** *maya*

Limitless are the manifestations of My **divine** attributes – My concise declaration is a mere example of My **detailed glories.**

Verse 41 (1,000)

yad yad **vibhutimat** *sattvam srimad urjitam eva va*
tat tad eva 'vagaccha tvam mama **tejomsasambhavam**

You should know that whatever is beautiful and **glorious** – be sure that it is **born from a fragment** of My Divine **Splendor.**

Verse 42 (1,000) Summary – *I pervade this entire world*

athava **bahunai** *'tena kim jnatena tava arjuna*
vistabhya 'ham idam krtsnam **ekamsena** *sthito* **jagat**

What use is it to know all these details of the **many** kinds of manifestations Arjuna? I pervade this entire **world** with just a **single**
portion of Myself.

I LONG TO SEE YOU

CHAPTER ELEVEN (999.3)

55 Verses

Primary Themes: Krishna and Consciousness

This chapter is unlike any of the other chapters in the *Bhagavad Gita* and one of the great moments in world literature. Krishna bestows upon Arjuna the full experience of consciousness, giving him *Divine sight*—crossing over from the observable world into the unobservable world. What if we could actually see consciousness—what would that look like, and beyond that, how could we possibly describe it? By the grace of God, Arjuna is given the direct experience of Krishna and there are no words to describe what Arjuna sees—it is beyond his understanding. During Arjuna's experience—everything suddenly changes, terrifying him. What Arjuna sees isn't what he expects when he asks Krishna to see His Divine form. The moment Arjuna starts feeling fear, he descends back to his mortal state. It's only our fear that separates us from the enlightened state. Krishna speaks in Verses 32 through 34 saying: *I am the world destroying time, annihilating the world.* This is the most potent truth Krishna reveals. Arjuna now understands who Krishna *really* is and surrenders himself—no longer having any doubts about His powers. In Verses 41 and 42, Arjuna becomes frightened—he remembers how casually he has treated Krishna in the past and asks Krishna for forgiveness in Verse 44: *Lord forgive me!* Krishna consoles Arjuna, telling him that no one has ever seen what he just saw—no one! Krishna concludes this chapter with what a devotee should do to reach Him. The final verse of this chapter may be the single most important verse in the entire *Bhagavad Gita*. It makes perfect sense for it to be the final verse in our most important chapter. As I presented in Chapter 10 a section uninterrupted by the verses in Sanskrit and commentary, I present this Chapter with little interruption.

Arjuna said:

Verses 1 through 4: (995)

(1) You have compassionately revealed to me the supreme secret of Your Existence and glory, removing my delusion.

(2) You have told me of the beginning and end of all beings in great detail, and also of Your inexhaustible greatness.

(3) Truly You have declared Yourself. Yet, I wish to see Your Divine form.

(4) If You think I am strong enough, worthy enough, show me Your Infinite Self!

Krishna said:

Verses 5 through 8: (999.4)

(5) Behold My divine forms, Arjuna, by hundreds and thousands – variously colored and of all shapes!

(6) Behold Arjuna, the Aditya, the Vasu, the Rudra, the Ashvin, the Marut, and many wonderful beings never seen before!

(7) Behold the entire universe, here and now, all that moves or is unmoving, and whatever else you wish to see.

(8) But you are unable to see Me with mortal eyes.
I give you Divine sight. *Behold My Divine power.*

Sanjaya now narrates to the blind King about what happened:

Verses 9 through 14: (995)

(9) With these words, Krishna, the great Lord of Yoga, revealed to Arjuna His highest divine form.

(10) Infinite in forms, shining in every direction, adorned with countless ornaments, and upraising divine weapons.

(11) Wearing countless celestial robes, garlands, fragrant with every lovely essence, His mouths and eyes turned in all directions!

(12) If a thousand suns appeared simultaneously in the sky, that might resemble the splendor of that Great Being.

(13) There, resting within the infinite Form of the God of gods, Arjuna beheld the entire universe with all its infinite manifestations.

(14) Arjuna, filled with amazement, his hair standing on end, his hands together in a prayerful gesture, bowed his head and addressed the Lord.

Arjuna said:

Verses 15 through 31: (997)

(15) Beloved Lord! Behold, all the gods in Your body and many types of beings. The serpent's nature, though fierce and subtle, is now tame; and Lord Brahma, god of gods, seated on the lotus.

(16) I behold Your infinite form everywhere, Your countless arms, stomachs, mouths, and eyes! My knowledge lies about Your birth and reign and ending. This day, O Lord, whose form is the entire universe, Your Name spreads everywhere.

(17) Gilded with a crown of stars and wielding mace and discus of sovereign power, shining on all sides, blazing everywhere with the radiance of the flaming sun and fire.

(18) You are what is to be known – the Supreme Reality. You are the treasure house of the universe, the refuge of all creatures, and the eternal guardian of Dharma. Now I understand You are Purusa, the ancient of the ancients.

(19) I see You without a beginning, middle, or end – infinite in power with many arms. With eyes that are the sun and moon, the blazing fire Your mouth, the entire universe scorched by Your radiance.

(20) This space between earth and the heavens, in all directions,
O Sovereign Soul, all high abodes and all encircling spheres,
is pervaded by You alone. The three worlds tremble with fear.

(21) In Thee the gods enter into You, some praise You in fear with
folded hands. The rishis and enlightened ones worship You and You
alone.

(22) The Rudra, the Aditya, the Vasu, the Sadhya, the Visvadeva,
the Ashvin, the Marut, the ancestral spirits and a host of
Gandharava, Yaksha, Asura, and enlightened beings,
all behold You in amazement.

(23) I behold, O Mighty-armed one, with eyes and endless hands,
and legs adorned with lotus feet. Your mouth with teeth yawns to
swallow worlds above, beneath, and leaves a joyous awe in me:
Your grandeur is wonder-struck to see!

(24) To view the bowels of the void filled with You - Your mouth
opened wide with many colors shining – O Vishnu, I am frightened,
I find neither courage nor peace.

(25) Seeing Your many mouths possessing ferocious teeth, resembling
the deadly fires at the end of the universe, I've lost my sense of
direction and find no peace. Lord of gods, please accept my pleading
words. Show mercy!

(26) The sons of Dhristarashtra, along with many kings of the earth,
Bhishma, Drona, Karna, as well as our own mighty warriors;

(27) They all ride the race of death, to fall and hide forever into Your
devouring mouth, adorned with crushing cruel teeth. The shattered
skulls of some are caught between Your greedy teeth and crushed to
powder.

(28) As the water currents flow toward the ocean, in the same way,
burnt by Your fire, these warriors enter into Your flame-licked mouths.

(29) As insects rush to flame, so do mortals rush to meet their own destruction.

(30) O Vishnu, with Your mouth ablaze, You lick the angry blood of strong and weak, swallowing entire worlds of living beings. Filling the entire world with Your splendor, You scorch the world with radiance.

(31) Tell me who You are, have mercy. I still not know Your purpose but I desire to know You. O Best of Gods, I ache to know who You are.

Krishna said:

Verses 32 through 34: (1,000)

(32) I am the world-destroying Time, annihilating the world. *Except for yourself, none of the warriors standing in hostile armies shall live.*

*(33) Arise and gain glory! Conquer the foe and enjoy the prosperous kingdom. **I have slain these warriors ages ago** – you are only My instrument, left-handed archer!*

*(34) Slay Drona, Bhishma, Jayadratha, Karna and other brave warriors – **My victims**. Do not be afraid! Fight and you shall conquer your enemies in battle.*

Sanjaya said to the King:

(35) After hearing the words of Krishna, Arjuna, trembling and terrified, joining his palms in worshipful gesture, again made humble homage and addressed Krishna in a quavering voice.

Arjuna said:

Verses 36 through 46 (991)

(36) O Krishna! Rightly are the worlds proud and gladdened to exude

Your glory! The demons, terrified, seek safety in distance; while the multitudes of siddhas bow down to worship You.

(37) And why should they not pay homage to You, O Great Spirit? For greater than all else, Brahma the Creator, who issued from Thee O Infinite One, O God of gods, O Shelter of the Universe, You are the Imperishable – the Manifested, the Unmanifested, and That beyond the Ultimate Mystery.

(38) You are the Original God! The Pristine Spirit, the Final Refuge of the universe, the Knower and the Known, the Supreme abode! O Being of Infinite Forms, Your Omnipresence shines in the universe!

(39) O Lord of Immeasurable Glory, O King of Death, O God of Flames, O Sovereign of Sea and Sky, O Lord of Night, O Divine Father of Countless Offspring, O Ancestor of All! To You praise, praise without end! To You my thousand-fold salutations!

(40) O God, I bow to You in front and behind, I bow to You on the left and the right, I bow to You above and beneath, You are everything and everywhere!

(41) Unaware of Your Glory, and thinking of You as a friend, often have I audaciously hailed You as "Friend" and "Krishna" and "Yadava." For all such words, whether spoken carelessly or with affection;

*(42) And for any irreverence I have displayed toward You, O Lord! In lighthearted mood at mealtimes or while walking or sitting or resting, alone with You or in the company of others – for all such unintentional slights, **I beg forgiveness**.*

(43) You are the father of this world, moving and unmoving. The whole world should adore and worship You, for You are the greatest guru, nothing is Your equal. How can there be another superior to You in the three worlds?

*(44) I humbly bow before You and ask You to **forgive me**. Even as a
father forgives his son, a friend his friend, a lover his beloved,
You should forgive me.*

*(45) I am thrilled to behold You as no one else has. I am terrified by
Your cosmic form. Mercifully show Your more familiar form to me
again.*

*(46) I wish to see You as You were before, with crown, four-armed
with mace, disc in Your hand. I long to see You in that form.*

Krishna said:

Verses 47 through 49 (999.4)

*(47) I have graciously revealed My own Yoga Power to you, Arjuna,
and to none other! No one before you has seen this unlimited
brilliant form.*

*(48) O Great Hero of the Kurus, this Supreme Primeval Form of
Mine, no mortal man, save only you, is able to be looked upon. My
Highest form cannot be seen by sacrifices or charity or works or
rigorous austerity or study of the Vedas.*

*(49) Don't be frightened or confused at seeing My fearsome form.
Be free from all disturbances and with heart rejoicing,
behold once more My familiar form!*

Sanjaya said to the King:

*(50) After speaking thus, Vasudeva, "the Lord of the World," **resumed
His own shape as Krishna**. He, the Great-Souled One, appearing to
Arjuna in the form of grace, consoled His fear-stricken friend.*

Arjuna said:

*(51) O Granter of All Wishes, as I gaze on You again in gentle
human shape, my mind is now calm and I feel more like my
natural self.*

Krishna said:

Verses 52 through 54 (999.7)

(52) It is very difficult to behold the Universal Vision, as you have done! Even the gods yearn to see it.

(53) But it is not unveiled through one's penance, or scriptural study, or gift-giving, or formal worship. One cannot see Me as I am by these means.

*(54) Arjuna, only by **undivided devotion** may I be seen as you have beheld Me in My Cosmic Form and recognized in reality **and finally embraced Oneness.***

Verse 55 (1,000) Summary

matkarmakrn *matparamo madbhaktah* **sangavarjitah**
nirvairah sarvabhutesu *yah sa mam eti pandava*

Work for Me, surrender to Me, free from attachments to whatever you do, leaving the results to Me. Love everyone as your own Self Arjuna, **without dislike or hatred**.

Verse 55 may be the single most important verse in the entire *Bhagavad Gita*.

*** There are editions that have 60 verses in this chapter.

DEAR TO ME

CHAPTER TWELVE (998)

....

20 Verses

Primary Themes: Krishna and Enlightenment
Secondary Themes: *bhakti*, Yoga, and *karma*

bhakti – devotion, faith, and reverence

Bhakti happens only after a spiritual experience, not before. A spiritual experience is any event that connects us to our souls—we are not the same as we were before, which is why this chapter follows Arjuna's experience in Chapter 11. Up until this chapter, we haven't read too many verses concerned with *bhakti*. People cannot express *bhakti* unless they've had a spiritual experience themselves. The story I told earlier in the book from being in Taos is an example of a spiritual experience—I was not the same afterwards.

Love is the quality of our soul—the shift from ego to soul happens only through love. Love has total freedom—freedom from conflict, desire, expectations, jealousy, and possessiveness. Love is the recognition of ourselves in others—unity—all One. It isn't until level 540 that we come to see God in everyone—the level of unconditional love. At level 500, the emotional, conceptual **linear** mind moves to a **non-linear** context. Meaning, significance, and value are reprioritized, profoundly influencing our choices. Love becomes the guiding principle—love serves above 499 whereas the ego seeks to be served below 500. Krishna says to Arjuna in Verse 54 of the last chapter, *only by undivided devotion may I be seen as you have beheld Me in My Cosmic Form and recognized in reality and finally embraced Oneness*—unity— the movement from the individual to the Universal—All One. Arjuna begins this chapter by asking two questions – *should the yogin worship the Unmanifested, or a personal God? And, which one* *is greater?* We return to the subject of duality and consciousness—God in duality as well as in unity.

Arjuna asked:

Verse 1: *What type of person is greater – is it the person who closes their eyes and sees God within themselves, or the person who opens their eyes and sees God in everyone? Who is greater?*

Krishna answers:

Verse 2 (1,000) Two types of devotion – both are the same

mayy avesya mano ye mam nityayukta **upasate**
sraddhaya parayo*petas te me* **yuktatma** *matah*

Those who meditate on Me, **worshiping** Me with **supreme devotion**, I consider them to be **perfect in Yoga**, ready to be united with Me.

Verses 3 and 4 (1,000)

ye tvaksaram anirdesyam **avyaktam** *paryupasate*
sarvatragam *acintyam ca kutastham* **acalam dhruvam**

*sam***niyamyendriyagramam** *sarvatra samabuddhayah*
te prapnuvanti mam eva **sarvabhutahite** *ratah*

But those who adore the Indestructible, the Indescribable, the **Unmanifested**, the **All-Pervading**, the Incomprehensible, the Immutable, the **Unmoving**, the **Ever-Constant**;

(4) who have **conquered all of the senses**, possessing even-mindedness in every circumstance, and devotes themselves to the **good of all beings** – they also attain Me.

Verse 5 (1,000) Enlightenment is nearly impossible

kleso 'dhikataras tesam avyaktasaktacetasam
avyakta *hi* **gatir duhkham dehavadbhir** *avapyate*

Those whose **goal** is the **Unmanifested** (enlightenment) increase the **difficulties** – arduous is the path of the Absolute **for embodied beings.**

Verses 6 and 7 (1,000) Enlightenment

*ye tu **sarvani karmani** mayi **samnyasya** matparah*
*ananyenaiva **yogena** mam dhyayanta **upasate***

*tesam aham **samuddharta mrtyusamsarasagarat***
*bhavami na **cirat** partha mayy avesitacetasam*

But those who **worship** Me with single-minded devotion, **renouncing** all activities unto Me, regarding Me as their supreme goal; (7) Indeed Arjuna, those whose consciousness has merged with Me, **before long**, I become their **Redeemer** to bring them **out of the sea of mortal births.**

Steps to Enlightenment – Primary Theme

Verse 8 (1,000) *Concentrate your intellect on Me*

*mayy eva **mana** adhatsva mayi **buddhim** nivesaya*
nivasisyasi** mayy eva ata urdhvam na **samsayah

Immerse your **mind** on Me alone – concentrate your **intellect** on Me – and beyond **doubt, you shall dwell** immortally in Me.

Verse 9 (1,000) *Seek to attain Me by constant Yoga practice*

*atha **cittam** samadhatum **na saknosi** mayi **sthiram***
***abhyasayogena** tato mam icchaptum dhanamjaya*

If you are **unable** to keep your **mind wholly** on Me, then seek to attain Me by **constant Yoga practice** Arjuna.

Verse 10 (1,000) *If you are unable to practice, then dedicate all actions to Me*

*abhyasa 'pyasamartho 'si mat**karma**paramo bhava*
*madartham api karmani kurvan **siddhim avapsyasi***

If you are **unable to practice** (continuous Yoga), be diligent in performing **actions** in the thought of Me. Even engaging in actions on My behalf **you will attain perfection** (enlightenment).

Verse 11 (1,000) *Do what you do for My sake*

*athaitad apy **asakto** 'si kartum madyogam asritah*
sarvakarmaphalatyagam** tatah kuru **yatamavan

If you are **unable** to even do this, then, remaining attached to Me as your Shelter, **relinquish the fruits of all actions** while continuing to strive for **Self-control**.

Verse 12 (1,000) Priorities

*sreyo hi **jnanam abhyasaj** jnanad **dhyanam** visisyate*
*dhyanat **karmaphalatyagas tyagac** chanter anantaram*

Knowledge is better than mere **practice; meditation** is superior to knowledge; better than meditation is the **relinquishment of the fruits of actions. Renunciation** of the fruits of actions is followed immediately by peace.

This may be the clearest statement of the superiority of *karma yoga* over *jnana yoga*.

Exceptional Human Behavior Described

Verses 13 and 14 (1,000) Human behavior

*advesta **sarvabhutanam maitrah karuna** eva ca*
*nirmamo **nirahamkarah samadukhasukhah** ksami*

*samtustah satatam **yogi yatatma** drdhaniscayah*
*mayy **arpitamanobuddhir** yo madbhaktah sa **me priyah***

Those who are free from hatred toward all creatures, who are **friendly and compassionate, devoid of the consciousness of "I-ness"** and possessiveness – are **even-minded in suffering and joy**, and patient; (14) always content, a regular Yoga practitioner, constantly **trying by Yoga to know the Self** and united to Spirit, possessed of firm determination, **with mind and discrimination** surrendered to Me – they are My devotees and **dear to Me.**

Verse 15 (1,000) Human behavior – *who does not disturb the world*

*yasman nodvijate **loko lokan** nodvijate ca yah*
*harsamarsabhayodvegair **mukto** yah sa ca **me priyah***

A person who does not disturb **the world** and who cannot be disturbed **by the world**, who is free from joy, envy, fear, and anxiety – they too are **dear to Me.**

Verse 16 (1,000) Human behavior

***anapeksah sucir daksa udasino** gatavyathah*
*sarvarambhaparityagi yo **madbhaktah** sa **me priyah***

Those who are **free from wants**, who are **pure** and **capable**, always ready to work, who remain **unconcerned** with and unafflicted by circumstances, who have abandoned all ego-initiated undertakings – they are **My devotees** and **dear to Me.**

God appoints the work we are called to do.

Verse 17 (1,000) Human behavior – dualities

*yo na **hrsyati** na **dvesti** na **socati** na kanksati*
subhasubhaparityagi** bhaktiman yah sa **me priyah

Those who neither **rejoice** nor **hate, grieve** or **desire, letting go of the consciousness of good and evil**, and are full of devotion – they are **dear to Me.**

Verses 18 and 19 (1,000) Human behavior

aniketah – doing whatever needs to be done.

samah satrau ca **mitre** ca tatha manapamanayoh
sitosna**sukhaduhkhesu** sama sangavivarjitah

tulyanindastutir mauni samtusto yena kenacit
***aniketah sthiramatir** bhaktiman **me priyo** narah

Who is the **same** before **friend** and enemy alike, and in
encountering adoration and insult, and during the experiences
of warmth and cold, **pleasure and suffering**; (19) **who regards
blame and praise in the same light** – who is **quiet** and easily
contented, not attached to domesticity, of **calm disposition**,
and devotional, that person is **dear to Me**.

Verse 20 (1,000) *Bhakti*

ye tu **dharmyamrtam** idam yathoktam paryupasate
sraddhadhana matprama bhaktas te tiva **me priyah**

But those who adoringly pursue this **undying *dharma* as
heretofore declared, saturated with devotion, supremely
engrossed in Me** – such devotees are extremely **dear to Me**.

REMEMBER TO REMEMBER

CHAPTER THIRTEEN (997)

....

34 Verses

Primary Themes: Krishna, Consciousness, *gunas*, Enlightenment
Secondary Themes: Soul, Yoga, and *jnana*

pasyati – to behold, to see, to perceive

Chapter 13 returns to earlier themes from Chapters Two and Three—the Soul, Yoga, enlightenment, *gunas*, *jnana*, consciousness, and reincarnation. This chapter is a little more challenging to understand because of the emphasis on *Purusha* and *Prakriti—the field and the knower of the field*. The human body is the *field* where Nature operates—the soul is the *knower of this field*, our guide. **Purusha** is the individual Soul, manifesting when the divine becomes a limited being. **Prakriti** is Nature or matter—the force that provides the material for creation. It's the yoga (union) of Spirit and matter that brings creation into being. *Purusha* is the cause and *Prakriti* is the effect. The cause and the effect are one, as neither can exist without the other. Think of *Purusha* as being the ocean and *Prakriti* as being the wave—neither exists separately.

The human ego is a distortion of the human soul and human nature. These distortions are created by the *gunas* (levels of consciousness), *malas* (impurities), *kanchukas* (cloaks), and *maya*—the power of illusion veiling the true nature of the Soul. *Maya* has two functions—to conceal the real and project the unreal. *Maya* can be defined as illusion, deceit, and fraud. *Anava-mala* gives us the illusion and misunderstanding that we are separate from God, incomplete, and unworthy. **Anava-mala serves as the catalyst for our desire to merge with God**. Our egos are unconscious to the fact that we are spiritual beings having a human experience—not human beings having a spiritual experience. Ego identifies with forms, primarily thought forms, but also included are physical forms and emotional forms. The result of ego being identified with forms (individual) is the total unawareness of being connected to Spirit (Universal).

We have the power to manifest our sense of being imperfect and incomplete into our lives. Whatever we believe about ourselves is what we project to the outside world and other people. Those beliefs are what the outside world and others believe about us. Our own misperception of our spiritual being becomes an act of creation. Our **doubts** rise out of *anava-mala*—which is an illusion because we're the only one's having the experience of doubt and lack of self-worth. No one else has the doubts we have about ourselves. We don't need anyone or anything outside ourselves to validate our existence. We are not separate from God, we are not incomplete, and we are not unworthy. Whatever our self-worth issues might be, they are nothing more than God calling us home to remind us that we are never alone.

At the beginning of Chapter Three, I wrote about the three main Yogas within the *Bhagavad Gita*: *Karma Yoga*—selfless service; *Jnana Yoga*—knowledge; and *Bhakti Yoga*—the heart or devotional aspect. One of the great American films of all time is *The Wizard of Oz*, based on the book, *The Wonderful Wizard of Oz*, by L. Frank Baum, published in 1900. John Algeo wrote a wonderful article entitled, *The Wizard of Oz, The Perilous Journey*, for the Theosophical Society interpreting this fairytale in great detail. My interpretation of John Algeo's allegory is slightly different—your interpretation may also be different from mine. The main characters within the story all relate to the *Bhagavad Gita*. Dorothy and Arjuna are each the protagonist for their stories and the three friends she meets in her dream are the three primary Yogas within the *Bhagavad Gita*. The scarecrow desperately wanting a brain represents *jnana Yoga*; the tin-man wanting a heart represents *bhakti Yoga*; and the cowardly lion wanting courage represents *karma Yoga*. Dorothy's dog Toto, always by her side, sometimes hiding in her basket, is Krishna, our guiding intuition who ultimately removes the veil of illusion *(maya, malas)* exposing the Wizard himself, a total fraud. Toto always seems to know what is happening throughout the movie—mostly unseen and certainly unsuspected, just like Krishna.

Anava-mala serves as the catalyst for our desire to merge with God – *there's no place like home. Anava-mala* gives us the illusion and misunderstanding that we are incomplete, and unworthy. Dorothy, the lion, tin-man, and scarecrow had everything they desired all along—what they believed about themselves was only in their minds, no one else's. The wicked witch is our fear of death and her flying monkeys represent our doubts—carrying us off to unknown lands if captured by them. Our fear of death and doubts are all based in future thoughts—easily dissolved when we become absolutely present and see them for what they truly are. The tornado is Duryodhana. And the mighty Oz himself, nothing more than all the illusions of life, hiding behind a curtain, making us believe all kinds of false things about ourselves and others. Dorothy's ruby slippers are the power of the present moment—where we have within us the way to find our way home, back to our true self, and back to God—if only we could **remember to remember** our inherent power.

Preface: Chapter 13 begins with Arjuna wanting to know about *Prakrit*i and *Purusha* – *the field and the knower of the field.*

Krishna answers:

New Subject – kshetra and kshetrajna

Verse 1 (1,000)

idam sariram kaunteya **ksetram** *ity abhidhiyate*
etad yo vetti tam prahuh **ksetrajna** *iti tadvidah*

This body is called the **kshetra** (the Field) Arjuna – likewise, that which has conscious recognition of the Field they call **kshetrajna** (the soul).

Conscious recognition *(purusa)* is when you look in the mirror and you know it's you.

Verse 2 (1,000) Non-dual – the soul in all bodies

*ksetrajnam capi mam viddhi **sarvaksetresu** bharata*
***ksetraksetrajnayor** jnanam yat taj **jnanam** matam mama*

Know Me to be the **kshetrajna** in all **kshetras**, Arjuna. The **understanding of kshetra** and **kshetrajna** that is deemed by Me, constitutes true **knowledge**.

Verses 3 and 4 (1,000)

*tat **ksetram** yac ca yadrk ca yadvikari yatas ca yat*
*sa ca yo yatprabhavas ca tat **samasena** me **srnu***

***rsibhir** bahudha gitam chandobhir vividhaih prthak*
***brahmasutrapadais** caiva hetumadbhir viniscitaih*

Hear briefly from Me about **kshetra**, its attributes, its cause-and-effect principles, and its distorting influences – and also who the knower is *(kshetrajna)*, and the nature of His powers.

(4) Truths that have been celebrated by the **rishis** in many ways – in various chants and in the definitive reasoned analyses of the **aphorisms about Brahman**.

Verses 5 and 6 (1,000) The *tattvas* define our material selves

*mahabhutany **ahamkara buddhir** avyaktam (prakriti) eva ca*
***indriyani** dasaikam ca **panca** cendriyagocarah*

*iccha **dvesah sukham duhkham** samghatas cetana dhrtih*
*etat **ksetram samasena** savikaram udahrtam*

(5) The **kshetra** and its modifications are composed of *Prakriti*, the **five** elements, the **ten senses**, plus the mind, **intelligence**, and **ego**:

(6) The five objects of the senses – desire, **hate, pleasure, pain**, the body, consciousness, and **persistence**. These briefly describe the Field with its modifications.

The *tattvas* influence humans – not the soul. All 24 *tattvas* (qualities) of a total 25 *tattvas* belong to Nature or *Prakriti*, the human body – not God, the Knower *(Purusa)*.

Qualities of Wisdom – Secondary Theme

All of the qualities listed in Verses 7 through 11 manifest wisdom qualities – those qualities opposed to them constitute ignorance.

Verse 7 (1,000) Higher levels of consciousness and human behavior.

*amanitvam adambhitvam **ahimsa** ksantir arjavam*
*acaryopasanam **saucam** sthairyam atmavinigraha*

The sage is marked by humility, integrity, **kindness**, forgivingness, uprightness, service to the teacher, **purity** of mind and body, steadfastness, self-control;

Verse 8 (1,000)

*indriyarthesu vairagyam **anahamkara** eva ca*
janmamrtyujaravyadhiduhkhadosanudarsanam (40 letters)

Indifference to sense objects, **absence of egotism, understanding of the pain and evils inherent in mortal life, birth, illness, old age, and death;**

Verse 9 (1,000)

asaktir anabhisvangah putradaragrhadisu
nityam *ca* **smacittatvam** *istanistopapattisu*

Non-attachment, non-identification of the Self with one's children, wife/husband, home and so on – **constant equal-mindedness** in desirable and undesirable circumstances;

Verse 10 (1,000) *avoidance of the company of worldly individuals*

mayi **cananyayogena bhaktir** *avyabhicarini*
viviktadesasevitvam aratir janasamsadi

Unwavering devotion to Me **by the Yoga of non-separateness**, abiding in solitary places, avoidance of the company of worldly individuals;

These last seven words in Verse 10 are easy to miss and not pay much attention to. Just who are these *worldly individuals?* I consider worldly individuals to be those who calibrate below 200—which are half of the people in the United States and four out of five people worldwide. Avoiding such a large percentage of the population isn't practical, but understanding worldly individuals gives us an immediate strategy on how not to create a conflict with them. There are many people in my life who do calibrate below 200, but I'm cautious in those relationships. What I mean by cautious is I don't put a lot of investment or trust in these relationships, which manifests in a variety of ways. The challenge is to not step into force with worldly individuals. One of the best strategies for avoiding a force-force situation is to simply agree with the force person—it completely disarms them and the situation. Perhaps we can interpret this part of the verse as staying in our power at all times—which is a great definition for Yoga.

Verse 11 (1,000) Contrast

adhyatmajnananityatvam tattvajnanarthadarsanam
etaj jnanam iti proktam ajnanam yad ato 'nyatha

Perseverance in Self-knowledge and the insight into the object of all learning – as well as the knowledge of reality: all of these qualities constitute **wisdom** (Power) – qualities opposed to them constitute **ignorance** (Force).

Brahman (Consciousness) – Primary Theme

The major contribution of *Vedanta* Philosophy is the additional category of *Brahman*, which causes the initial impulse in nature—the *causeless cause*. Only the existence of an intelligent agent *(Brahman)* can account for the mysterious super-imposition of *Purusa* and *Prakriti*. The primal cause cannot be a modification of *Prakriti*, for then it would be an effect—and an effect cannot affect itself, no more than fire can burn fire. The primal cause must be separate and apart from *Purusa* and *Prakriti*.

Verse 12 (1,000) *Brahman* – The Causeless Cause

*jneyam yat **tat** pravaksyami yaj jnatvamrtam asnute*
*anadimat **param brahma** na sat tan **nasad ucyate***

I will describe *That* which is to be known, **the beginningless Spirit** *(Brahman)* – said to be neither **existent** nor **non-existent**.

Verse 13 (1,000) *Brahman*

sarvatahpanipadam tat sarvatoksisiromukham
sarvatahsrutimal loke sarvam avrtya tisthaty

Hands and feet, enveloping all – eyes and ears, mouths and heads present on all sides, dwelling in the world, embracing everything in the universe;

God is not a person, but Consciousness itself,
aware of the thoughts of every human being.

Verse 14 (1,000) A paradox

*sarvendriyaguna**abhasam** sarvendriyavivarjitam*
*asaktam sarvabhrc caiva **nirgunam gunabhoktr***

Seeming to possess all the functions of the senses, yet
transcending the senses – unattached to creation, yet the
Mainstay of all – free from the *gunas*, yet **experiencing them**.

abhasa – false appearance

Verse 15 (1,000) A paradox

bahir *antas ca* **bhutanam acaram caram** *ca*
suksmatvat tad avijneyam durastham cantike ca tat

Without all that exists, yet within; **inanimate** yet **animate**;
so subtle It is imperceptible; so far and yet so near.

Verse 16 (1,000) *Brahma – Vishnu – Shiva*

avibhaktam ca bhutesu vibhaktam iva ca sthitam
bhutabhartr *ca taj jneyam grasisnu **prabhavisnu** ca*

The **Indivisible One**, yet appearing as **countless beings** – Main-
taining and destroying those forms, then creating them anew.

Krishna is the eighth and supreme incarnation of Lord *Vishnu*.
Rama is the seventh incarnation of Lord *Vishnu*, whose story is
told in the *Ramayana* – The story of Ram. (935)

Verse 17 (1,000) *In the hearts of all*

jyotisam api taj jyotis *tamasah param **ucyate***
*jnanam jneyam jnanagamyam **hrdi** sarvasya visthitam*

The Light of All Lights, said to be beyond darkness.
It is knowledge itself, That which is to be known, the Goal of all learning, seated in the **hearts** of all.

Verse 18 (1,000) The field *(ksetra)*, knowledge *(jnana)*, and the object of knowledge *(jneya)*

*iti **ksetram** tatha **jnanam jneyam** coktam samasatah*
*madbhakta etad **vijnaya madbhavayopapadyate***

I have briefly described the **Field** (consciousness), the nature of **knowledge**, and the **Object of knowledge. Understanding these, My devotees enter My being**.

Purusha and Prakriti – Spirit and Matter

Verse 19 (1,000) Both are aspects of the same God

***prakrtim purusam** caiva **viddhi** anadi ubhav api*
*vikarams ca **gunams** caiva **viddhi prakrtisambhavan***

Know that both ***Purusha*** and ***Prakriti*** are beginningless – and also **know** that all modifications and **qualities *(gunas)*** are **born of *Prakriti***.

Verse 20 (1,000) *hetuh* – cause; *ucyate* – is said

*karya karana kartrtve **hetuh prakrtir ucyate***
purusah sukhaduhkhanam** bhoktrtve **hetur ucyate

Prakriti is **said** to be the **cause** in the creation of effects from causes. ***Purusha*** is **said** to be the **cause** in the experience of **happiness and sorrow**.

Prakriti is the direct cause of the human body and its activities. Our Soul then interprets its contact with experiences in terms of good or bad. Because *Purusha* is dominant between the two, it is the enjoyer of *Prakriti*.

Verse 21 (1,000) Is this why we are born with our specific level of consciousness?

*purusah prakrtishtho hi bhunkte **prakrti**jan **gunan***
*karanam **guna**sango 'say sadasad**yoni**janmasu*

Purusha, abiding in **Prakriti**, experiences the **gunas** born of **Prakriti**. Attachment to the **gunas** is the cause of birth in good and evil **wombs**.

The conditions of each new incarnation—for better or worse—is the direct result of the degree of our desires and influences of the *gunas*.

Verse 22 (1,000) God is present in our bodies and minds

upadrasta**numanta ca bharta bhokta **mahesvarah
*paramatmeti capy ukto dehe 'smin **purusah** parah (beyond)*

The Great Lord, also called the Supreme Spirit (consciousness), is the transcendent **Purusa**, who is the **Witness**, Consenter, Sustainer, and Experiencer.

Verse 23 (1,000) Those who attain enlightenment will never be misguided by reason.

*ya evam vetti **purusam prakrtim** ca **gunaih** saha*
sarvatah vartamano 'pi na sa bhuyo 'bhijayate

Those who know the true nature of **Spirit** and **matter**, together with its **gunas**, are free from the cycle of births and deaths, no matter how they may live.

Three Yogas to Enlightenment – Secondary Themes

Verse 24 (1,000) *Raja Yoga* (meditation), *Samkhya* (theory), *Yoga* (practice), and *Karma Yoga*.

***dhyane**natmani **pasyanti** kecid atmanam atmana*
***anye samkhyena yogena karmayogena** capare*

To behold the Self (Soul) in the self (ego) by the self, some follow the path of **meditation, others** follow **the path of knowledge** (theory) **and Yoga**, and some **the path of selfless action**.

Verse 25 (1,000) *Bhakti Yoga*

*anye tv evam **ajanantah** srutvanyebhya upasate*
*te 'pi catitaranty eva mrtyum **srutiparayanah***

Yet **others, ignorant** of these paths, **accept what they hear from others**. Following the path of worship *(Bhakti Yoga)*, regarding ancient teachings as the Highest Refuge, they also attain immortality (enlightenment).

Verse 26 (1,000) Whatever exists, cannot remain outside the field of consciousness.

yavat samjayate kimcit sattvam sthavarajangamam
***ksetraksetrajnasamyogat** tad viddhi bharatarsabha*

Whatever exists – every being and every object – animate or inanimate, **is born from the union** (yoga) of ***Kshetra*** (field) and ***Kshetrajna*** (knower of the field), Arjuna.

Not only is consciousness the cause, but also the material from which it is made – non dual.

The Soul – Secondary Theme

Verse 27 (1,000) God is present in everyone – every human being has a Soul.

samam sarvesu bhutesu tisthantam paramesvaram
*vinasyatsv avinasyantam yah **pasyati** sa **pasyati***

Perceiving the Supreme Lord equally present in all creatures, the Imperishable (God) in the perishable (humans), they truly **see**.

And when a person sees God in them is the same God in all that is, they hurt not themselves by hurting others.

Seeing ourselves as less than divine is the source of whatever our life experience is giving us, or not giving us. God is present in everyone, only the unenlightened sees distinctions, where in reality, none are present. We are all One.

Verse 28 (1,000) Therefore

*samam pasyan hi **sarvatra samavasthitam isvaram**
na hinasty **atmanatmanam** tato yati **param gatim***

Those who perceive the **omnipresence of God** do not injure (ignorance, humiliation) **the Self** (Soul) **by the self** (ego) – that person reaches the **Supreme Goal** (enligtenment).

Verse 29 (1,000) The Soul, *Purusha* – the actionless witness

***prakrtyaiva** ca **karmani** kriyamanani sarvasah
yah **pasyati** tathatmanam akartaram sa **pasyati***

Those who see all actions performed in their entirety by *Prakriti* alone, and not the Soul *(atman)*, are indeed the **beholder** of truth.

All actions originate in their entirety from *Prakriti*.

Verse 30 (1,000) One source, many Souls – all sustained by God.

*yada **bhutaprthagbhavam ekastham** anu**pasyati**
tata eva ca vistaram **brahma** sampadyate tada*

When a person **beholds** all separate beings **existing in the One**, from which **all expand into the many**, they become one with *Brahman* (enlightenment).

Verse 31 (1,000) The Soul is an actionless witness

*anaditvan **nirgunatvat paramatmayam** avyayah*
*sarirastho 'pi kaunteya na karoti **na lipyate***

Because the **Supreme Self** is unchanging, beginningless, and **free from attributes** *(gunas)*, it neither performs actions **nor is affected by them** Arjuna, even though dwelling in the body.

Verse 32 (1,000) Our Soul is never polluted by material contact

*yatha sarvagatam sauksmyad **akasam nopalipyate***
*sarvatravasthito dehe tathatma **nopalipyate***

Just as the all-pervading **ether** is **beyond taint** because of its subtlety, similarly the Soul, though present everywhere in the body, is **not affected**.

Verse 33 (1,000) Light metaphor

*yatha **prakasayati ekah** krtsnam **lokam** imam ravih*
***ksetram ksetri** tatha krtsnam **prakasa**yati bharata*

Just as the **one** sun **illuminates** the entire **world**, so does the **Lord of the Field illuminate** this entire field, Arjuna.

The sun lights the entire world, God and His reflection as the Soul enlightens all of creation.

Verse 34 (1,000) Summary

ksetraksetrajnayor** evam antaram **jnanacaksusa
***bhutaprakrtimoksam** ca ye vidur yanti te param*

Those who perceive with the **eye of wisdom** the distinctions between the *Kshetra* (Field) and the *Kshetrajna* (Knower of the Field), and the methods (secrets) of **liberation of beings** from *Prakriti*, attains the Supreme.

ETERNAL DHARMA

CHAPTER FOURTEEN (995)

27 Verses

Primary Themes: Krishna, Enlightenment, and the *gunas*
Secondary Themes: *jnana* and *bhakti*

About ten percent of the entire *Bhagavad Gita* involves the *gunas*, making the *gunas* an integral part of the text. The *gunas* were first introduced in Chapter Two, Verse 45. Up until now, we've only had 15 verses over the last 13 chapters involving the *gunas*, with five chapters having no mention of them at all. In this chapter, 21 out of 27 verses relate to the *gunas*—which is the most time that Krishna has spent teaching us about them. *Jnana*, enlightenment, Krishna, and *bhakti* will also be discussed in this chapter—keeping us connected to our primary and secondary themes. We also have two verses contrasting light and dark, a familiar metaphor by now.

Verse 1 (1,000) Enlightenment and *jnana*

*param bhuyah pra**vak**syami **jnananam jnanam** uttamam*
*yaj **jnatva** munayah sarve param siddhim ito gatah*

I will **speak** again about the highest **knowledge** which transcends all **knowledge**, the **knowledge** with which all sages have attained the highest Perfection (enlightenment).

Verse 2 (1,000) Enlightened people are not reborn

*idam **jnanam** upasritya mama sadharmyam agatah*
sarge 'pi nonpajayante pralaye na vyathanti ca

Absorbing this **knowledge**, established in My Being, sages are not reborn, even at the start of a new cycle of creation – nor do they suffer at the time of dissolution.

Verse 3 (1,000) Let there be a universe, and a universe came into existence.

*mama **yonir mahad brahma** tasmin **garbham** dadhamy aham*
*sambhavah **sarvabhutanam** tato bhavati bharata*

My **womb** is the **Great *Brahman***, into which I deposit the seed of My imagination – this is the cause of **birth** of **all beings**, Arjuna.

Verse 4 (1,000) Therefore

***sarvayonisu** kaunteya murtayah sambhavanti yah*
*tasam **brahma mahad yonir** aham **bijapradah** pita*

All forms, Arjuna – produced in any **wombs** – The **Great *Brahman*** is their original **womb,** and I am the **seed-giving** Father (of this universe).

The Gunas – Primary Theme

Verse 5 (1,000) The *gunas* are different levels of consciousness.

sattvam rajas tama** iti **gunah prakrtisambhavah
***nibadhnanti** mahabaho dehe **dehinam** avyayam*

The *gunas* are called *sattva, rajas,* and *tamas*, and are **inherent in *Prakriti*.** They keep the Imperishable Dweller (Soul) **bound** to the **body**.

Verse 6 (1,000) *sattva* – consciousness from 500 to 599

*tatra **sattvam** nirmalatvat **prakasakam** anamayam*
***sukhasangena** badhnati **jnanasangena** canagha*

Of these, the pure nature *sattva* gives **light** and healing. It binds through **attachment to happiness** and attachment to **knowledge**.

Verse 7 (1,000) *rajas* – consciousness from 200 to 499

*tajo **raga**tmakam viddhi trsnasangasamudbhavam*
*tan **nibadhnanti** kaunteya **karmasangena dehinam***

Know that *rajas* is characterized by passion, the source of desire and attachment, Arjuna – it **binds** the **embodied** soul by **attachment to action**.

Verse 8 (1,000) *tamas* – consciousness below 200

***tamas tv ajnanajam** viddhi **mohanam** sarvadehinam*
***pramadalasyanidrabhis** tan **nibadhnanti** bharata*

Know that *tamas* arises from **ignorance**, **deluding** all embodied beings. It **binds** them by **heedlessness** *(pramad*)*, **laziness** *(alasya)*, and **sleep** *(nidra)* Arjuna.

*pramadi – someone who misuses their life

Verse 9 (1,000) Review – Human behavior

***sattvam sukhe** sanjayati **rajah karmani** bharata*
*jnanam avrtya tu **tamah pramade** sanjayaty uta*

Sattva binds one to **happiness** – *rajas* to activity, Arjuna; *tamas* attaches to **heedlessness** by concealing discrimination and good judgment.

sanjayati, used twice in this verse, means to attach, bind, or join.

Verse 10 (1,000) Varieties of human consciousness

***rajas tamas** cabhibhuya **sattvam** bhavati bharata*
***rajah sattvam tamas** caiva **tamah sattvam rajas** tatha*

Sometimes *sattva* is predominant, overpowering *rajas* and *tamas*, Arjuna. Sometimes *rajas* prevails, not *sattva* or *tamas*. And sometimes, *tamas* obscures *sattva* and *rajas*.

Verse 11 (1,000) The light of knowledge

*sarvadvaresu dehe 'smin **prakasah** upajayate*
***jnanam** yada vidyad vivrddham **sattvam** ity uta*

When the **light of knowledge** shines through all the **sense gates** of the body, one may know that ***sattva*** is prevalent.

Verse 12 (1,000) Human behavior

lobhah pravrttir arambhah karmanam asamah sprha
***rajasy** etani jayante vivrddhe bharatarsabha*

When ***rajas*** dominates Arjuna, it causes greed, vigorous activity, enterprise, restlessness, and desire.

Verse 13 (1,000) Human behavior

***aprakaso** 'pravrttis ca **pramado moha** eva ca*
***tamasy** etani jayante vivrddhe kurunandana*

Darkness (depression), sloth, **heedlessness**, and **delusion** are evidence when ***tamas*** rules, Arjuna.

Verse 14 (1,000) We are born with our level of consciousness.

*yada **sattve** pravrddhe tu pralayam yati **dehabhrt***
*tadottamavidam lokan amalan **pratipadyate***

If the **embodied** soul dies when ***sattva*** prevails, they **reach** the pure worlds of those who have the highest knowledge.

Verse 15 (1,000) Continuation from previous verse

rajasi** pralayam gatva **karmasangisu jayate
*tatha pralinas **tamasi** mudha**yonisu jayate***

When ***rajas*** prevails at the time of death, a person is **reborn** among those **attached to activity**. Those who die in ***tamas*** **are born** in the **wombs** (environment, family) of the deluded.

Verse 16 (1,000) Actions and levels of consciousness

karmanah sukrtasyahuh **sattvikam nirmalam phalam**
rajas *as tu* **phalam duhkham ajnanam tamasah phalam**

The fruit of *sattvic* actions is said to be virtuous. **The fruit** of *rajas* actions is **pain**, and **the fruit** of *tamas* is **ignorance.**

Verse 17 (1,000) Knowledge, greed, and ignorance

sattva *samjayate* **jnanam rajaso lobha** *eva ca*
pramadamohau **tamaso** *bhavato* '**jnanam** *eva ca*

From *sattva* rises **knowledge** and from *rajas* **greed** – heedlessness, delusion, and **ignorance** are born from *tamas*.

Verse 18 (1,000) The Map of Consciousness

urdhvam *gacchanti* **sattvastha** *madhye tishanti* **rajasah**
jaghanyagunavrttistha adho *gacchanti* **tamasah**

Those abiding in *sattva* go **upward** – those in *rajas* stay in the middle. Those who **abide** in *tamas*, **the lowest** *guna*, **descend**.

In my book *Warrior Self*, I spent a great deal of time discussing this particular verse in relationship to the *chakra* system. In this book, my focus has been on levels of consciousness, which this verse clearly shows. The *chakra* system came out of *Tantric* philosophy around 600 to 700 C.E. The *Bhagavad Gita* dates long before *Tantra* and is grounded in the philosophies of *Samkhya, Yoga,* and *Vedanta*—which is why Krishna is teaching the *gunas*. The **purpose** of *Tantra, Samkhya, Yoga,* and *Vedanta* philosophy is to attain enlightenment. *Going upward* implies the rising of consciousness toward spirituality. *Descending* implies a lowering of consciousness toward materialism, ego, and survival.

Enlightenment – Primary Theme

Verse 19 (1,000) Transcend – no power over me

*nanyam gunebhyah kartaram yada drastanu**pasyati***
*gunebhyas ca param vetti **madbhavam** so 'dhigacchati*

When a person of insight **perceives** no other acts but the *gunas* –
knowing That which transcends the *gunas*, they attain
My Being.

Verse 20 (1,000) Enlightenment

***gunan** etan atitya trin dehi dehasamudbhavan*
***janmamrtyujaraduhkahair** vimukto 'mrtam asnute*

Having transcended the ***gunas*** (above 599) – the cause of
physical embodiment – that person is ***released from the
sufferings of birth, old age, and death***, becoming immortal.

Arjuna now asks three logical questions.

Arjuna asked:

Verse 21: *What distinguishes someone who has transcended the
gunas? What is their behavior? How do they transcend the gunas?*

Krishna answers:

Verse 22 (1,000) *Illumination* – light, knowledge, and wisdom

***prakasam** ca pravrttim ca **moham** eva ca pandava*
na dvesti sampravrttani na nivrttani kanksati

Arjuna, those who do not abhor **illumination** (*sattva*), activity
(*rajas*), and delusion (*tamas*) – when they arise, nor desires them
when they cease;

Verse 23 (1,000) Continuing

*udasinavad asino **gunair** o no vicalyate*
***guna** vartanta ity eva yo 'vatisthati nengate*

Remaining unconcerned and undisturbed by the **gunas** –
unmoved in the mind and always Self-controlled,
knowing that it is only the **gunas** that operate;

Verse 24 (1,000) Continuing

***samaduhkhasukhah** svasthah samalostasmakancanah*
tulyapriyapriyo dhiras tulyanindatmasamstutih

Unaffected by joy and sorrow, always even-minded in praise and
blame – regarding earth, stone, and gold of equal worth;
the same toward pleasant or unpleasant experiences and secure
in their Divine nature;

Verse 25 (1,000) Conclusion

*manapamanayos tulyas tulyo **mitrarip**aksayoh*
*sarvarambhapari**tyagi gunatitah** sa **ucyate***

Uninfluenced by respect or insult – treating **friend** and **enemy**
alike – abandoning all delusions of personal doership *(karma-
mala)* – that person **is said** to have **transcended the gunas**!

Verse 26 (1,000) *Bhakti Yoga*

*mam ca yo 'vyabhicarena **bhaktiyogena** sevate*
*sa **gunan** smatityaitan **brahmabhuyaya** kalpate*

Those who serve Me alone with absolute necessity and with
bhakti yoga, transcends the **gunas** and are **worthy to become
Brahman** (enlightened).

Verse 27 (1,000) Krishna – the foundation of *Brahman*

brahmano *hi* **pratisthaham** *amrtasyavyayasya ca*
sasvatasya ca **dharmasya sukha**syaikantikasya ca

I am the **foundation of *Brahman***, Immortal and Indestructible –
I am **eternal *Dharma*** and infinite **Bliss**.

THERE EXISTS ANOTHER

CHAPTER FIFTEEN (997)

···

20 Verses

Primary Themes: Krishna, Consciousness, Enlightenment, and the *gunas*
Secondary Themes: *jnana*, Reincarnation, and the Soul

The *Ashvattha* tree used metaphorically in the first four verses of Chapter 15 refers specifically to the creative principles of *Prakriti* and consciousness. The *tree of life – with roots in heaven and boughs earthward*, is the human mind and human body. The one who understands the *tree of life* is a knower of all wisdom, the *Vedas*. Extending *upward* they give knowledge of **consciousness** and stretching *downward* they limit perception to the ego and materialism. Using *the powerful axe of non-attachment* to destroy the *Ashvattha* tree within, we transcend the ego, elevating our consciousness toward **enlightenment** and ending **reincarnation**.

Anything we say or do that is an attempt to make ourselves appear greater than we are, or anything that creates some form of separation, is a root connected to ego. If we take away one form of ego identification, our ego will quickly find something else with which to identify. The content of the ego may have changed, but the thoughts keeping it alive have not changed. We must stop comparing ourselves, judging ourselves, and trying to make ourselves look better than others. Most importantly, stop pretending to be someone we are not. These are the roots that keep us connected to our false self, the individual, and separate from the Universal. In Chapters 13, 14, and 15, Krishna uses metaphors not easily understood. *The Field and the Knower of the Field*, The *Gunas*, and the *Asvattha* tree, are teachings unlike anything we encounter in today's world. Chapters 16 through 18 are among the easiest to understand in the entire text. The remainder of this short chapter covers three of our primary themes—enlightenment, consciousness, and Krishna.

Verse 1 (997) *mulam* – Highest Reality; *urdhvam* – above everything else

urdhvamulam adhahsakham asvattham *prahur avyayam*
chandamsi yasya parnani yas tam **veda** *sa* **vedavit**

The wise speak of an eternal *asvattha* tree, with **roots in heaven** and **boughs earthward** – each of its leaves is a hymn of the **Vedas**. Those who know it **know all the** **Vedas**.

In the *Mahabharata*, Krishna was fatally shot by an arrow while He sat beneath an *asvattha* tree. A hunter mistakenly thought Krishna was a deer.

Verse 2 (999) *gunapravrddha* – the unfolding of the universe

adhas *cordhvam prasrtas tasya sakha* **guna***pravrddha visayapravalah*
adhas *ca* **mulany** *anusamtatani* **karma***nubandhini manusyaloke*

Its branches spread above and **below**, nurtured by the *gunas* – its buds are the sense objects. Extending **downward** into the world are the **roots** that are the consequences of **action** (ego).

Verses 3 and 4 (998.6) *Find the path which does not come back.*

na rupam asyeha tathopalabhyate nanto na cadir na ca sampratistha
asvattham *enam* **suvirudhamulam** *asangasastrena drdhena chittva*

tatah padam tat parimargitavyam yasmin gata na nivartante bhuyah
tam eva cadyam **purusam** *prapadye yatah pravrttih prasrtas purani*

The true nature of this tree, its **beginning, end**, and **foundation** – none of these can ever be known here. The wise destroy the **firmly rooted** *Asvattha* with the powerful axe of non-attachment.

(4) Seeking the Supreme Goal (enlightenment), take refuge in the Primordial *Purusha* from who has issued this ancient process of creation, finding the path which does not come back (ending reincarnation).

Verse 5 (1,000) *Without craving for honor*

nirmanamoha jitasangadosa **adhyatmanitya** *vinvrttakamah*
dvandvair vimuktah **sukhaduhkhasamjnair** *gacchanty*
amudhahpadam **avyayam** *tat*

Without craving for honor, free from delusion and malignant attachment, free from all desires, disengaged from the pair of opposites such as **pleasure and pain – they live in constant union with the Self**, the undeceived attain the highest **imperishable** reality (enlightenment).

Verse 6 (1,000) Reincarnation ends

na tad **bhasayate suryo** *na sasanko na* **pavakah**
yad gatva na nivartante tad dhama paramam mama

Where no **sun**, moon, or **fire shines**, that is My Supreme Abode. Those who arrive there are never reborn.

The highest reality transcends the sun, fire, and moon, because the highest reality transcends time and space.

The Soul – Secondary Theme

Verse 7 (1,000) The individual Soul, a fragment of God, is part of the totality of consciousness.

mamaivamso jivaloke jivabhutah **sanatanah**
manah *sasthanindriyani* **prakrti***sthani karsati*

A fragment of My **eternal** Self takes the form of an individual soul within every creature; attracting to itself the senses, including the **mind** as the sixth sense, which rests in *Prakriti*.

Individual souls *(jiva)*, eternal *(sanatanah)* and existing in the order of souls *(jivabhutah)*, are a fragment *(amso)* of God *(Brahman)* from whom they receive their qualities *(prakriti)* as souls.

Verse 8 (1,000) The Soul

sariram yad **avapnoti** *yac capy* **utkramati***svarah*
grhitvaitani samyati **vayur** *gandhan ivasayat*

When the Lord (as the *jiva*) **acquires a body,** He brings with Him the mind and senses. When He **leaves that body**, He takes them and goes, just as the **wind** steals scents from flowers.

Verse 9 (1,000) It's God who enjoys our senses, experiencing His creation through us.

srotram caksuh sparsanam ca rasanam ghranam eva ca
adhisthaya **manas** *cayam visayan upasevate*

He enjoys the sensory world, using hearing, sight, touch, taste, and smell – including the **mind.**

Consciousness – Primary Theme

Verse 10 (1,000) Contrast of consciousness

utkramantam sthitam vapi bhunjanam va **gunanvitam**
vimudha **nanupasyanti pasyanti** *jnanacaksusah*

Whether He departs from or remains in the body, or experiences the **world of the** *gunas* – the deluded **do not perceive** Him: only those with the **eyesight of knowledge** do.

Verse 11 (1,000) Contrasting levels of consciousness

yantanto **yoginas** *caiman* **pasyanti** *atmany avasthitam*
yantanto 'py akrtatmano nainam **pasyanti** *acetasah*

Yogins striving for enlightenment **see** Him existing in themselves – but those who are not purified and lack insight are unable to **perceive** Him, even when they struggle to do so.

Krishna – Primary Theme

Verse 12 (1,000) Krishna – Three forms of light *(tejas)*: sun, moon, and fire.

*yad **adityagatam tejo** jagad bhasayate 'khilam*
*yac **candramasi** yac cagnau tat **tejo** viddhi mamikam*

The **light that lives in the sun, illuminating** the whole world, and also the **light from the moon,** as well as the fire – know this **radiance** to be Mine.

Verse 13 (1,000) Krishna

*gam avisya ca **bhutani** dharayamy aham **ojasa***
*pusnami causadhih sarvah somo **bhutva** rasatmakah*

Permeating the earth, I support **all creatures** with My powers – I become the **watery** moon, nourishing **all** plants.

Verse 14 (1,000) Krishna

*aham **vaisvanaro bhutva** praninam deham asritah*
pranapana**samayuktah pacamy annam **caturvidham

Having become *Vaisvanaro* (the heat that digests food), I exist in the body of **living creatures** – and with the aid of *prana* and *apana*, I digest food in **four** ways.

The four ways are masticating, sucking, licking, and swallowing.

Verse 15 (1,000) Krishna

*sarvasya caham **hrdi** samnivisto mattah **smrtir jnanam***
apohanam ca*
***vedais** ca sarvair **aham** eva **vedyo vedantakrd vedavid** eva caham*

I am seated in the **hearts** of all. From Me comes **memory, knowledge**, and **differentiation**. **I am** the one the *Vedas* tell. **I am** the Author of the *Vedanta*, **I know** the *Vedas*.

* *apohanam* – If this is not accomplished, then this will happen.

Verse 16 (1,000) *Kutastha* – the changeless Divine Consciousness that informs the universe.

*dvav imau **purusau loke** ksaras caksara eva ca*
*ksarah sarvani **bhutani kutastho** 'ksara ucyate*

There are two Beings *(Purushas)* in this **world**, the perishable and the imperishable. The **creatures** are the perishable (form) – the *kutastha* is the imperishable (formless).

Consciousness is imperishable, it never changes.

Verse 17 (1,000) *The three worlds* – physical, astral (stars), and ideational (ideas or thoughts).

uttamah purusas *tv anyah paramatmeti **udahrtah***
*yo **lokatrayam** avisya bibharty avyaya **isvarah***

But there exists Another, the **Highest Being** *(Purusottama)*, **who they call** the Supreme Spirit – **the Eternal Lord**, who permeates and sustains *the three worlds*.

Verse 18 (1,000) Krishna, Supreme Consciousness, *Purushottama*

yasmat ksaram atito **'ham aksarad** *api cottamah*
*ato 'smi **loke vede** ca prathitah **purusottamah***

I transcend the perishable (*Prakriti* - form) and am also **higher than the imperishable** (*Kutastha* - formless). I am known in this **world** and in the *Vedas* as *Purushottama* (the Supreme Spirit).

Verse 19 (1,000) Krishna

*yo mam evam asammudho janati **purusottamam***
*sa sarvavid bhajati mam **sarvabhavena** bharata*

Whosoever is freed from delusion (enlightened),
knowing Me as ***Purusottamam***, knows all that can be known.
They worship Me with their whole being, Arjuna.

Verse 20 (1,000) Final verse

*iti **guhyatamam sastram** idam uktam mayanagha*
etad buddhva buddhiman syat krtakrtyas ca bharata

I have taught you this most **mysterious doctrine**.
Realization of this knowledge brings about the accomplishment
of everything that is to be accomplished *(krtakrtyas)*, Arjuna.

UNDERSTAND FIRST – THEN ACT

CHAPTER SIXTEEN (996)

....

24 Verses

Primary Themes: Krishna, Consciousness, and Enlightenment

Chapter 16 is perhaps the easiest chapter to understand—everything Krishna intended to teach Arjuna concluded in Chapter 15. We hear only from Krishna in the previous chapter as well as this one, beginning with 26 **power** qualities that calibrate over 200. Krishna then contrasts the **force** qualities that calibrate below 200—making this chapter a contrast of human consciousness and human behavior. The final verse is one of the most important verses in the entire *Bhagavad Gita – understand first – then act*. This teaching from Krishna tells us to stop making assumptions. We make **assumptions** because our ego has to know everything in order to feel safe. We make assumptions because we don't have the courage to ask questions to find out the truth. This links our assumptions to our survival, behavior, and level of consciousness. If there is something the ego doesn't know, it will create a story and make an assumption. Nothing strengthens the ego more than the belief that it is right. In order for the ego to be right, the ego believes it has to make something or someone wrong by making an assumption—making us feel safe. The biggest assumption we make is that everyone sees life the same way we do. Now that we know more about consciousness, we know that isn't true. We learned in Chapter Four that one of the ways we learn is by asking questions. Arjuna only asks questions until the very end of Chapter 18 when Krishna asks Arjuna two questions, making sure Arjuna understands His teachings. Krishna doesn't assume that Arjuna does, so He asks Arjuna if he truly understands everything he's been taught. Arjuna's final words to Krishna at the end of Chapter 18 are: *I understand and will act accordingly.*

If we want to create the future we desire, we need to ask questions and stop making assumptions. Whenever we make an assumption, we invite conflict into our lives. Assumptions cause conflicts when we misunderstand—then the ego interprets everything personally. We don't allow ourselves to see things as they *truly* are. Because the ego interprets everything personally, we often *re-act*—making the assumption that everything is about us—it's not! What other people do or say is never about us—it's about them! They are dealing with their own feelings, beliefs, assumptions, lies, opinions, and self-worth issues that are all related to their specific level of consciousness, which has nothing to do with us. If we could learn to communicate truthfully with one another—by **understanding first**—we would end all conflicts and misunderstandings. If we constantly protect and hide parts of ourselves, we will never be completely truthful in our relationships and will continue making assumptions.

26 Power Qualities above 200

Verse 1 (1,000) Human behavior

abhayam sattvasamsuddhir jnanayogavyavasthitih
danam damas ca yajnas ca svadhyayas tapa arjavam

Fearlessness, purity of heart, perseverance in acquiring wisdom and in practicing Yoga, charity, self-restraint, performance of holy rites, study of the scriptures, self-discipline, straight-forwardness;

Verse 2 (1,000) Human behavior

ahimsa satyam akrodhas tyagah santir apaisunam
daya bhutesv aloluptvam mardavam hrir acapalam

Non-harming, truthfulness, freedom from anger, spirit of dedication, peacefulness, non-slanderousness, **compassion** for all creatures, absence of greed, **gentleness, modesty, reliability**;

Verse 3 (1,000) Human behavior

*tejah ksama **dhrtih saucam adroho** natimanita*
*bhavanti sampadam **daivim** abhijatasya bharata*

Radiance of character, forgiveness, **patience, cleanness, freedom from hate**, and absence of conceit – these qualities are the wealth of those born with **divine** heritage, Arjuna.

Force Qualities below 200

Verse 4 (1,000) Human behavior

dambho darpo 'bhimanas ca krodhah parusyam eva ca
ajnanam cabhijatasya partha sampadam asuram

Pretentiousness, arrogance, conceit, anger, harshness, and ignorance – these qualities mark the person who is born with a demonic nature, Arjuna.

Verse 5 (1,000) Contrast

daivi sampad vimoksaya nibandhayasuri mata
*ma sucah sampadam **daivim** abhijato 'si pandava*

The **divine** qualities bestow enlightenment – the demonic qualities lead to bondage (rebirth). Fear not, Arjuna, you are endowed with the **divine** traits.

Verse 6 (1,000) Two types of people

dvau bhutasargau loke 'smin daiva asura eva ca
daivo vistarasah prokta asuram partha me srnu

Two types of **people** exist in this world – the **divine** and the **demonic**. I have told you fully about the divine qualities, now

Arjuna, hear about the demonic.

Consider what this verse is telling us—*two types of people*. This is the one verse that encouraged me to write this book—it calibrates as absolute Truth.

Verses 7 through 20 all calibrate at 1,000 and relate to human behavior below level 200. The contrasts between power and force qualities are very clear—there really is a distinction between those who calibrate above and below 200.

Verse 7 – The demonic lack purity, truth, and proper conduct (integrity).

Verse 8 – They say, "The world has no moral foundation, no truth and no God."

Verse 9 – They are enemies of the world (problem people).

Verse 10 – All their actions are impurely motivated (ego-driven).

Verse 11 – These people are engrossed in earthly concerns until the moment of death.

Verse 12 – Bound by selfish hopes and expectations, enslaved by anger and passion.

Verse 13 – "This is my present wealth – however, more shall also be mine."

Verse 14 – "I have killed this enemy. I am successful, strong, and happy."

Verse 15 – "I am rich and well-born – can any others be compared to me?"

Verse 16 – Harboring bewildering thoughts, they sink into a foul hell.

Verse 17 – Vain, stubborn, and intoxicated by pride in wealth.

Verse 18 – Egotistical and prone to rage, these people despise Me.

Verse 19 – I hurl them again into demonic wombs (below 200) for rebirth.

Verse 20 – Deluded birth after birth, they descend to the very lowest depths of the soul.

Three Gates of Hell

Verse 21 (1,000) Lust, anger, and greed – 135 to 150

trividham *narakasyedam dvaram nasanam atmanah*
kamah **krodhas** *tatha lobhas tasmad etat trayam* **tyajet**

Lust, **anger**, and greed – these constitute the **threefold** gates of hell, leading to destruction of the Soul's welfare. Therefore, these three should be **abandoned**.

Verse 22 (1,000) Highest good

etair vimuktah **kaunteya** *tamodvarais* **tribhir** *narah*
acarati atmanah sreyas tato yati param gatim

By turning away from these **three entrances** of darkness (ignorance), **Arjuna**, mankind behaves according to their highest good and therefore reaches the Supreme (enlightenment).

Verse 23 (1,000) Warning

yah **sastravidhim** *utsrjya vartate kamakaratah*
na sa siddhim avapnoti na **sukham** *na param gatim*

Those who ignore the **scriptural teachings** and follow their own foolish desires will not find **happiness** or success.

Verse 24 (1,000) **Understand first – then act**

tasmac chastram pramanam te karyakaryavyavasthitau
jnatva **sastra**vidhanoktam karma kartum iharhasi

Therefore, let the scriptures be your guide in deciding what to do and what not to do. **First understand** the path of action as the **scriptures** teach it, and **then act** accordingly.

WHATEVER
THEIR FAITH

CHAPTER SEVENTEEN (997)

....

28 Verses

Primary Themes: *gunas*
Secondary Themes: *yajna* and *karma*

tapas – learning to behave

Here in Chapter 17, Krishna gives clear examples regarding our behaviors and actions in categories related to the *gunas*. More than half of the verses in this chapter relate to the *gunas*. In addition to teachings regarding faith, food, and giving—Krishna returns to earlier secondary themes of *yajna* and *karma*, as well as *tapas* and *sraddha*. *Tapas* is one of the *niyamas* from Patanjali's *Yoga Sutras*. In this chapter, the essence of *tapas* is learning to behave. As with so many Sanskrit words, there are multiple definitions for a single word. I teach *tapas* as service to others—an appetite for life—gratitude—no longer needing to be our false selves—the desire to explore the will of God—and the force to end suffering. All of these definitions align with exceptional behavior. *Tapas* will be discussed further at the conclusion of the *Bhagavad Gita*.

Arjuna asked:

Verse 1: *There are those who worship with faith, and yet they reject the scriptures. Which of the gunas prevails in them?*

Krishna answers:

Verse 2 (999)

trividha *bhavati* **sraddha** *dehinam sa svabhavaja*
sattviki rajasi *caiva* **tamasi** *ceti tam* **srnu**

The natural **faith** of everyone is threefold – *sattvic, rajasic*, and *tamasic.* **Hear** about it now.

Verse 3 (1,000) We behave according to our level of consciousness.

*sattvanurupa sarvasya **sraddha** bhavati bharata*
***sraddha**mayo 'yam puruso yo yacchraddhah sa eva sah*

The **devotion** of each person is in accord with their inborn nature (level of consciousness). Everyone's **faith** conforms to their nature – whatever their faith is, that is their state.

Verse 4 (1,000)

*yajante **sattvika** devan yaksaraksamsi rajasah*
*pretan bhutaganams canye yajante **tamasa** janah*

The **sattvic** pay homage to the **Devas**, the **rajasic** worship the **Yakshas** and **Rakshasas** – the **tamasic** worship the spirits of the dead.

People with *sattvic shraddha* learn for their own personal growth and development.Reading this book and studying the teachings of the *Bhagavad Gita* is *sattvic shraddha*.

Verse 5 (1,000)

asastravihitam ghoram tapyante ye tapo janah
***dambha**hamkarasamyuktah kamaragabalanvitah*

Hypocrites and egotists – possessed by desire and passion, perform terrible austerities that are a product of their imagination and not ordained by the scriptures *(sastra)*;

Verse 6 (1,000) *acetasah* – lack of discrimination

*karsayantah sarirastham bhutagramam **acetasah***
*mam caivantah sarirastham tan viddhi **asura**niscayan*

They offend Me because their actions contradict *sastric* teachings. Know those to be of **asuric** (demonic) nature.

Food as an expression of God

Verse 7: Not only do the *gunas* influence faith, but also the food we eat, how we perform our duties, as well as our generosity.

Verse 8: Our diets show which of the *gunas* is prevalent in our food choices. Foods that promote longevity, vitality, strength, and health are *sattvic*.

Verse 9: *Rajasic* foods are hot and spicy.

Verse 10: *Tamasic* foods are unwholesome.

Food is an interesting consideration in regards to consciousness. What we ingest into our bodies matters—whether it's foods, liquids, drugs, or other substances. Commercial cigarettes calibrate at 82, whereas organic tobacco calibrates at 742. Marijuana calibrates at 87; heroin – 65; cocaine – 66; methamphetamine – 59; and LSD – 56. Although I have no scientific proof, it's my belief that low consciousness substances have the potential to lower an individual's level of consciousness to harmful levels. It seems Krishna supports this premise. Food is very personal—I don't appreciate being told how I should eat and I never tell anyone how they should eat. In Native American culture, it's believed the bear taught man how to eat. Bears are omnivores—calibrating at 266. The omnivore diet calibrates at 835. A vegetarian and paleo diet both calibrate at 766—and a vegan diet at 686. We like the numbers when they work in our favor, but watch how ego desperately wants to discredit the numbers when we don't like the results.

Yajna – Selfless Actions – Secondary Theme

Verse 11 (1,000) *manah samadhaya* – firmly believe

*aphalakanksibhir **yajno** vidhidrsto ta ijyate*
*yastavyam eveti manah samadhaya **sa sattvikah***

Sattvic individuals **worship** (act) without any desire for a reward.

Verse 12 (1,000) *dambha* - hypocrisy

abhisamdhaya tu phalam dambhartham api caiva yat
*iyate bharatasrestha tam **yajnam** viddhi **rajasam***

Rajasic individuals **worship** (act) in hope of a reward.

Verse 13 (1,000) *vidhihinam* – *tamasic* sacrifice

vidhihinam asrstannam mantrahinam adaksinam
***sraddha**virahitam yajnam **tamasam** paricaksate*

Tamasic individuals have no regard for the scriptures –
they never offer appreciation and have no **devotion** to God.

Tapas

The next five out of six verses uses the word *austerity*. To help understand these five verses, think of austerity as human behavior.

Verse 14 (1,000) Higher levels of consciousness of the body

***devadvijaguruprajnapujanam saucam** arjavam*
brahmacaryam ahimsa** ca sariram **tapa ucyate

Reverence for the ***Devas***, the **twice**-born, the ***gurus***,
and **the wise** – **purity**, sincerity, **self-control**, and **non-harming**
are **considered** the penance (voluntary acts of devotion)
or **austerity** of the body.

Verse 15 (1,000) Speech as related to higher levels of consciousness

*anudvegakaram **vakyam satyam** priyahitam ca yat*
*svadhyayabhyasanam caiva vanmayam **tapa ucyate***

To **speak** without ever causing pain to another, to be **truthful**, to always say what is kind and beneficial, and to **study the scriptures** regularly: this practice is **called austerity** of speech.

Verse 16 (1,000) The mind related to levels of consciousness

manahprasadah saumyatvam maunam atmavinigrahah
*bhavasamsuddhir ity etat **tapo manas**am **ucyate***

A calm contented mental clarity, kindness, silence, self-control, and purity of character **constitute** the **austerity** of the **mind**.

Verse 17 (1,000) *sattvic*

***sraddhaya** paraya taptam **tapas** tat **trividham** naraih*
***aphalaka**nksibhir yuktaih **sattvikam** paricaksate*

This **threefold penance** (voluntary acts of devotion), *sattvic* in nature, is practiced by persevering individuals possessing great **devotion**, desiring **no fruit** of actions.

Verse 18 (1,000) *rajasic*

*satkaramanapujartham **tapo** dambhena caiva yat*
*kriyate tad iha proktam **rajasam** calam adhruvam*

Austerities (behaviors) are said to be *rajasic* when practiced for the purpose of selfish pride and for gaining recognition, honor, and homage. Its effect is unstable and fleeting.

Verse 19 (1,000) *tamasic* – destruction of one's enemies

*mudhagrahenatmano yat pidaya kriyate **tapah***
*parasyotsadanartham va tat **tamasam** udahrtam*

Tamasic **austerities** (behaviors) are those based on ignorance, foolishness, self-torture, or in order to harm another person.

We harm others when we make assumptions, when we judge, and when we discredit others. Our behavior can be very subtle when it comes to our relationships with other people. Anything we do to diminish someone else to make ourselves appear greater is *tamasic* behavior.

Giving as related to consciousness

Verse 20 (1,000) *sattvic*

*datavyam iti yad **danam** diyate 'nupakarine*
*dese kale ca patre ca tad **danam sattvikam** smrtam*

The ***sattvic* gift** is made for the sake of righteousness, without expecting anything in return, and is **bestowed** in the proper time and place on a deserving person.

Verse 21 (1,000) *rajasic*

yat tu pratyupakarartham phalam uddisya va punah
*diyate ca **pariklistam** tad **danam rajasam** smrtam*

A ***rajasic* gift** is offered with **reluctance**, or with the thought of receiving a return gift or gaining merit.

Verse 22 (1,000) *tamasic*

*adesakale yad **danam** apatrebhyas ca diyate*
*asatkrtam avajnatam tat **tamasam** udahrtam*

A ***tamasic* gift** is given at the wrong time and place on an unworthy person, contemptuously or without goodwill.

Yajna, Karma, and Tapas

Verse 23 (1,000) *In the beginning*

aum tat sad *iti nirdeso* **brahmanas trividhah** *smrtah*
brahmanas *tena* **vedas** *ca* **yajnas** *ca vihitah pura*

Aum-Tat-Sat: these **three words designate** *Brahman* (God –
Consciousness). In the beginning, this power created the
Brahmins, the *Vedas*, and the **sacrificial rites**.

Verse 24 (1,000) *Aum* – the first sound of God in the universe

tasmad **om** *ity udahrtya* **yajnadanatapahkriyah**
pravartante vidhanoktah satatam **brahmavadinam**

Therefore, **aum** is always chanted by the **followers of Brahman**,
as the scriptures direct, before undertaking any act of **sacrifice,
gift-giving, or austerity**.

Verse 25 (1,000) *tat* – the Absolute

tad *ity anabhisamdhaya* **phalam yajnatapah**kriyah
danakriyas ca vividhaih kriyante moksakanksibhih

Repetition of the word **tat** also ensures **all acts and rituals**
contain no taint of desires for **personal results**.

Verse 26 (1,000) All actions dedicated to *Brahman* are *Sat*

sadbhave sadhubhave ca **sad** *ity etat prayujyate*
prasaste **karmani** *tatha sacchabdah partha yujyate*

The word **Sat** is the designation of the Supreme Reality
(beyond creation) and also goodness. **Sat** refers to the
higher forms (levels of consciousness) of spiritual **actions**.

Verse 27 (1,000) Human behavior

yajne tapasi **dane** ca **sthitih sad** iti cocyate
karma caiva tadarthiyam sad ity evabhidhiyate

Sat describes the **steady** and continuous **self-sacrifice** (action),
self-discipline, and selfless **giving**.

Verse 28 (1,000) *asat* – non-effective action

asraddhaya hutam dattam tapas taptam krtam ca yat
asad ity **ucyate** partha na ca tat pretya no iha

Arjuna, whatever sacrifice (action) is offered, gift bestowed,
or austerity performed, **without faith** it **is called *asat***,
unreal – it is worthless here and in the hereafter.

REMEMBER
ME ALONE

CHAPTER EIGHTEEN (999.6)

....

78 Verses

Primary Themes: Krishna, Enlightenment, Consciousness, and *gunas*
Secondary Themes: Renunciation, *jnana*, Soul, Reincarnation,
Yoga, karma, yajna, and *bhakti*

Our final chapter is the longest of all and serves as a summary for
everything that's been presented—with nearly one-third of Chapter
18 concerning the *gunas*. Verse 47 is one of the most quoted teachings from the *Bhagavad Gita*: *It is better to do your own duty imper-
fectly than to perfectly do another's.* This teaching relates directly back
to the Ralph Waldo Emerson quote from earlier. *To be yourself in a
world that is constantly trying to make you something else is the greatest
accomplishment.* We can think of our lives as actors in a play—we
may not have the lead role or a lot of lines, but our character is extremely important and no one else can play our role and speak our
lines. The Universe went to a lot of trouble to manifest each of our
lives and create a part for us to play in the universal drama. We are
all here for the Divine purpose of the universe to unfold and we ALL
have something great to offer the world. We must never compare
ourselves to others and we must never compromise our integrity.

Why do so many people try to *make us something else*? We looked
at assumptions in Chapter 16, discussing the ego having to know everything in order to feel safe, and when it doesn't know something, it
makes assumptions, forms opinions, judges, and discredits others. To
feel safe relates directly to survival. We may not have large predators
trying to eat us, but we are still hardwired to survive in the world.
Those above 200 become more selfless, and the higher the level of

consciousness, the less desire there is in controlling others—we're far less concerned with survival as we ascend higher in consciousness. By the time consciousness reaches 600, the fear of death has been transcended. Those below 200 are selfish and their survival instincts are on high alert—being able to control others as well as their environment makes those with lower levels of consciousness feel safe. Part of controlling their environment includes defining, discrediting, and diminishing those they feel threatened by.

My experience with people calibrating below 200 is they want to make those who calibrate higher *less than* or *something else* in order to feel safe in their presence. This happens in very subtle ways and sometimes not so subtle ways. We have enough doubts in our heads without letting others add to those doubts. One of the characteristics of those who calibrate in the 400's is a sense of humor—most great comedians calibrate at this level. It makes me wonder if they subconsciously developed their sense of humor to such a degree in order to make others feel safe in their presence. It's all very interesting to consider.

In Verse 63, Krishna warns us not to misuse our power of free choice. He just told us how everything in life works—we now *know better*, so we must *do better*. We make so many choices in our lives, taking us to where we find ourselves at this very moment. We now have the choice to incorporate the teachings of Krishna into our lives or continue doing what we've always done. Keep the *Bhagavad Gita* close, it will serve you well and never fail you—it's the Truth. The chapter concludes with five final verses from Sanjaya—ending how the *Bhagavad Gita* began. Perfect!

Renunciation – Secondary Theme

Arjuna said:

Verse 1: *I desire to know the true meaning of renunciation (samnyasa) and non-attachment (tyaga). What is the difference between these two?*

Krishna answers:

Verse 2 (1,000) *tyaga* – letting go of the results from actions.

kamyanam karmanam *nyasam* **samnyasam** *kavayo viduh*
*sarva**karmaphalatyagam** prahus **tyagam** vicaksanah*

Sages call **samnyasa** the renunciation of all **actions performed with desire** *(kamyanam)*. The wise declare that **tyaga** is the renunciation of the **fruits of actions**.

tyaga – surrendering with generosity what one may have kept.

samnyasa – surrendering entirely.

Verse 3 (1,000) *dosavad* – "as an evil" – acts that involve killing.

tyajyam *dosavad ity eke* **karma** *prahur manisinah*
yajnadanatapahkarma *na* **tyajyam** *iti capare*

Some philosophers say that all actions should be **renounced** as an evil, while others believe certain actions such as **yajna** (selfless actions), **dana** (philanthropy) and **tapas** (self-discipline) should **not** be **renounced**.

Verse 4 (1,000) Three levels of non-attachment

niscayam **srnu** *me tatra* **tyage** *bharatasattama*
tyago *hi purusavyaghra* **trividhah** *samprakirtitah*

Hear from Me My decision regarding **renunciation**, Arjuna. **Renunciation** is said to be of **three kinds**.

Verse 5 (1,000) *yajna* – selflessness; *dana* – charity; *tapas* – self-discipline

yajnadanatapahkarma *na* **tyajyam** *karyam eva tat*
yajno *danam* **tapas** *caiva pavanani manisinam*

Actions involving **yajna**, **dana**, and **tapas** should not be **renounced** – their performance is necessary. **Selflessness, philanthropy**, and **self-discipline** purify the wise.

Verse 6 (1,000)

etany api tu karmani sangam tyaktva phalani ca
kartavyaniti me partha **niscitam** *matam uttamam*

But even these actions should be performed, forsaking attachment and the desire for a certain outcome. Arjuna, this is My supreme and **definite** conviction.

Renunciation and Karma – Secondary Themes

Verse 7 (1,000) Not doing something we're supposed to do or should do are *tamasic* actions.

niyatasya tu **samnyasah karmano** *nopapadyate*
mohat *tasya pari***tyagas tamasah** *parikirtitah*

The **relinquishment** of dutiful **actions** is improper. **Renunciation** of such actions through **delusion** is spoken of as *tamasic*.

Verse 8 (1,000) *Rajasic* actions are those we avoid because we think they're too difficult.

dukham *ity eva yat* **karma** *kayaklesabhayat tyajet*
sa krtva **rajasam tyagam** *naiva* **tyga***phalam labhet*

Those who relinquish **actions** as being intrinsically difficult, for fear of physical **pain**, are performing *rajasic* **renunciation** and are unable to gain the reward of **renunciation**.

Verse 9 (1,000) Performing actions without regard for the outcome are *sattvic* actions.

karyam ity eva yat **karma** *niyatam kriyate 'rjuna*
sangam **tyaktva** *phalam caiva sa* **tyagah sattviko** *matah*

When a dutiful **action** is performed solely because it should be done Arjuna, **forsaking** attachment to it and the results, that **renunciation** is considered *sattvic*.

Verse 10 (1,000)

*na **dvesti** kausalam **karma** kusale nanusajjate*
***tyagi sattva**samavisto medhavi chinnasamsayah*

The wise **renunciant** inspired by ***sattva***, having a calm
understanding and free from doubts, neither **abhors**
unpleasant **actions** nor delights in pleasant ones.

Sattvic actions are performed with a calm understanding,
regardless of whether we like what we're doing.

Verse 11 (1,000) Renunciation is not being attached to the outcome of our actions.

*na hi **dehabhrta** sakyam tyaktum **karmany** asesatah*
*yas tu **karmaphalatyagi** sa **tyagity** abhidhiyate*

It is truly impossible for the **embodied being** to completely
abandon **actions**, but those who **relinquish the results from
actions** are called **renunciants** *(tyagi)*.

Verse 12 (1,000) Transcending *karma*

*anistam istam misram ca **trividham karmanah phalam***
*bhavaty **atyaginam** pretya na tu **samnyasinam** kvacit*

The **fruits of action** are **three types** – good, harmful, and mixed
– it accrues in **non-renunciants** after their death for those who
have not abandoned their desire for results, but not for those
who have **renounced**.

Those who have renounced ego and desire accrue no further
karma – either in this world or the next.

Part Two – Karma – Secondary Theme

Verse 13 (1,000) *krtante* – philosophical theory where a
conclusion has been reached.

pancaitani mahabaho karanani nibodha me
samkhye krtante proktani siddhaye sarvakarmanam

Learn from Me the **five** factors necessary for the performance of all actions, chronicled in the **Samkhya doctrine** for the accomplishment of **all action**.

Verse 14 (1,000) Destiny – *daivam*, unpredictable forces influencing actions.

adhisthanam tatha karta karanam ca prthagvidham
vividhas ca prthakcesta daivam caivatra pancamam

The human body, the ego (the *doer*), the sense organs, mind, and intelligence – the actual functioning of the body and mind – and the **fifth**, the presiding **destiny**.

Destiny is the predetermined course of events in our lives and a very *important teaching here and in the Mahabharata*. In my book *Warrior Self*, I gave this chapter the title, *The Yoga of Destiny*. Krishna is about to finish His teachings to Arjuna at the end of this chapter—and then the Pandavas and Kauravas are going to fight to the death. After the war, when so many have died, typically someone is held responsible for all the devastation. Before King Dhritarashtra leaves his kingdom, he speaks to his subjects about his role in the war. The King says: *Pardon me that I did not destroy my son Duryodhana myself – I had more than the strength to do it. Duryodhana caused this Great War from his pride, but whether or not this action was good or bad, I do not know.* A spokesperson from the King's subjects answered Dhritarashtra saying: *The destruction of the Kurus was not caused by Duryodhana and it was not caused by you. Such devastation could never happen without the influence of destiny. In your presence, we absolve your son for what he did.*

Near the end of the *Mahabharata*, Krishna meets a Holy man who asks Him about preventing the war. Krishna tells the stranger that the war was not prevented and was the work of the gods. Krishna says: *The knot of destiny is hard to untie. Born as a man, I must act as a man – I did all I could. All my effort could not overreach the time and place – bound by their own deeds, they called it **destiny**.* Every choice we make creates our future—not even God can change the destiny we choose for ourselves. In our discussion at the beginning of the book about *karma*, I defined *karma* as the force that propels our destiny. Our minds are inherently defective, the blind king rules us all—everyone sees truth from different perspectives because of our levels of consciousness; which is directly related to the choices we make for ourselves—whether right or wrong, as Krishna will tell us in the next verse.

Verse 15 (1,000)

*sariravanmanobhir yat **karma** prarabhate narah*
*nyayyam va viparitam va **pancaite** tasya hetavah*

Whatever the **action**, right or wrong, whether of speech, mind, or body – **These five** are the cause of all actions.

Verse 16 (1,000) Continuing

tatraivam sati kartaram atmanam kevalam tu yah
pasyaty akrtabuddhitvan** na sa **pasyati durmatih

This being the case, those of **insufficient understanding sees** themselves as the sole agent (doer) of action, they are **in error**, and do not **see**.

Verse 17 (1,000) Evil (force) eventually causes its own destruction

*yasya nahamkrto bhavo **buddhir** yasya **na lipyate***
*hatvapi sa imaml lokan na **hanti** na **nibadhyate***

Those who are free from all sense of "I" (enlightened), whose **motives** are **untainted**, though they slay *(hanti)*, they slay not – nor are they bound *(nibadhyate)* by such an act.

This verse is difficult to unravel—another paradox of God, who does nothing, yet is doing everything—who is non-violent, yet kills. Arjuna was incarnated to help Krishna set things right in the world—his actions at Kurukshetra were karmically ordained, Arjuna was an instrument of God, carrying out the Divine law. Krishna told Arjuna at the end of Chapter 11 that karmic law has already killed Arjuna's foes—long before the battle ever began. Duryodhana's actions came from his ego, not from God—he alone was held liable for his evil actions by the law of karma. As an allegory, Arjuna plays an important role in the battle ahead—he's the only one who can kill Bhishma and Karna—ego and desire. Without self-control and will power, we are defenseless against these two powerful forces. Allegory aside, God is the only one who can slay and not be bound by such an act—never humans.

Verse 18 (1,000) *Knowledge unites knower with that which is known.*

jnanam jneyam parijnata **trividha karmacodana**
karanam karma karteti **trividhah karmasamgrahah**

There are **three things** which **motivate actions: knowledge**, the **knower**, and that which is **known**. There are **three constituents of action**: the means, the doer, and the purpose.

Knowledge, knower, and *known* are the real sources of all action. If we want to make tea, we need the *knowledge* (the means) of how to make tea, bringing together everything we (*the knower* – the *doer*) need to make the tea (*that which is known* – the purpose).

Part Three – Gunas – Primary Theme

Verse 19 (1,000)

jnanam karma *ca* **karta** *ca* **tridhaiva gunabhedatah**
procyate **gunasamkhyane** *yathavac chrnu tany api*

Samkhya philosophy describes **knowledge, action,** and **doer** as being of **three kinds** only, related to the *guna* (levels of consciousness) which predominates in each. Please listen as I explain.

Verses 20 through 28 describe various levels of consciousness and human behavior.

Verse 20 (1,000) *sattva* – 500 to 599

sarvabhutesu *yenaikam bhavam avyayam iksate*
avibhaktam vibhaktesu taj **jnanam viddhi sattvikam**

Sattvic knowledge sees God in **everyone.**

Verse 21 (1,000) 200 to 400 – *prthaktvena* – dominated by *rajas*

prthaktvena tu yaj jnanam nanabhavan prthagvidhan
vetti sarvesu **bhutesu** *taj* **jnanam viddhi rajasam**

Rajasic knowledge sees differences in **people.**

Verse 22 (1,000) Below 200 – *ahaitukam* – acting without thinking about the consequences.

yat tu krtsnavad ekasmin karye saktam ahaitukam
atattvarthavad alpam ca tat **tamasam** *udahrtam*

Tamasic knowledge sees us above everyone else.

Krishna begins His explanation on the relationship of the *gunas* to *karma*.

Verse 23 (1,000) 500 to 600 – *niyatam* – morally binding actions.

niyatam sangarahitam aragadvesatah krtam
aphalaprepsuna **karma** *yat tat* **sattvikam** *ucyate*

Sattvic actions know what to do, how to do it, and the reason for doing it.

Verse 24 (1,000) 200 to 499

*yat tu kamepsuna **karma** sahamkarena va punah*
*kriyate bahulayasam tad **rajasam** udahrtam*

Rajasic actions imply doing something motivated by self-interest.

Verse 25 (1,000) Below 200

anubandham ksayam himsam anapeksya ca paurusam
*mohad arabhyate **karma** yat tat **tamasam** ucyate*

Tamasic actions always take the easy way out, never fully understanding the consequences of the actions.

Verse 26 (1,000) 500 to 600 – *karta* – *"I am the doer of this action."*

muktasango 'nahamvadi dhrtyutsahasamanvitah
*siddhyasiddhyor nirvikarah karta **sattvika** ucyate*

The characteristic expressions (ego) of **sattva** are acting without ego, without attachment, and without regard for success or failure.

Verse 27 (1,000) 200 to 499

ragi karmaphalaprepsur lubdho himsatmako 'sucih
*harasokanvitah karta **rajasah** parikirtitah*

Characteristic **rajasic** expressions (ego) include attachment to the outcome, desire for recognition, greed, and being easily pleased or discouraged by the outcome.

Verse 28 (1,000) Below 200 – *naikrtiko* – lacking compassion

ayuktah prakrtah stabdhah satho naikrtiko 'lasah
*visadi dirghasutri ca karta **tamasa** ucyate*

Tamasic expressions (ego) are lazy, malicious, stupid, mean, deceitful, and easily depressed.

Intelligence (buddhi), Will (dhrtih), and Happiness (sukham)

Verse 29 (1,000)

buddhir bhedam dhrtes caiva gunatas trividham srnu
procyamanam asesena prthaktvena dhanamjaya

Listen Arjuna, as I explain separately and extensively, the **three kinds** of **conscience** and **determination**, according the *gunas.*

Verse 30 (1,000) Contrast of actions

pravrttim ca nivrttim ca karyakarye bhayabhaye
*bandham **moksam** ca ya vetti **buddhih** sa partha **sattviki***

Intelligence is *sattvic* when it correctly understands the differences between desireful actions and renunciation – non-dutiful actions are the cause of apprehension, fear, and **bondage,** Arjuna.

Verse 31 (1,000) *rajasic* – 200 to 499

*yaya **dharmam adharmam** ca **karyam cakaryam** eva ca*
*ayathavat prajanati **buddhih** sa partha **rajasi***

Intelligence is *rajasic* Arjuna, when someone cannot distinguish between **right** and **wrong**, or know what **should** or **should not be done.**

Verse 32 (1,000) *tamasic* – Below 200 – Problem people

adharmam dharmam iti ya manyate tamasavrta
*sarvarthan viparitam ca **buddhih** sa partha **tamasi***

Tamasic **intelligence** mistakes **wrong from right** – looking upon all things in a perverted way.

Tamasic consciousness is unpredictable, unreasonable, and can potentially be harmful to others. This is the realm of force, where people can be destructive of life.

Verse 33 (1,000) *sattvic* will is not affected in any way by either good or bad activities.

dhrtya *yaya dharayate* **manahpranendriyakriyah**
yogenavyaabhicarinya dhrtih *sa partha* **sattviki**

The **determination** which **sustains the functions of the mind, prana, and senses – strengthened through Yoga practice –** that **will** is **sattvic** Arjuna.

Verse 34 (1,000) *rajasic* will is always attached to the outcome.

yaya tu **dharma**kamarthan dhrtya dharayate 'rjuna
prasangena **phala**kanksi **dhrtih** *sa partha* **rajasi**

Rajasic **will** is attached to **righteousness**, desire, and wealth, while longing for the **results**, Arjuna.

Verse 35 (1,000) *tamasic* will is full of fear, grief, despair, conceit, and laziness.

yaya svapnam bhayam sokam visadam madam eva ca
na vimuncati durmedha **dhrtih** *sa partha* **tamasi**

The will by which a stupid person does not forsake too much sleep, fear, sorrow, despair, and pride, Arjuna, is **tamasic will**.

Happiness

Verse 36 (1,000) There are three kinds of happiness influenced by the *gunas*.

sukham *tv idanim* **trividham srnu** *me bharatarsabha*
abhyasad *ramate yatra* **duhkhantam** *ca nigacchati*

And now Arjuna, I will **tell** you about the **three kinds** of

happiness: **Transcendent happiness** enjoyed by repeated practice, which **ends all sorrows**.

Verse 37 (1,000) *sattvic* – sacrifice and hardship in the beginning

yat tad agre visam iva pariname 'mrtopamam
*tat **sukham sattvikam** proktam **atmabuddhiprasadajam***

That **happiness** which is born of the **clear perceptive discrimination of Self-realization** is called *sattvic*. It seems like poison *(visvam)* at first *(agre)*, but like nectar afterward.

Verse 38 (1,000) *rajasic* – satisfaction of our desires is temporary

visayendriyasamyogad yat tad agre 'mrtopamam
*pariname visam iva tat **sukham rajasam** smrtam*

The **happiness** which springs from the contact of the senses and their objects is termed *rajasic*. It seems like nectar in the beginning *(agre)* and like poison *(visvam)* in the end.

Verse 39 (1,000) *tamasic*

*yad agre canubandhe ca **sukham mohanam atmanah***
*nidralasyapramadottham tat **tamasam** udahrtam*

That elusive **happiness** which originates *(agre)* and ends in **self-delusion**, stemming from too much sleep, slothfulness, and miscomprehension, is called *tamasic*.

Part Four – Duty in Life – Karma and Dharma

Verse 40 (1,000) Only the enlightened are free

na tad asti prthivyam va divi devesu va punah
*sattvam **prakrtijair** muktam yad ebhih syat tribhir **gunaih***

There are no unenlightened beings that are free from the **gunas**, born of *Prakriti*.

Verse 41 (1,000) The last verse about the *gunas*

brahmanaksatriyavisam sudranam *ca paramtapa*
karmani pravibhaktani **svabhavaprabhavair gunaih**

The duties of **Brahmins, Kshatriyas, Vaishyas**, and **Sudras** are allocated *(pravibhaktani)* according to the **gunas**, arising from **their own nature** (level of consciousness).

The caste system in India has been greatly misunderstood—I believe it is based on levels of consciousness, not on birth. In Krishna's descriptions of the four castes below, He lists human behavior qualities for the *Brahmins* and *Kshatriyas*. Krishna then describes *Vaishyas* and *Sudras* much differently. Clearly nothing is said by Krishna regarding tradition, family origin, or heredity.
Brahmins -- 500 and up
Kshatriyas -- 400 to 499
Vaishyas --   200 to 399
Sudras   --   Below 200

Verse 42 (1,000) *Brahmins* – 500 and up – Human behavior described

samo damas **tapah saucam** *ksantir arjavam eva ca*
jnanam *vijnanam astikyam* **brahmakarma** *svabhavajam*

Serenity, self-control, **austerity, purity**, forgiveness, honesty, insight, and **knowledge** are the natural duties
(level of consciousness) of **Brahmin's**.

svabhavajam – born of one's own nature (level of consciousness).

Verse 43 (1,000) *Kshatriyas* – 400 to 499 – Human behavior described

sauryam tejo dhrtir daksyam yuddhe capy apalayanam
danam *isvarabhavas ca* **ksatram** *karma svabhavajam*

Kshatriyas have (level of consciousness reflects) valor, radiance, endurance, skillfulness, courage, **generosity**, and leadership.

Verse 44 (1,000) Human behavior is not described here, an interesting contrast.

krsigauraksyavanijyam **vaisya***karma svabhavajam*
paricaryatmakam karma **sudras***yapi svabhavajam*

Tilling the soil, cattle breeding, and business are the natural duties of the *Vaishyas* (200 – 399). Actions characterized by service are the natural duties of the *Sudras* (below 200).

paricarya – behavior, conduct
atmakam – having or consisting of the nature or character of
vanijyam – commerce
gaura – earth
krsi - agriculture

Verse 45 (1,000) Everyone is born for enlightenment

sve sve karmany abhiratah samsiddhim labhate narah
svakarma*niratah siddhim yatha vindati tac chrnu*

Each one attentive to their **own duty**, people gain the highest success. Now hear how to gain perfection (enlightenment) by devotion to that duty.

We all have our own level of consciousness and it is in our best interest to raise our level of consciousness so we can increase our happiness, personal power, and better serve the world.

Verse 46 (1,000) We all have something great to offer to the world.

yatah pravrttir **bhutanam** *yena sarvam idam tatam*
svakarmana *tam abhyarcya siddhim vindati manavah*

People will reach perfection (enlightenment) by **doing their duty** as an act of worship to the Lord, whom **all beings** are evolved and by whom this entire world is permeated.

Verse 47 (1,000) *svadharma – one's own duty is better than another's.*

*sreyan **svadharmo** vigunah **paradharmat** svanusthitat*
svabhavaniyatam karma kurvan napnoti kilbisam

Better than the well-accomplished ***dharma* of another** is **one's own *dharma***, even though somewhat imperfect. Those who perform the duty decreed by their inborn nature (level of consciousness) contracts no sin.

Verse 48 (1,000) Each person's highest *dharma* is to express their soul qualities.

*sahajam karma kaunteya **sadosam** api **na tyajet***
*sarvarambha hi dosena dhumen**agnir** ivavrtah*

Therefore, no one should **abandon** one's duty, even though it has **some imperfection**, Arjuna, for all actions, in the beginning, are covered by imperfections, as **fire** is by smoke.

Part 5 – Summary on the Bhagavad Gita's Message

Verse 49 (1,000) Renunciation, Enlightenment, and the Soul

***asaktabuddhih** sarvatra **jitatma** vigatasprhah*
***naiskarmyasiddhim** paramam **samnyase**nadhigacchati*

Keeping their intellect always detached from worldly ties and passions, victorious in regaining **their soul**, and free from desires through **renunciation** – one reaches the ultimate perfection (enlightenment) – **the actionless state of realization.**

Verse 50 (1,000) Enlightenment

*siddhim prapto yatha **brahma** tathapnoti nibodha me*
*samasenaiva kaunteya nistha **jnanasya** ya para*

Learn from Me in brief, Arjuna, how those who attain such perfection finds **Brahman**, the supreme culmination of **knowledge**.

Verses 51 through 53 specify the Yoga practices necessary to reach the state of *Brahman* (enlightenment).

Verse 51 (1,000) Enlightenment

buddhya visuddhaya yukto dhrtyatmanam niyamya ca
sabdadin visayams tyaktva ragadvesau vyudasya ca

Absorbed in a completely purified **intellect**, subjugating the body and the senses by resolute **patience**, forsaking sound and the other objects of the senses, without regretting, without aversion;

Verse 52 (1,000) continuing

viviktasevi laghvasi yatavakkayamanasah
dhyanayogaparo nityam vairagyam samupasritah

Seeking solitude *(viviktasevi)*, **eating lightly**, controlling body, **speech**, and **mind – always absorbed in the Yoga of contemplation – cultivating dispassion**;

Verse 53 (1,000) Human behavior

ahamkaram balam darpam kamam krodham parigraham
vimucya nirmamah santo brahmabhuyaya kalpate

Without **pride, violence, arrogance**, lust, **anger**, possessions, the "me and mine" consciousness (duality) and **peaceful** in mind – they are qualified to become *(kalpate)* one with **Brahman**.

Verse 54 (1,000) Unconditional love – regarding all beings alike

brahmabhutah prasannatma na socati na kanksati
samah sarvesu bhutesu madbhaktim labhate param

By becoming **absorbed in Brahman** and at **peace with**

themselves, neither grieving nor craving – regarding **all beings** alike – they attain *(labhate)* **supreme devotion** to Me.

Verse 55 (1,000) *By devotion they realize Me – the truth that I am.*

bhaktya mam abhijanati *yavan yas casmi tattvatah* *tato mam tattvato* **jnatva** *visate tadanantaram*

By **devotion** they **realize Me**, My innermost nature – the truth that I am – through this **knowledge** – they quickly make entry into Me (enlightenment).

Verse 56 (1,000) *It is by My grace*

sarvakarmani *api sada kurvano madvyapasrayah* *matprasadad avapnoti sasvatam padam avyayam*

Over and above performing **one's duties** faithfully, taking shelter in Me, it is by My grace a devotee finds the eternal, unchanging state (enlightenment).

God is the sole judge as to whether we fulfill the laws of spiritual conduct required for enlightenment.

Verse 57 (1,000) *buddhi* – to understand the meaning of right knowledge.

cetasa **sarvakarmani** *mayi samnyasya matparah* **buddhiyogam** *upasritya* **maccittah** *satatam bhava*

Mentally dedicate **all your actions** to Me, regard Me as your Supreme Goal, embrace the **yoga of the spirit**, and always absorb **your heart** in Me.

Verse 58 (1,000) A word of caution

maccittah *sarvadurgani matprasadad tarisyasi* *atha cet tvam* **ahamkaran** *na srosyasi vinanksyasi*

With heart united in Me and by My grace, you shall overcome all difficulties. But if you are too **self-centered** to heed My advice, you will meet destruction.

Verse 59 (1,000) As a born *Kshatriya*, Arjuna is compelled to do what is right.

*yam **ahamkaram** asritya na yotsya iti manyase*
*mithyaisa vyavasayas te **prakrtis tvam** niyoksyati*

If you **self-centeredly** decide that you will not fight, your decision is meaningless. Your inborn **nature** (level of consciousness) will force **you** to fight (do the right thing).

Verse 60 (1,000) *karma* and Consciousness

svabhavajena** kaunteya nibaddhah svena **karmana
*kartum necchasi yan **mohat** karisyasi avaso 'pi tat*

Shackled by your own **karma** and **inborn nature**, Arjuna, what through **delusion** you wish not to do, you will helplessly be compelled to do.

Krishna is encouraging Arjuna to do what needs to be done— saying, if you follow the instructions that I've been explaining to you, then you will be free of any *karma* from this war.

Verse 61 (1,000) The power of God keeps everything in motion

***isvarah sarvabhutanam hrddese** 'rjuna tisthaty*
*bhramayan **sarvabhutani** yantrarudhani **mayaya***

The Lord lives in the **hearts** of **all creatures** Arjuna,
and by **His cosmic delusion,** *(maya)* compels **all beings**
to rotate as though attached to a wheel.

Verse 62 (1,000) *Bhakti* and Enlightenment

***tam eva saranam gaccha** sarvabhavena bharata*
***matprasadat** param **santim** sthanam prapsyasi sasvatam*

Take shelter in Him with all the eagerness of your heart, Arjuna. And **by His grace**, you shall reach the Eternal Shelter (enlightenment) which is ultimate **peace**.

Verse 63 (1,000) Don't misuse your power of free choice.

*iti te **jnanam** akhyatam **guhyad guhyataram** maya*
vimrsyaitad asesena yatecchasi tatha kuru

Now that I have taught you this **knowledge**, the most **secret of all secrets**, and **after exhaustively reflecting on it**,
act as you think best.

Verse 64 (1,000) Once more

*sarva**guhya**tamam bhuyah **srnu me paramam vacah***
*isto 'si me drdham iti tato **vak**syamy te hitam*

Listen again to My **supreme word**, the most **secret** of all. Because you are dearly loved by Me, I **speak** for your own good *(hitam)*.

Verse 65 (1,000) *You shall attain Me*

***manmana** bhava **madbhakta** madyaji mam namaskuru*
*mam evaisyasy **satyam** te pratijane priyo 'si me*

Occupy your mind in Me – honor Me with **devotion** and sacrifice. **So in truth** I promise – you shall attain Me, as you are dear to Me!

Verse 66 (1,000) **Entire *Bhagavad Gita* summarized!**

*sarva**dharman** parityajya mam **ekam saranam vraja***
*aham tva sarvapapebhyo moksayisyami **ma sucah***

Forsaking all other *dharmas*, **remember Me alone,**
Do not grieve, for I will free you from all sins.

Our highest *dharma* is to discover that we are sustained by God.

Verse 67 (1,000) This knowledge is not meant for everyone.

*idam te **natapaskaya** na**bhaktaya** kadacana*
*na casusrusave **vacyam** na ca mam yo 'bhyasuyati*

Never voice *(vacyam)* these truths to **one who is without self-control** or **devotion** (faith), nor to one who doesn't serve or does not care to hear – nor to one who speaks ill of Me.

Verses 68 and 69 (1,000) *There shall be none dearer*

*ya idam paramam **guhyam madbhaktesv** abhidhasyati*
***bhaktim** mayi param krtva mam evaisyaty asamsayah*

na ca tasman manusyesu kascin me priyakrttamah
bhavita na ca me tasmad anyah priyataro bhuvi

Whosoever shall impart to **My devotees** the supreme **secret** knowledge, with utmost **devotion** to Me, shall without a doubt come to Me. No one performs a more priceless service to Me than they – in all the world there shall be none dearer to Me.

Verse 70 (1,000) *Those who study and know*

***adhyesyate** ca ya imam dharmyam samvadam avayoh*
***jnanayajnena** tenaham istah syam iti me matih*

Those who study and know this sacred dialogue between us will be worshiping Me through the **sacrifice of knowledge**. This is My holy word.

Verse 71 (1,000) *Those who simply listen*

***sraddhavan** anasuyas ca **srnuyad** api yo narah*
*so 'pi muktah subhaml **lokan** prapnuyat punya**karma**nam*

Even those **who simply listen** to these words with **faith**, and do not doubt them, they will be free from *karma* and reach the **heaven** of the righteous.

Part Six – The Dialogue Concludes

Krishna now asks Arjuna two questions:

Verse 72 (1,000) *Do you truly understand?* Krishna's final verse.

kaccid etac chrutam partha tvayaikagrena cetasa
kaccid **ajnanasammohah** *pranastas te dhanamjaya*

Have you listened to this wisdom with concentrated heart, Arjuna? Has your **confusion caused by ignorance** been annihilated, Arjuna?

Arjuna answers:

Verse 73: *Yes, my confusion is gone! I will act according to what you have taught me.*

Sanjaya said:

Verses 74 through 78: Sanjaya closes with five final verses, saying he has listened to this amazing conversation between Krishna and Arjuna. He feels blessed to experience this truth through his own intuition—feeling a deep, encouraging conviction within his soul, knowing all the wisdom, love, and powers of God.

At the conclusion of Krishna's sermon, Arjuna picks up his bow and tells Krishna he will fight.

Make Your Own Light

Another important text in Yoga philosophy is the *Yoga Sutras* (895), compiled about 400 CE by Patanjali. One of the more practical aspects of the *Yoga Sutras* is the moral precepts—the **yamas** and **niyamas**—the methods for internal and external purification. These precepts will be the framework for organizing Krishna's teachings in the *Bhagavad Gita* into an everyday practice to elevate our consciousness. The ten single Sanskrit words

Patanjali uses to organize the *yamas* and *niyamas* are actually found within the *Bhagavad Gita* itself. As we discovered reading the *Bhagavad Gita* and learning many Sanskrit words, they have multiple meanings. We'll look at each of these ten words in a different context from how we typically understand these precepts. We'll begin with the five *yamas*. We learned this word when we discussed *pranayama* – *yama* can be defined as control or restraint.

Ahimsa is the first *yama*, often understood as non-harming or even non-violence. My favorite understanding of *ahimsa* is not judging ourselves and others—any negative thoughts we have about ourselves violates this precept. *Ahimsa* can also mean consideration and attention to ourselves and others—not to cause injury—compassion and love for ourselves. *Ahimsa* is really about being kind to everything and everyone, including ourselves, at all times, and with no exceptions. Successful people are considerate to all, treating everyone as equals—they have no inclination to act arrogantly and never consider themselves better than others, just more fortunate. Kindness toward everyone can ensue only when we stop condemning, fearing, judging, discrediting, and hating each other—we're always the victims of our own vindictiveness (Duryodhana learned this the hard way). Four verses within the *Bhagavad Gita* that relate to *ahimsa* are as follows:

Those who feel for others – even as the feel for themselves.
Chapter Six, Verse, 32

Love everyone as your own Self, without dislike and hatred.
Chapter Eleven, Verse 55

And when a person sees God in them is the same God in all that is, they hurt not themselves by hurting others.
Chapter Thirteen, Verse 27

Speak without ever causing pain to another.
Chapter Seventeen, Verse 15

These four verses are another way to express what we know as *The Golden Rule – Do unto others as you would have them do unto you.* Not only is this a teaching about *ahimsa*, it's also a teaching about *karma* and destiny—**how we treat ourselves and others determines our future.**

Satya means truth—the bedrock of this entire book has been about truth. In our examination of truth and how to measure it, we discovered that our ability to speak and comprehend truth is largely based on our level of consciousness. What is true for one person may not be true for someone else. *Satya* is about letting go of pretense and our false self—which boils down to humility. Truth and humility are connected in that the human mind is intrinsically incapable of discovering truth—primarily because of its own structure and engineering. Humility gives us the attitude of inquiry, which results in becoming a student of truth. In the last verse of Chapter One, Arjuna lays down his bow and arrows. This action by Arjuna is an act of humility. Only now can Arjuna hear the truth that Krishna has to offer—the truth that has been with Arjuna all along but couldn't be revealed until Arjuna became humble. Catastrophic events in our lives will certainly make us humble—we have to surrender our weapons of anger, judgment, reactiveness, victimhood, and knowing in order to discover truth—which exists in another paradigm beyond facts. Only facts can be proven—truth is not subject to proof. Our ego sees Truth as its ultimate enemy, which is why Bhishma fought for the Kauravas and not the Pandavas. Lack of humility, pretense, and trying to appear greater than we actually are is in direct conflict with Truth. By making our lives a **living prayer** through intention, alignment, humility, and surrendering our false selves and pretenses, we enter into a true spiritual reality and authentic way of being in the world.

Never think about personal gain or impressing others.
Perform all your actions without beingattached to the
outcome, whether of success or failure.
Chapter Two, Verse 47

Our third *yama* is **asteya** – non-stealing. The problem with one word definitions like non-harming and truth, we can easily think we're on our spiritual path and living all these precepts perfectly— but it's not that easy. As humans, we suffer because we think we don't have enough—and when we have something, we suffer because we think we have to protect it. We came into this world with nothing and we'll leave with nothing. We worry about money and acquiring more and more stuff—we think we need more to be more. We don't! We're the only species that seeks more than it needs. *Asteya* is about letting go of the desire to acquire and possess as well as not living beyond our means. Our ego tells us *the more we have the more we are* – and *if I win, you lose*. A minimum of want is a common characteristic of true success in general— there's no need to get when you already have. The basis of non-materiality is a radical understanding of the nature of consciousness itself. That which supports life is supported by life. Anything we are going to lose, we should lose—it's not the real thing.

When you reside in My Consciousness, whatever you lack,
I give. And whatever you have, I preserve.
Chapter Nine, Verse 22

Brahmacharya may be my favorite precept—it literally means *to walk with God* or behaving like a disciple of *Brahma*. I teach this *yama* as personal responsibility, which everyone can understand. This precept is often interpreted as celibacy—which is why I prefer personal responsibility instead. We learned the big difference between people calibrating either above or below 200 is personal responsibility. People below 200 won't take responsibility for their thoughts, words, and actions—they will use a well disguised form of blame and distortion of truth instead. We all know people who are never wrong and who know everything about everything. For someone calibrating below 200, taking responsibility for their actions will take them over 200—but that isn't so easy to do if you calibrate below 200. Self-centered motivations for personal gain draw us into the kingdom of force. Commitment to a higher principle *(dharma)* provides the only protection from our ego. Force always shows off, originating from self-doubts. Believing the source of power lies outside ourselves, we become powerless and vulnerable, and therefore, defensive and possessive. When we take responsibility for all our thoughts, words, and actions—it places us squarely in the kingdom of power. Below is the verse in sanskrit that shows the word *brahmacaryam* in context.

yad aksaram vedavido vadanti visanti yad yatayo vi-
*taragah yad icchanto **brahmacaryam** caranti tat te*
padam samgrahena pravaksye

That abode, which the knowers of the Vedas declare as
Unchanging, in which renunciants free from attachments
***lead a life of self-discipline** – the method for attaining*
That, I will explain to you in brief.
Chapter Eight, Verse 11

Stand up, Arjuna! Take shelter in Yoga, slashing with the
sword of knowledge this doubt born of ignorance existing
in your heart about yourself.
Chapter Four, Verse 42

Krishna commanding Arjuna to *stand up* is really about Arjuna living up to his responsibility of setting things right in the kingdom. Sooner or later, we all have to *stand up* and take responsibility for our lives—overcoming our doubts and imagined lack of self-worth, setting things right in our personal kingdom.

Our final *yama* is **aparigraha**, often interpreted as non-hoarding. My interpretation of this complicated word is living as truthfully with ourselves as we can. Non-hoarding is about letting go of our "stuff"—the stuff that no longer serves us, and I'm not talking about all the junk out in the garage. Letting go implies renunciation, surrendering our *outside reflections*, the foundation of Truth throughout the *Bhagavad Gita*. Letting go leaves room for impartial objectivity and clarity to reveal itself. In regards to *ahimsa*, it's letting go of the desire to cause harm to someone who may have hurt us in the past. In other words—get over it. *Satya*, letting go of pretense; *asteya*, letting go of desire; *brahmacharya*, letting go of blame and the need to always be right. These five powerful *yamas* are all interrelated to one another covering a lot of ground in our personal growth, which when practiced truthfully, will raise our level of consciousness. The one common thread shared with all five *yamas* is ego. Not being able to forgive, our pretense in all its forms, all of our desires, not wanting to be wrong and admitting we made a mistake, and finally, *aparigraha* itself—**living truthfully** on all levels.

*nirasir yatacittatma tyaktasarv**aparigrahah***
sariram kevalam karma kurvan napnoti kilbisam

They incur no sin performing mere bodily actions,
having **renounced all sense of possession**, free from
hopes, and whose heart is controlled by the soul.
Chapter Four, Verse 21

The words *niyama* and *niyamya* are found within the *Bhagavad Gita* and defined in the verses below as patience, discrimination, conquering, and taking control. **Patience** is exactly what's needed as we work with our *yamas* and *niyamas*.

buddhya visuddhaya yukto dhrtyatmanam **niyamya** *ca*
sabdadin visayams tyaktva ragadvesau vyudasya ca

Absorbed in a completely purified intellect, subjugating the body and the senses by resolute **patience**,
forsaking sound and the other objects of the senses,
without regretting, withoutaversion;
Chapter Eighteen, Verse 51

kamais tais tair hrtajnanah prapadyante 'nyadevatah
tam tam **niyama***m asthaya prakrtya niyatah svaya*

Led by their own inclinations (levels of consciousness),
their **discrimination** stolen by this or that craving, pursuing this or that obsessive desire, many seek lesser gods.
Chapter Seven, Verse 20

tasmat tvam indriyanyadau **niyamya** *bharatarsabha*
papmanam prajahi hyenam jnanavijnananasanam

Therefore, Arjuna, **take control** of the senses, and
then destroy desire,the annihilator of knowledge and
discrimination.
Chapter Three, Verse 41

*sam***niyam***yendriyagramam sarvatra samabuddhayah*
te prapnuvanti mam eva sarvabhutahite ratah

Those who have **conquered** all of the senses, possessing
even-mindedness in every circumstance, and devotes
themselves to the good of all beings.
Chapter Twelve, Verse 4

Our first *niyama* is **Sauca**, commonly defined as purity—but a broader definition is the maintenance of our bodies and environment as a spiritual duty. We did our yoga practice on the mat, took a shower, and put our recycles in the bin—check *sauca* off the list for the day—we're so spiritual. Not so fast, it isn't that easy—getting on the mat, showering, and recycling are what I would call *outside reflections*. What about the *reality within*? We always have to go deeper with our *yamas* and *niyamas* in order to affect positive change in our lives. The *reality within* is made up of our intentions, commitments, motivations, and thoughts. Is our kindness pure? Is our truth pure? Are our desires pure? Are we pure in our personal responsibility? Is our entire life pure? The dictionary defines *pure* as being free from contaminants and impurities; free from faults; containing nothing inappropriate or unnecessary. *Free from* sounds like renunciation—*free from outside reflections*. Did your ego stumble a moment ago when you read *free from faults? Sauca* just became a little more interesting than taking a shower.

Our thoughts, feelings, and interpretations are being reflected back to us constantly. When we try to make ourselves appear greater than we actually are, it's because of our own self-worth issues—we don't think we're enough as we are. Our upbringing and education has made us afraid to be different from others. No one else has the doubts we have about ourselves. Our doubts are contaminants, impurities, inappropriate, and unnecessary. The greatest renunciation is surrendering all of the attachments and impurities that keep us from speaking our truth. If we think we have to protect and hide some part of ourselves, some impurity about ourselves, we will never be completely truthful with others. Consciousness responds to each and every thought, reflecting our thoughts, feelings, and interpretations back to us. What we think matters even more than what we say. We have to be careful—pure—in what we think, how we talk to others, and how we talk to ourselves.

Our next *niyama* is **santosa**—often defined as contentment, but we now know it's more than a single word definition. *Santosa* is about things being enough and reverence *(bhakti)*, especially toward others. With *santosa* being defined as things being enough, it directly relates to four of our *yamas*—*satya, asteya, brahmacharya,* and *aparigraha*. With *satya*, content with who we are; with *asteya*, content with what we have; with *brahmacharya*, content with being moderate and walking the middle path; with *aparigraha*, content with not wanting more than what we really need. *Santosa* asks the questions, *Do I have everything I need? Do I really need everything I have?* We have our possessions, but they don't have us. Simplicity lightens our load—the layers of complexity in our life keeps us from seeing ourselves as we truly are—perfect and whole. The more we simplify our lives, the more honest and straightforward we become. There's simplicity to *sauca*—purity; the letting go of *aparigraha* lightens our load; *brahmacharya* reminds us to live a balanced life; truth in all its forms is simple; and finally, kindness is simple too, when we surrender our fears. **Contentment destroys the ego**. The war in the *Mahabharata* is really the war between *I am this* versus *I should be that*. The war is a personal show-down with ourselves—learning to make peace and be content with who we truly are—divine and perfect. When we experience true contentment, God is present.

> *Those who receive with **contentment** whatever befalls them, unaffected by dualities (likes and dislikes), devoid of jealousy, envy, or enmity, looking equally on success and failure, that person is free from karma.*
> Chapter Four, Verse 22

Tapas is used often in the *Bhagavad Gita*—it means self-discipline, learning to behave, and no longer needing to be our false self. *Tapas* can be expanded to mean enthusiasm for health, an appetite for life, gratitude, the force to end our suffering, to find out what happens next, service to others, and finally, the desire to explore the will of God. *Tapas* is commonly defined as *burning zeal*. Reading this book falls into the category of *tapas*—it takes a certain type of energy to read a book like this. *Tapas* is also **the fire of change**. When Krishna commands Arjuna to *stand up and fight*—the energy to *stand up* and change our lives for the better is the very essence of *tapas*. Commitment and *tapas* are connected to one another. The biggest part of our transformational work— our *learning to behave*, is to look honestly at our actions and behaviors. Learning about ourselves takes a patient *(niyamya)* effort *(tapas)* on a deeper level of understanding—an introspective level—and this can't happen without a powerful commitment.

tyajyam dosavad ity eke karma prahur manisinah
yajnadanatapahkarma na tyajyam iti capare

Some philosophers say that all actions should be renounced as an evil, while others believe certain actions such as *yajna* (selfless actions), *dana* (philanthropy) and *tapas* (self-discipline) should not be renounced.
Chapter 18, Verse 3

The *introspective* level of understanding I just wrote about is **svadhyaya**, also found in the *Bhagavad Gita* in the context of study of the scriptures. Reading this book is an example of *svadhyaya*. Another common definition is the **education of the self,** but beyond these definitions are non-attachment, staying connected to inspiration, inspiring others, humility, and letting go of results and embracing the process. Every choice of who and how to be is of great consequence—consciousness doesn't forget. Our range of choice is limited by our perception (level of consciousness). Eventually we will have to accept responsibility for every thought, word, and action we generate, and will re-experience exactly the same suffering we've caused *(karma)*. Our decisions resonate throughout the universe of consciousness to affect the lives of everyone—each **individual** is accountable to the **universal**. Until we, in our relationships with others, understand ourselves first, we will be the cause of all our conflicts. How we react to people and situations, especially when we have conflicts, is the best indicator of how well we know ourselves. The better we know ourselves the better our lives flow. Unless we deeply know and understand ourselves, we will be the cause of all our future conflicts.

Those who ignore the scriptural teachings and follow their own foolish desires will not find happiness or success.
Chapter 16, Verse 23

*Therefore, let the **scriptures** be your guide in deciding what to do and what not to do. First understand the path of action as the **scriptures** teach it, and then act accordingly.*
Chapter 16, Verse 24

dravyayajnas tapoyajna yogayajnas tathapare
svadhyaya*jnanayajnasca yatayah samsitavratah*

Other devotees offer wealth, self-discipline, and the methods of Yoga – while other individuals offer self-control and keeping strict vows, offer as sacrifices **self-study** and the acquirement of **scriptural** wisdom.
Chapter Four, Verse 28

Our final *niyama* is **Isvara-pranidhana**, surrender to God, practicing reverence, and experiencing the joy of devotion. This definition of *Isvara-pranidhana* defines *Bhakti Yoga* perfectly. If we only had one precept to practice, this is the one—because if we truly surrender to God, we automatically practice all the other precepts. In Chapter Nine, Krishna tells Arjuna that the Divine always protects. Krishna says, *On Me fix thy mind*. When we are thinking of the Divine, we become the Divine. The moment we understand this truth, the Divine takes care of us. The whole point of Yoga is to create a greater connection with the Divine—the Universal. When Arjuna was ready, grace descended upon him in Chapter 11—Arjuna didn't have to do anything, except surrender to God. Grace always finds us worthy—our only sin (mistake) is not **recognizing we are Divine**. Seeing ourselves as less than Divine is the source of whatever our life experience is giving us, or not giving us.

> *Work for Me, **surrender to Me**, free from attachments*
> *to whatever you do, leaving the results to Me.*
> Chapter 11, Verse 55

> *By using free choice to **put God first**, we receive the*
> ***grace** of God.*
> Chapter 18, Verse 62

> *Forsaking all other dharmas, **remember Me alone**,*
> *Do not grieve, for I will free you from all sins.*
> Chapter 18, Verse 66

As we discovered earlier in the book, many of the verses contain multiple themes—the same technique occurs with our *yamas* and *niyamas*. In Chapter 12, Verses 13 and 14 – all ten precepts are accounted for in these two verses.

*Those who are free from hatred toward all, who are friendly and compassionate to all – **ahimsa***

*Devoid of the consciousness of "I-ness" and possessiveness – **asteya** and **aparigraha***

*Is even-minded in suffering and joy – **brahmacharya***

*Forgiving – **ahimsa***

*Ever content – **santosa***

*A regular Yoga practitioner – **tapas** and **sauca***

*Constantly trying by Yoga to know the Self – **svadhyaya***

*United to Spirit – **isvara-pranidhana***

*Possessed of firm determination – **brahmacharya** and **tapas***

*With mind and discrimination surrendered to Me – **satya** and **isvara-pranidhana***

They are My devotees and dear to Me.

In the opening of Chapter 16, Verses 1, 2, and 3, Krishna lists extensively the qualities of higher consciousness related directly to the *yamas* and *niyamas*. Six of our precepts are specifically listed, but we can easily see many more in varying forms.

> *abhayam sattvasamsuddhir jnanayogavyavasthitih*
> *danam damas ca yajnas ca **svadhyayas tapa** arjavam*

> (1) Fearlessness, purity of heart, perseverance in acquiring wisdom and in practicing Yoga, charity, subjugation of the senses, performance of holy rites, **study of the scriptures, self-discipline**, straightforwardness;

> ***ahimsa satyam** akrodhas tyagah **santir** apaisunam*
> *daya bhutesv aloluptvam mardavam hrir acapalam*

> (2) **Non-harming, truthfulness**, freedom from anger, renunciation, **peacefulness,** non-slanderousness, compassion for all creatures, absence of greed, gentleness, modesty, lack of restlessness;

tejah ksama dhrtih **saucam** *adroho natimanita*
bhavanti sampadam daivim abhijatasya bharata

Radiance of character, forgiveness, patience,
cleanliness, freedom from hate, andabsence of conceit
– these qualities are the wealth of a divinely inclined
person, Arjuna.

Asana

In *Paths to God*, Ram Dass tells the story of a conversation he
had with his guru, Neem Karoli Baba, about *hatha-yoga*. "Nobody
does *hatha-yoga* anymore. I was surprised; I said, No? But it's very
big in America. He said, No, nobody does it anymore, because
hatha-yoga assumes that you've already finished with the first
two practices of *yama* and *niyama*, and nobody does that now."

Before we ever step on the mat to learn the physical practice
of yoga, we are to master all ten of the *yamas* and *niyamas* first.
The same thing goes for the fourth limb of the eight total limbs,
pranayama. We begin the study of *pranayama* only after we master
the third limb, *asana*. *A Tribute* is a book about the legendary
yoga teacher Pattabhi Jois, in which the question is asked whether
Krishnamacharya ever taught him *pranayama*. He answers: "Yes,
but before doing *pranayama*, you first have to practice yoga *asana*.
When you practice perfectly, then you can be taught *pranayama*.
Before that, *pranayama* should not be taught—it's too difficult."
We move through the eight limbs in order. The last four limbs
are all concerned with meditation—*pratyahara, dharana, dhyana*,
and *samadhi*. These last four limbs are the *internal* practices of
Yoga—the mental path from the individual to the Universal.

How do we know when we've mastered the *yamas* and *niyamas*? In truth, I don't think we ever master all ten precepts.
These teachings weave an intricate web for us to easily get caught
in—it's our ego that makes the web so sticky. A lot of fake spiritu-

ality exists in yoga these days—people love to tell us how spiritual they are, telling us about their diets and posting photos on social media of themselves along with many other things they do to try and look like great *yogins*. They actually weave a web of their own making, never realizing they got tangled up in the *yamas* and *niyamas*. *Satya*, letting go of pretense; *aparigraha*, truthful living; *tapas*, no longer needing to be our false self—these teachings are challenging to say the least. Living our lives with the highest level of truth and integrity is not so easy to do—especially if we try and live a "yogic" life. To me, that means truthful living on all levels and nothing else. What is true for me may be completely different than what is true for you. There is far too much projection on people who practice and teach yoga. I wouldn't presume to know what is best for anyone, and I'm certainly not going to try and tell someone how to live their life—not even Krishna does that. In Verse 63 of Chapter 18, Krishna says, *act as you think best*. One of the purposes of a yogic life is to move us toward our own truth within, so that we can express our truth out into the world. Expressing our truth has nothing to do with expressing our *outside reflections* and trying to make ourselves look better than others—or to make ourselves *look* like a yoga teacher.

By having a deeper understanding of the *yamas* and *niyamas*, before we begin our *asana* practice, helps us better understand the physical practice itself. Perhaps the biggest cause for injury in *hatha-yoga* is our ego. On the mat we must practice unconditional kindness toward our bodies and minds—never judging what we can or cannot do. We must always stay humble, respecting our limitations, not pushing ourselves beyond our abilities. We are responsible for our practice—not the teacher. *Aparigraha* reminds us to let go of our ambition of being able to do certain poses. Our intention for practicing on the mat must remain pure. Can our practice be enough—just as it is? Staying committed to going to class may be one of the harder practices to learn. *Svadhyaya* shows up on the mat as letting go of results and embracing the process.

One of the biggest teachings of the *Bhagavad Gita* is for us to learn to pay attention to our actions, not the results. Had Yudhisthira paid attention while he was gambling, he wouldn't have lost his kingdom, but his ego got the better of him—he countered force with force. We will injure ourselves by not paying attention on our mat. *Isvara-pranidhana* is the attitude of gratitude for being able to step onto a yoga mat and practice. These are some ideas as to why I think we should have a thorough understanding of the *yamas* and *niyamas*, first. We typically go to a yoga class without any knowledge of these ten precepts, and over time, we learn all these lessons from the *yamas* and *niyamas* the hard way—often through injury.

Stepping onto the path of Yoga takes **courage**. Staying on the path of Yoga requires **commitment**. Teaching yoga demands **humility**. Living the teachings of Yoga takes **patience**. Just as we fall in any balance pose at any given moment, we fall in these ten practices at any given moment. This is where we remind ourselves about *ahimsa*—not standing in judgment of ourselves. Having the awareness that we fell is what's important. Just as in our *asana* practice, we get back up and try again.

We can embody the philosophy of Yoga in our *hatha-yoga* practice in several different ways. We learned the **universal** is unseen whereas the **individual** is seen—the front of our body represents the individual and the back of our body the universal. Not only do I think of the *Bhagavad Gita* as having primary and secondary themes, I also think of the physical practice as having primary and secondary aspects of importance. For example, students in downward facing dog almost always look at their feet and collapse in their shoulders and backs. What makes down dog so challenging is we can't see the pose. If we begin to think of the hand of grace on our back supporting us—even though we can't see it, we connect to the Universal. By connecting to our back body and making that the primary importance, our practice begins to take on a whole new dimension of understanding. The universe always has our back—grace always remembers us, even though we often forget grace. Bringing our awareness to that which we cannot see—moving toward the hand of grace in our poses helps connect us to the universal.

Aligning our values with the positive attractors of the *yamas* and *niyamas* is more associated with success than anything else. Success comes as the consequence of aligning our lives with kindness, humility, patience, courage, concentration, commitment, perseverance, integrity, and truth. We are successful when we act without personal desire, regardless of success or failure. The underlying desire is to feel worthy, appreciated, wanted, heard, seen, loved, and valued. The feeling of emptiness in our lives comes from failing to align with the principles *(yamas-niyamas)* from which power originates.

Buddhism and the Bhagavad Gita

Many of our themes throughout the *Bhagavad Gita* are related to themes found within Buddhism—there are many parallel truths to what Krishna teaches us in the *Bhagavad Gita* and what the Buddha also taught. At the core of Buddhist teachings are **The Four Noble Truths**. The First Noble Truth is life is difficult. The Second Noble Truth is life is difficult because of our desires and attachments. The Third Noble Truth is the possibility of enlightenment—the liberation from our suffering exists for everyone. The Fourth Noble Truth is how we become enlightened through the teachings of the **Eightfold Path**. The first two Noble Truths are the diagnosis—the second pair of truths are the cure. The Eightfold Path is an eight-step recovery program to end suffering. Hopefully the Eightfold Path sounds similar to Patanjali's Eight Limbs of Yoga mentioned earlier. I'll break down those parallels in a moment.

Arjuna in the middle of the battlefield represents the First Noble Truth—life is hard. Arjuna reminiscing to Krishna about all the good times he's had with his friends, relatives, and teachers opposing him on the battlefield represents the Second Noble Truth—all of Arjuna's attachments that are making him suffer.

The Third Noble Truth is enlightenment exists for everyone — Arjuna found this out in Chapter 11 when Krishna gave him divine sight, losing his fear of death, and becoming present to the now. In other words, Arjuna had a spiritual breakthrough when he woke from the dream of illusion. In Buddhism, enlightenment is often referred to as *nirvana*—which means extinction of desire and the annihilation of suffering. The Fourth Noble Truth is known in Buddhism as the Eightfold Path—which is everything Krishna has been teaching Arjuna throughout the *Bhagavad Gita*.

Chapter Six, Verse 15 (1,000) *nirvana* – extinguishment of ego

yunjann evam sadatmanam yogi niyatamanasah
santim nirvanaparamam matsamstham adhigacchati

When yoked continuously, the yogin of restrained thought attains the peace of My being, the final *nirvana*.

Buddhism teaches that within each of us is the **fire of desire**. Sometimes the fire is under control and sometimes the fire rages out of control, causing untold destruction. We generate friction when we counter force with force. Power is the attitude of to be and to let be. One stick of wood can't create enough friction to start a fire without another stick of wood. The fire within each of us is caused by the friction of duality. We learned earlier that duality is a basic component of creation—we all have likes and dislikes. Krishna taught Arjuna about desire at the end of Chapter Three.

> **Desire** *is full of unappeasable craving and great evil.*
> Verse 37

> *The eternal enemy of the wise, is in the form of **desire**,*
> *the insatiable fire.*
> Verse 39

*Take control and destroy **desire**.*
Verse 41
*Annihilate the enemy in the form of **desire**.*
Verse 43

The friction between what we **want** and what we can't **have** creates the fire of suffering. We also learned this duality as linear and non-linear. When we cross over into the non-linear world of enlightenment—the fires of duality go out and we experience complete freedom. Our fire of suffering (second Noble Truth) has the potential to become the light of consciousness (Third Noble Truth). Our freedom from desire becomes true peace and contentment—***santosa***!

Third Noble Truth

Verse 32 (1,000) Everyone has the opportunity to become enlightened.

*Anyone who takes shelter in Me, Arjuna, women, Vaishyas, Sudras or even sinners – **all beings** can achieve the Supreme Destination (enlightenment).*

The Eightfold Path is also known in Buddhism as the *Middle Path*. In my discussion about **brahmacharya**, I defined it as personal responsibility, *walking with God*, and the *middle path*. Remember, all Yogas (not *hatha-yoga*) are paths to God—paths to enlightenment and *nirvana*. The *Middle Path* is the path of balance—perhaps my favorite one word definition of Yoga. The eight steps to enlightenment on the Noble Eightfold Path are as follows: Right View, Right Intention, Right Speech, Right Action, Right Livelihood, Right Effort, Right Mindfulness, and Right Concentration. The Buddha's intent was for these eight teachings to be thought of as circular—interconnected to help us develop the three essential values of Buddhism: wisdom, ethics, and awareness.

All eight of these practices begin with the word *right*—meaning **ethical**. In our exploration of the *yamas* and *niyamas*, we could easily apply our words *satya* (truth) and *sauca* (purity) to the word *right*; True View, Pure Intention, True Speech, Pure Action, etc. Our first two steps, Right View and Right Intention fall under the larger category of **wisdom**, or *Jnana Yoga*—one of our three primary Yogas in the *Bhagavad Gita*. The next three steps are Right Speech, Right Action, and Right Livelihood. These three are our **ethical** practices, which we could place in the *brahmacharya* and *aparigraha* categories. In this instance, I would apply the definition of living as truthfully and consciously with ourselves as we can to *aparigraha*. Right Speech is *ahimsa – speak without ever causing pain to another*. Krishna defines Yoga as the art of proper action. Right Action is *Karma Yoga*, our second of three primary Yogas. Right Livelihood aligns with *dharma*. Our final three practices fall under the category of concentration and meditation. Awareness is *Bhakti Yoga*—the awareness that we are always connected to God.

Remember the Ram Dass passage I included earlier in the book about making tea? Ram Dass describes meditation as *being present with every step and acting out of the total harmony of each moment*. I believe this is the true essence of Right Effort, Right Mindfulness, and Right Concentration. Meditation is not concentration—it is something much more profound than concentration. Meditation imposes order and freedom in our lives, making us aware of what we're doing and able to see the constant, ever-changing movement of life. Thus meditation becomes a way of life! The intention of the Eightfold path and the *yamas* and *niyamas*—is for them to also become a way of life. Not only do we have to expand our understanding of single Sanskrit words, we also have to expand our understanding with English words too. We commonly think of meditation as sitting quietly with our eyes closed, but how Ram Dass described making tea is also meditation. Being on our yoga mats can be meditation in motion. We can make everything we do, even making our tea, a meditation.

The Eightfold Path and the Bhagavad Gita

Right View: There is nothing to believe and everything to discover.

That which is night (maya) for all creatures is wakefulness to the one of self-mastery. And what is wakefulness to an ordinary person – that is night to the divinely perceptive sage.
Chapter Two, Verse 69

Enlightened beings are spiritually awake and materially asleep – whereas most people are materially awake and spiritually asleep.

Right Intention: Think of what you want, and realize we all want and need the same things.

Those who feel for others even as they feel for themselves.
Chapter Six, Verse 32

Right Speech: Speak the Truth – our words must be used to help, not to harm.

*To speak without ever causing pain to another, to be **truthful**, to always say what is kind and beneficial.* Chapter 17, Verse 15

Right Action: Doing what needs to be done.

Those who follow their inner-guidance will always do what's right and treat everyone with respect. Chapter Three, Verse 17

Right Livelihood: Our true vocation is serving others.

When we discover the true purpose of our existence, our dharma, we've made the first step toward enlightenment.
Chapter Two, Verse 51

Right Effort: Non-doing, yielding, and going with the flow.

Relinquishing attachment to the fruits of work, always content, and independent of material rewards. Chapter Four, Verse 20

Right Mindfulness: What are we doing and why are we doing it?

They are true renunciants and yogins who perform dutiful and spiritual actions without desiring their fruits. Chapter Six, Verse 1.

Right Concentration: Fully inhabiting the present moment.

By becoming absorbed in Brahman and at peace with themselves, neither grieving nor craving – regarding all beings alike. Chapter 18, Verse 54

And one example from Chapter 12, Verse 16, combining five of the eight practices.

Those who are free from wants, **Right View**

who are pure and capable, **Right Intention**

always ready to work, **Right Action**

who remains unconcerned with and unafflicted by circumstances, **Right Effort**

who have abandoned all ego-initiated undertakings. **Right Mindfulness**

In Patanjali's Eight Limbs, outlined in his *Yoga Sutras*, the sixth and seventh limbs are exactly the same as Buddha's seventh and eighth steps on the Eightfold Path—*dharana* is concentration and *dhyana* is meditation. The eighth limb is termed *samadhi*, ecstasy, complete integration, absolute union, enlightenment, and *nirvana*.

Another cornerstone of Buddhist teachings are the **Three Jewels**—*Buddha, Dharma,* and *Sangha. Buddha* represents **knowing** the truth; *Dharma* is knowing the truth and **speaking** the truth; *Sangha* is **being** the truth—living and embodying the truth in all aspects of life, especially in our communities. It's not enough to *be the truth* alone at home—we have to *be the truth* out in the world.

Life is difficult due to our attachments and desires—the *yamas* and *niyamas* deal with desire directly. Letting go of all that doesn't serve us is the bedrock of transformation. *Satya*, letting go of pretense; *asteya*, letting go of the desire to acquire and possess; *brahmacharya*, the middle path of moderation; *aparigraha*, letting go of our possessiveness and greed; *santosa*, things being enough; *tapas*, the very force to end suffering; *svadhyaya*, letting go of results and embracing the process—a major teaching in the *Bhagavad Gita*. All of these practices take great patience *(niyamya)*, a pure intention to spiritually grow *(sauca)*, and an overwhelming kindness and compassion toward ourselves *(ahimsa)* as we walk our path toward a more awakened life. And finally, we surrender it all to God, *isvara-pranidhana* and *Bhakti Yoga*.

Buddhism was a reaction to Hinduism, which is far older than Buddhism. The Buddha was born about 563 and died circa 483 BCE. One of the ways Buddhism differs from Hinduism is in regards to reincarnation. The word *rebirth* is more precise in Buddhism. Reincarnation implies a constant, never-changing, eternal soul that is reborn time and again. Each new lifetime brings with it a new outer identity, but the soul remains the same until enlightenment is achieved. Rebirth in Buddhism describes an innate soul that constantly evolves and changes. This subtle difference is one of the ways Buddha broke with Hindu tradition. In Buddhism, belief is secondary—direct experience is primary. We don't have to believe in anything to progress on our unique path of awakening.

> *This Self is never born nor does it ever die; nor having*
> *come into existence will it again cease to be. It is*
> *birth-less, eternal, changeless, and always the same.*
> Chapter Two, Verse 20

Levels of Consciousness

At some point during the reading of this book, I suspect you've wondered where you and others in your life calibrate. No one wants to be below 200, but you've seen the statistics. If you've read this far into the book, I seriously doubt you calibrate below 200. I measure people all the time, whether they know it or not—I almost never tell someone their number unless asked. If you calibrate below 200, you can't measure consciousness—you won't have enough power. Between 200 and 400 the accuracy of your findings will vary due to varying levels of power. The 400's have more power and are more accurate—the upper 400's even more so. Just like anything else, it takes practice. The next question may be, *how do you measure consciousness?* As I wrote earlier, it's measured by an all or nothing muscle response to levels of Truth—I must refer you to Dr. Hawkins for an explanation on how to calibrate consciousness. When you first learn how consciousness can be measured, it may seem impossible, but it works. Remember, Truth is not subject to proof. Its human nature to dismiss something we know nothing about—human reason can never explain the inexplicable. The research Dr. Hawkins has provided is enormous and he's written many books on the subject. Until you read and study his work, stay open, humble, and don't dismiss it all out of ignorance. *Understand first!*

Try not to think of the numbers as better or worse—it's hard to keep the ego from judging the numbers—it is information to primarily explain human behavior. It doesn't mean you are smarter or more successful or any of that ego stuff. We are all unique in every other way—it only makes sense that we would all have different levels of consciousness. On the path of spiritual evolution, some people are ahead of us and others behind. Our past lives may have everything to do with our level in this life. It's challenging not to get caught up in the number—it is what it is and we do have the power to change it for better or worse—it really is our choice. Your level of consciousness will rise having read this book and having a deeper understanding of the teachings within the *Bhagavad Gita*—I have no doubt about that truth. Going beyond just reading this book toward fully embodying Krishna's teachings will truly affect positive change in your life, on all levels. The price of this book and the time reading it is a small price to pay for any increase in your personal power and happiness! On the logarithmic scale, one-tenth of a point increase is a huge shift in power.

The most powerful action we can do to raise our level of consciousness is to **take responsibility** for every thought, word, and action in our lives. The attitude of blame and *it's not my fault* are sure signs of someone calibrating below 200. The second most powerful way to raise consciousness is through **unconditional kindness** to everything and everyone. *Our duty – our dharma*, is to figure out what we're here to do—without attachment—letting go of all our expectations of what we think our life is about. The 20th century American philosopher Joseph Campbell said: *We must let go of the life we have planned, so as to accept the one that is waiting for us.* Each of us has to figure out for ourselves what our *dharma* might be. Our *dharma* is waiting for all of us— we only have to have the courage to *stand up* and discover it.

The possibility exists for our level of consciousness to drop— too much loss can lead to devastating consequences. Earlier in this book I wrote about the *malas* and how they are part of *maya*. *Anava-mala* is the source of incompleteness and separation we feel deep inside ourselves—creating the illusion of a lack of self-worth so powerful—we believe it to be true. We've all felt at some point in our lives unworthy, inadequate, unappreciated, unwanted, unheard, unloved, and under-valued. *Anava-mala* is an inherent quality within each of us—but we are not separate and incomplete. No one is free from these feelings that are fundamental to our being. Through divine will, God stays separate from human beings and only through God's will can *anava-mala* be dissolved. Krishna built His own city, *Dwaraka, (gateway to heaven)* where He lived separate and apart from the Pandavas and Kauravas. In order to enter His city, you had to have His permission.

Our consciousness must be cared for and nurtured daily, similar to caring for our teeth. My suspicion is *anava-mala* may be the cause for the lowering of consciousness leading to the feelings of depression. We typically treat the effects of depression with low consciousness drugs—rather than trying to understand and treat the cause. In *Warrior Self*, I write in more detail about *anava-mala* and my personal experience—but before I discovered my specific *anava-mala* in 2007, I would sometimes become depressed. Fortunately, with my level of consciousness, I could pull my level back up and come out of my depression rather quickly. I never had to take medications to cope with life, but many do. There are many ways to nurture consciousness—to feed our souls. Serving others is one great way—this may be Krishna's favorite way for us. Feeding our souls through great music and books is another example. I'm fortunate to play in a symphony orchestra—most classical music calibrates very high. Take time to appreciate the beauty of nature—it's all around us all the time. Use the time on the yoga mat to feed your soul—don't let any of your *asana* practice be an ego trip. Develop the *attitude of gratitude*. Find your own ways—but most importantly, begin to think of nurturing your consciousness daily.

Patient Effort

Many definitions of the word *Yoga* have been offered throughout this book—but one of my personal favorites is *patient effort*. Learning about ourselves takes a patient effort on a deeper level of understanding—an introspective level. The thirteen year exile of the Pandavas in the *Mahabharata* is an allegory for the patient effort it takes to transform one's life. Transformation is not some extraordinary event—paying close attention to our thoughts, words, and actions and changing our negative tendencies to more positive tendencies is transformation. It takes faith, courage, commitment, humility, and patience to *know* ourselves and *to be* ourselves. It takes time—most likely the rest of our lives. There are no shortcuts on our journey to God.

Krishna teaches Arjuna how to use the battles of life to come to God—uniting the individual to the Universal. Our suffering produces the strong desire for spiritual enlightenment—we need the desire for a better life to motivate us along our unique path of awakening—greater suffering summons higher consciousness. Suffering forces us to realize things as they are. We all experience loss in some form—creating change and suffering—it's our suffering which helps us recognize happiness. We will most likely live in the forest as the Pandavas did, but in time, we will all find our *true north* that leads us out of the darkness to find our true purpose in life—our Soul's purpose. The fire of suffering truly becomes the light for higher consciousness.

Some have said that we are every character in the *Mahabharata*—I disagree. There will always be Duryodhana's and weak kings in the world who have the desire to hurt others, but I'm not so fearful of life that I have to control, manipulate, and lie to make myself feel safe at the expense of others. I can't imagine living life at that level of consciousness, but many do. We all have the full range of emotions, including the emotions we may not like to admit—so from that perspective, we just might be every character. Krishna is everyone's charioteer—our intuition—always driving our chariot, whether we know it or not. Inside each of us is Arjuna—our *inner* warrior, ready to stand up and fight for ourselves and others, setting things right in our sovereign kingdom. He is us, about to go into battle, facing reality, and reclaiming his kingdom with God by his side. The common thread connecting all these teachings is **Truth**. Bhishma tells us in the *Mahabharata* that *there is Truth where Krishna is, and there is victory where Truth is*. Sooner or later, we'll all be called to battle, and then we too will become the great warriors we are meant to be, fighting for our **Warrior Truth**.

The one who has conquered himself is a far greater hero than he who has defeated a thousand times a thousand men.
The Buddha

Dharma Warrior

Krishna taught us everything we need to know about life in the *Bhagavad Gita*—but truly understanding His teachings and applying them to our everyday lives isn't so easy to do. One of our inherent human attributes is freedom—we have the freedom to decide which choice may be best for us. We learned that the human mind is inherently defective—so we can't always distinguish truth from falsehood, right from wrong, and we sometimes make the wrong choice. One of the dualities in society is success and failure—but who's to judge whether or not we've succeeded or failed? This leads to judgment and opinion—but what are those judgments and opinions based on—the truth? Judgments and opinions are rooted in ego, not the soul – *I'm right, you're wrong – I win, you lose* – are all expressions from ego, creating more and more separation with life, others, and God. Where there is division, it is the law that there must be conflict.

Part of any *hatha-yoga* class is standing balance poses—tree pose for example. Newer students to yoga typically fall out of tree pose and often get frustrated, believing they have somehow failed. With time, patience, and practice, we're able to stand strong on one leg with greater ease. Falling is part of learning—I encourage my students to embrace their "failure" when they fall—that's how I know they're playing their edge and expanding their balance. If we fall in our balance poses, it's mostly due to not being present and not engaging—many students stop breathing when they try to balance. Couldn't we say the exact same thing about life? If we don't give life our full attention and engage, we'll sometimes fall. By playing our edge and taking some risks in life, we move toward *dharma*—one of the foundational words in the *Bhagavad Gita*. The life that's waiting for us is most likely our *dharma*—but how do we know whether we're living our *dharma*? My belief is we are all moving toward our *dharma* every choice of every day. I'll help people answer their *dharma* question with another question. ***When in your life are you completely present and your most authentic self?*** For me, it's teaching, whether it's *asana* or something else. My *dharma* isn't necessarily teaching a yoga class, it's just teaching—which also includes writing. When I'm teaching, I'm completely present *and acting out of the total harmony of each moment.* Our earlier quote from Ram Dass about making tea is perfect for our understanding of *dharma.*

> *While you're making the tea, you're just making the tea – nothing else. You're not worrying about how the tea will turn out, and you're not wondering whether you're good enough to make the tea correctly, and you're not thinking about whether you should serve it with honey. You're just right there, making the tea – being present with every step and acting out of the total harmony of each moment.*

Success in life is the result of aligning with our *dharma.* The *life I planned* since I was in High School was to be a professional musician in a symphony orchestra. As of the writing of this book, I've enjoyed that profession for over 30 years. However, my *dharma* is not being a musician, that's just something I do. I serve others through teaching—playing in a symphony orchestra isn't the best way for me to serve others. We are taught to set goals in life—but goals actually become the very obstacles to our happiness. Goals themselves create models of finished and unfinished—success and failure. Goals can actually be limiting because we are capable of much more than we can ever imagine for ourselves. Goals align with the future—not the present.

Many judgments are rooted in fears—which are based on future thoughts, *worrying about how our tea will turn out, and wondering whether we're good enough to make the tea correctly.* Also from fear comes jealousy—we learned how Duryodhana's jealousy of his cousins ultimately destroyed him. Duryodhana's choices were motivated by his imagined fears about the future.

My music teaching career didn't end on my terms—I too had a metaphorical Duryodhana whose jealousy tried to destroy me. His birth level is 156—anger, hate, and aggression. When I departed from my last university job, I made the choice to never work for anyone ever again—all of it was a risk. I started my own business and learned a new career—stepping more fully into *the life that was waiting for me*—my *dharma*. I've felt a divine guidance my entire life—I know without a doubt that I'm doing exactly what I'm supposed to be doing right now—my *dharma* is evolving each and every day to where I'll serve more people.

One of the men I admire is baseball legend Jackie Robinson. He said, you don't steal the base behind you—you steal the base in front of you. Stealing bases in baseball is risky—you could be thrown out—but without risk, there's no reward. When you decide to steal a base, you make a split second decision and run—which are present moment choices. You don't stand on the base and say to yourself, "someday I'm going to steal a base"—which ends up being a goal set in the future. Arjuna risks his life reclaiming his kingdom. In Chapter One, he isn't so sure he should take the risk, trying to convince Krishna (and most likely himself) with his lame arguments which are all based in the future. My entire life has been one risk after the other—one stolen base at a time. It was a risk to want to make my living as a musician. It was a risk to quit a profession at age 44 and begin a new career in a different profession. It's a risk to write a book, especially this one. Moving toward the life that is waiting *in front* of each of us requires a certain amount of risk—and in order to take that risk, we have to overcome our fears and doubts, learning to live in the present moment and thereby moving closer to our edge. None of us knows what the future holds—if we think too much about the future, none of us will ever challenge ourselves to steal the next base. We'll stand on our safe base and ask the question, *what if? Dharma* is now—*karma* is now—risk is now—success is now—truth is now. What can you do today to make tomorrow better? That's *karma*!

What is success and what is failure—who decides? Only Krishna decides. Hurting others is failure. Having negative thoughts about ourselves is failure. Comparing ourselves to others is failure. Judging ourselves, looking outside ourselves for validation, trying to make ourselves look better than someone else, pretending to be someone we are not, lying, and finally, trying to prove ourselves to others—all of which are failures on our part. We fail ourselves when we believe we're not enough as we are.

Good *karma* is no *karma*. The **first** of three steps in not accruing *karma* is to align ourselves with our *dharma*. **Our purpose in life is to discover the Truth**, our best definition of *dharma*. I clearly remember asking myself, *is this all there is to my life?* I asked that question when I was teaching music at the university, prior to changing careers. Krishna was listening, He's always listening (He only pretends to be asleep)—and He answered with a resounding, No! If you've asked a similar question, chances are you are not aligned with your *dharma* and Krishna will answer in time—be patient, and get ready, your *dharma* ride may be a bit bumpy.

Step two is to not be attached to the outcome—just make the tea—the outcome is based in future thought. Years ago, one of my teachers asked me to do a project for him—I accepted because he asked me. I never once asked, *what's in it for me?* I spent a year completing the project to the best of my abilities. Upon completion, the project was published and I made a little bit of money, but that is not what motivated me to accept the project. I accepted before I even knew what the project was. Acting without any self-interest or ego attachment isn't so easy to do—we're not worrying about how the tea will turn out, and we're not wondering whether we're good enough to make the tea correctly, and we're not thinking about whether we should serve it with honey. We're just right there, making the tea.

Step three is even more challenging than the first two steps. This is where we turn it all over to Krishna—surrendering ourselves to faith. When my teacher asked me to do the project, I was the one who did the work, but the project wasn't my idea—it was his idea. This entire book is Krishna's, not mine—He needed someone to sit down and write this all out for Him. When my friend's son's consciousness was raised to rid him of his schizophrenic behavior—Krishna did that too, not me. Krishna showed me how I could help through the *Mahabharata*, instructing me what to do. This is the state of mind we begin to develop through practice, awareness, and faith. I remember being extremely present with the problem in front of me. *How can I help my friends' son?* Krishna heard that thought (which was actually His thought) and answered. We are not the *doers* of our thoughts and actions—but we're not always willing to accept that fact—our ego desperately wants to take credit. Of course, if we "fail," we're not always so eager to accept that fact either. The only way I can explain how I discovered to ask Krishna to raise someone's level of consciousness to help them was through Krishna Himself. Had I not been so immersed in writing this book, it may have never been discovered. How many lives will possibly be changed from this one event?

There will always be those who will tell us we aren't making the tea correctly—there will also be people who will be jealous of our tea—judging, criticizing, and discrediting our tea. By taking the risk of writing this book, there may be those who criticize and discredit *my* tea. It's easy to sit on the side-lines and tell someone how to make the tea—there's no risk. We are all faced with the choice and duality of being a victor or a victim of life—the exact same choice Arjuna faced in no-man's-land. What would we do in life if we knew we wouldn't fail? The answer to that question just might be our *dharma*. The fear of failure potentially keeps us from doing what we are here to do—but true alignment with our *dharma* never fails. That big step toward the next base, *the life that is waiting for us*, certainly takes the courage of a great warrior. Krishna told Arjuna in Chapter 11 that he will not fail if he engages with life (fights the Kauravas)—He already killed all of Arjuna's enemies long ago. Krishna is telling us the exact same thing! Our *dharma* and destiny waits for each of us—all we need is a little courage to act.

Until we're no longer attached to our egos in any way, every act we do will have our ego present in it. When our ego is present, we create *karma* for ourselves. We learned that *yajna* erases *karma*— our selfless acts that benefit others. *Karma Yoga* is supposed to be selfless actions, but unless we're enlightened, every act we do will most likely have an ego attachment in some form creating more and more *karma* for ourselves. *If you're going to make a cup of tea right, you can't be busy trying to make the cup of tea right, because while you're busy trying, you're not present with making the tea. You can't be doing both.*

True *dharma* involves serving others—alignment with *dharma* is the first step toward higher levels of consciousness and more enlightened living. Simply knowing we are alive is enlightenment— **enlightenment is where we are now!** If you don't believe you are aligned with your *dharma*, what are you waiting for? Krishna is indifferent—He's not going to tell you when to steal the base—that's for you to decide. Maybe you'll fall—maybe you'll get thrown out—what then? Will you stop trying and be a victim, or will you stand back up and try again, becoming a victor of your destiny? The *life we've planned* is most likely not *the life that is waiting for us.* What our ego perceives as failure is only Krishna helping us to align with our *dharma.* If that's true (which it is), how can we judge *the life we've planned* as failure? *Stand up now* and become a **Warrior of Truth!**

BIBLIOGRAPHY

Buck, William (1973) *Mahabharata*. Los Angeles:
University of California Press.

Bernard, Theos (1947) *Hindu Philosophy*. Delhi:
Motilal Banarsidass Publishers.

Cox, T. (2014) *Warrior Self – Unlocking the Promise of the
Bhagavad Gita*. Oklahoma City: Spirit House Yoga Publishing.

Dale, Ralph Alan. (2002) *Tao Te Ching*. Barnes and Noble.

Das, R. (2010) *Be Love Now: the path of the heart*. New York:
Harper One.

Das, R. (2004) *Paths to God – Living the Bhagavad Gita*.
New York: Three Rivers Press.

Das, Surya. (1997) *Awakening the Buddha Within*. New York:
Broadway Books.

Das, Surya. (2007) *Buddha is as Buddha Does*. New York:
Harper Collins.

Desikachar, T.K.V. (1998) *Health Healing and Beyond*.
New York: Aperture Foundation Inc.

Gandhi, Mohandas. (2000) *The Bhagavad Gita*.
Berkeley, California: Berkeley Hills Books.

Hawkins, D. (1995) *Power vs. Force – The Hidden Determinants of
Human Behavior*. Sedona, Arizona: Veritas Publishing.

Hawkins, D. (2006) *Transcending the Levels of Consciousness*:
Sedona, Arizona: Veritas Publishing.

Hawkins, D. (2005) *Truth vs Falsehood – How to Tell the Difference:* Toronto, Canada: Axial Publishing Company.

King, Stephen. (2000) *On Writing – A Memoir of the Craft*: New York, NY: Scribner Publishing.

Marjanovic, B. (2002) *Abhinavagupta's Commentary on the Bhagavad Gita.* Portland, OR: Rudra Press.

Shantananda. (2003) *The Splendor of Recognition.* South Fallsburg, NY: SYDA Foundation.

Stern, Eddie and Summerbell, Deirdre. (2002) *Sri K. Pattabhi Jois: A Tribute.* New York, NY: Eddie Stern and Gwyneth Paltrow.

Vanamali. (2000) *The Complete Life of Krishna*: Rochester, Vermont: Inner Traditions.

Vivekananda. (1997) *Practical Vedanta*: India, Advaita Ashrama.

Yogananda, P. (1995) *The Bhagavad Gita.* Los Angeles: Self-Realization Fellowship.